Word 6 for Windo

QuickStart,
Second Edition

Susanne Weixel

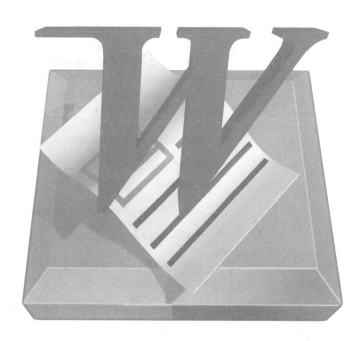

Publisher: David P. Ewing

Associate Publisher: Michael Miller

Managing Editor: Michael Cunningham

Product Marketing Manager: Ray Robinson

About the Author

Suzanne Weixel is a self-employed writer and editor specializing in the technology industry. Her experience with computers began in 1974, when she learned to play football on the Dartmouth Time Sharing terminal her brother installed in a spare bedroom.

For Que, Suzanne has written and revised numerous books, including *AmiPro 3 Quickstart, Easy PCs,* Second Edition, *I Hate Word 6 For Windows, DOS 6 QuickStart,* and *Everyday DOS.* She also writes about non-computer-related subjects whenever she has the chance.

Suzanne graduated from Dartmouth College in 1981 with a degree in art history. She currently lives in Marlborough, MA with her husband, their sons, Nathaniel and Evan, and their Samoyed, Cirrus.

Acknowledgements

Thanks to my sister and brother-in-law, Julie and Doug Weisman, for helping to keep the kids and dogs out of the way when the deadlines got tight, and to my brother and sister-in-law, Jeff and Joyce Sudikoff, for reminding me to take time for fun, too.

Publishing Manager
Don Roche, Jr.

Acquisitions Editor
Thomas F. Godfrey III

Product Director
Joyce J. Nielsen

Production Editor
Jill D. Bond

Technical Editor
Chris Pichereau

Technical Assistance
Rolf A. Crozier

Book Designer
Amy Peppler-Adams

Cover Designer
Dan Armstrong

Production Team
Stephen Adams
Angela D. Bannan
Cameron Booker
Paula Carroll
Aren Munk
G. Alan Palmore
Nanci Sears Perry
Caroline Roop
Michael Thomas
Tina M. Trettin
Donna Winter
Lillian Yates

Indexer
Greg Eldred

Composed in *Stone Serif* and *MCPdigital by* Que Corporation.

Contents at a Glance

Table of Contents

Introduction

Word 6 for Windows is a powerful word processing software package that takes full advantage of the easy-to-use Windows environment. The program combines basic text entry and editing capabilities with sophisticated layout, formatting, and document management features. In addition, the Windows version of Word 6 is almost identical to the Macintosh version; once you learn to use Word for Windows, you also will know how to use Word for the Macintosh.

Word 6 is an ideal choice for beginners trying to produce a simple memo as well as for experienced computer users creating complex reports and presentations.

Word 6 for Windows QuickStart covers the fundamentals of using Word 6. The text is supported by step-by-step instructions, on-your-own exercises, and clearly labeled illustrations, all designed to get you up and running with Word 6 quickly and easily.

What Does This Book Contain?

Each lesson in *Word 6 QuickStart* is built around a set of related tasks. The lessons, and the sections within the lessons, are organized so that you can use the information presented to accomplish the tasks that follow. In addition, the lessons are grouped into parts. You don't have to read the book sequentially, however, to learn to use Word 6. Feel free to jump around from lesson to lesson and section to section to find the information you want.

From beginning to end, the lessons move from the basics—such as creating and revising documents—through paragraph and page design, and then into more advanced tasks, such as customizing and automating the program; incorporating graphics, tables, and charts into documents; and using Word 6 with other Windows applications.

The book begins with a Visual Index of documents you can create with Word 6 for Windows. The Visual Index illustrates the wide range of projects you can produce with this program.

Part I: Creating and Editing Basic Documents

Lesson 1, "Learning the Basics," begins with an overview of Word 6's features. The lesson covers such essentials as starting Windows and using a mouse and a keyboard, and then you move on to learn how to start Word 6, understand the Word 6 screen, and get help.

Lesson 2, "Creating a Document," introduces you to document templates and styles. You learn how to start a new document and use Word's typing conventions to enter text. Finally, you learn how to save and print the document.

In Lesson 3, "Revising a Document," you learn how to open an existing document and use basic editing skills such as moving and copying text to make revisions. You learn how to correct mistakes by deleting text, and by using Undo. You also learn how to prevent some mistakes before you make them using Word's AutoCorrect feature. Finally, you learn how to open multiple document windows.

In Lesson 4, "Checking Your Document," you learn how to improve your document by using Word's proofing tools—Spelling Checker, Grammar Checker, and the Thesaurus, and you learn to find and replace characters and formatting in a document.

Part II: Formatting for a Professional Look

In Lesson 5, "Dressing Up Your Text," you learn how to use character formatting to format your text. You learn to apply fonts and character effects, change character spacing, and enhance the appearance of text with dropped capital letters and WordArt.

In Lesson 6, "Dressing Up Your Paragraphs," you learn how to use paragraph formatting to format paragraphs. You learn to align text and set line and paragraph spacing, and to use the horizontal ruler to indent paragraphs and to set tabs. You also learn to enhance paragraphs by adding borders and shading and by creating bulleted and numbered lists.

Lesson 7, "Setting Up Your Pages," provides information on controlling the document view and on setting up an effective page layout. You learn to choose a page size and orientation, set margins, create headers and footers, number pages, and divide a page into newspaper columns. You also learn to insert breaks for sections, pages, and columns, and to insert footnotes or endnotes.

Part III: Customizing and Adding Nontext Elements to Documents

In Lesson 8, "Customizing Word for Windows," you learn how to make Word 6 suit your own needs. You learn more about templates and styles, customizing keys, menus, and toolbars, and you learn how to change Word start-up options.

Lesson 9, "Making Your Work Easier," is filled with information about using Automatic Formatting, Wizards, AutoText, and Macros to automate and simplify your work.

Lesson 10, "Working with Frames," explains the concept of frames and describes how to create, format, and manipulate frames in a document and place a picture in a frame.

In Lesson 11, "Drawing with Word for Windows," you learn how to use Word's built-in drawing features to create and edit a drawing.

Lesson 12, "Working with Tables," covers creating, formatting, and editing tables.

Lesson 13, "Working with Graphs," describes how to use the different types of charts available in Word.

Part IV: Advanced Features and Integration

In Lesson 14, "Using Mail Merge," you learn about the merge operation and how to create and merge form letters, envelopes, and labels.

Lesson 15, "Working with Forms," provides information about using Word to create and fill out forms.

In Lesson 16, "Managing Your Document and Files," you learn how to use Word's document notation tools, including revision marking, annotations, bookmarks, and cross-references, and how to create outlines, tables of contents, and simple indexes. Finally, you learn to use Word to find misplaced files on a disk.

In Lesson 17, "Working with Other Windows Applications," you learn the ins and outs of using Word 6 for Windows with other Windows applications. You learn to share and link data between applications, including the other programs in the Microsoft Office series.

Who Should Use This Book?

Word 6 for Windows QuickStart is a useful guide for anyone who wants to use Word 6. The book presents enough basic information to get a first-time user started, and then builds on that user's growing understanding by introducing more advanced topics. If you're an experienced user, the book covers features and tasks to expand your knowledge and increase your proficiency. You also can use this book as a reference tool.

Where to Find More Help

After you master the features in this book, you may want to learn more about Word's advanced capabilities. If so, Que also publishes *Using Word Version 6 for Windows*, Special Edition and *Word Version 6 for Windows Quick Reference*. To learn more about using Windows, you may want to consult Que's *Using Windows 3.1*, Special Edition.

Word 6 for Windows also provides extensive on-line Help to answer many of your questions. To learn about getting help with Word 6, see Lesson 1, "Learning the Basics."

Microsoft also provides customer assistance and support for registered users.

What You Need to Use Word 6 for Windows

To use Word 6 for Windows, you must have the following computer hardware and software:

- A computer with an Intel 286 microprocessor, or greater, capable of running Windows 3.0 or higher

- A minimum of 4M of random access memory (RAM)

- An EGA monitor, or better, compatible with Windows version 3.1 or higher

- Microsoft Windows version 3.1 or higher

- DOS version 3.1 or higher

- A high-density floppy disk drive

- A hard disk with at least 6M of free space (to install the basic program) or 24M of free space (to install the complete package). This space must be available after installing DOS, Windows, and any other applications you use.

- A Windows-compatible mouse is highly recommended, but not required.

Conventions Used in This Book

Word 6 for Windows QuickStart uses certain conventions to help you use and understand the information in this book:

- Text that you type appears in **boldface** type.

- Key combinations, such as Ctrl+Enter, indicate that you should press and hold the first key as you press the second key.

- Important words or phrases appear in *italic* the first time they are discussed.

■ Screen displays and messages appear in a special typeface.

■ Menu commands are shown like this: Choose **F**ile, **R**un, which means use the mouse to click the **F**ile menu, and then click the **R**un item on that menu. You also can press Alt+F and then press R.

■ If toolbar button alternatives to menu commands are available, the icon appears in the margin of this book.

■ *Notes* describe information that might help you avoid problems or accomplish the task in a more efficient manner.

■ *Keywords* in the margins briefly define new terms that you encounter as you read this book.

■ *If You Have Problems...* paragraphs provide troubleshooting information to help you avoid—or escape—problem situations.

Visual Index

Word provides tools for creating a wide range of documents. This section illustrates some of the documents you can create using Word's document templates and wizards. Each sample has labels that briefly describe the relevant tasks and refer you to the appropriate sections of the book.

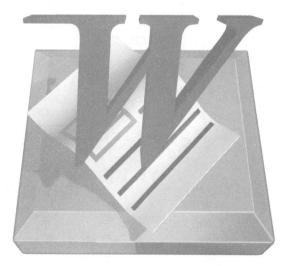

Headlines with different character effects, "Enhancing the Appearance of Text," p. 104

Borders around paragraphs, columns, and frames, "Adding Borders and Shading," p. 138

Water EveryWhere

Volume 1 Issue 1 ———————————————— **August 1994**

Different text alignments, "Aligning Paragraphs," p. 125

H2O ENHANCER

Enhancer Arrives!

The long awaited Enhancer from H_2O Products has finally hit the market. The waves stirred up by this product have long promised to overwhelm the industry. The buzz and rumors surrounding this advanced purification system have kept all watchers waiting eagerly.

No disappointment here! This product is truly a giant leap forward in water purification technology. Its simple design hides a major breakthrough that water specialists around the globe are bound to emulate.

Even the dingiest, smelliest, chemical-filled tap water glistens when this system is installed.

And somehow, it even makes heavily chlorinated

water taste like it just came from the well! These gems are going to fly off the shelves. If you can get your hands on an authorized dealership, take our advice and lock on!

WELL LABS

Well Labs Seeks Funds for Search

Well Labs has announced that it is applying for government funding to pursue an experimental water-finding, or dowsing, system. According to a laboratory spokesperson, Well Labs has been researching this particular system for some time now, and believes it is finally at a point where field research will yield important findings.

Additional funds are needed at this time to provide for new hires, lab costs and travel to field sites.

Text flows before and after the frame, "Positioning a Frame," p. 226

Dropped capital letter, "Emphasizing Text with Dropped Capital Letters," p. 112

Imported clip art graphics in a frame, "Importing Graphics," p. 400

A column break is used to be sure the headline starts at the top of the next column, "Customizing the Column Format," p. 172

Three newspaper-style columns, "Dividing a Page into Columns," p. 170

Landscape mode, "Setting Up Your Pages," p. 151

Borders added to top and bottom of frame, "Working with Frames," p. 221

Imported clip art border, "Importing Graphics," p. 400

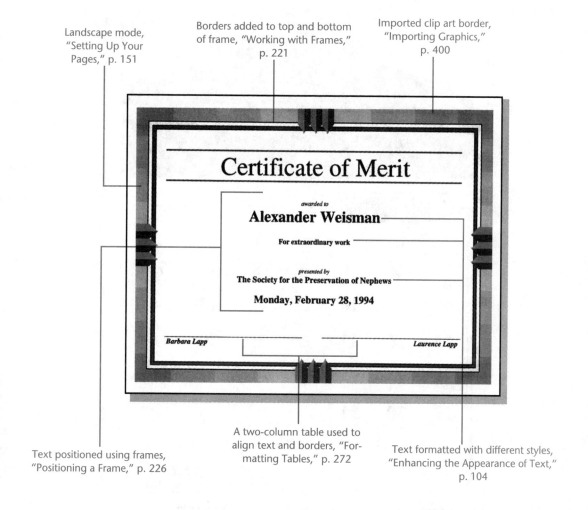

Certificate of Merit

awarded to

Alexander Weisman

For extraordinary work

presented by
The Society for the Preservation of Nephews

Monday, February 28, 1994

Barbara Lapp

Laurence Lapp

Text positioned using frames, "Positioning a Frame," p. 226

A two-column table used to align text and borders, "Formatting Tables," p. 272

Text formatted with different styles, "Enhancing the Appearance of Text," p. 104

Text positioned using a frame, "Positioning a Frame," p. 226

Imported clip art, "Importing Graphics," p. 400

Custom tab stops used to align numbers across the page, "Setting Tabs," p. 131

Frames enhanced with borders, lines and shading, "Adding Simple Borders and Shading," p. 139

Characters formatted with different font sizes and styles, "Enhancing the Appearance of Text," p. 104

Section break changes the page layout from a 2-column to a 1-column, "Dressing Up Your Paragraphs," p. 121."

Built-in forms can be customized, "Using Words Sample Forms," p. 344

Today's date is automatically inserted into the date form field, "Inserting Form Fields," p. 352

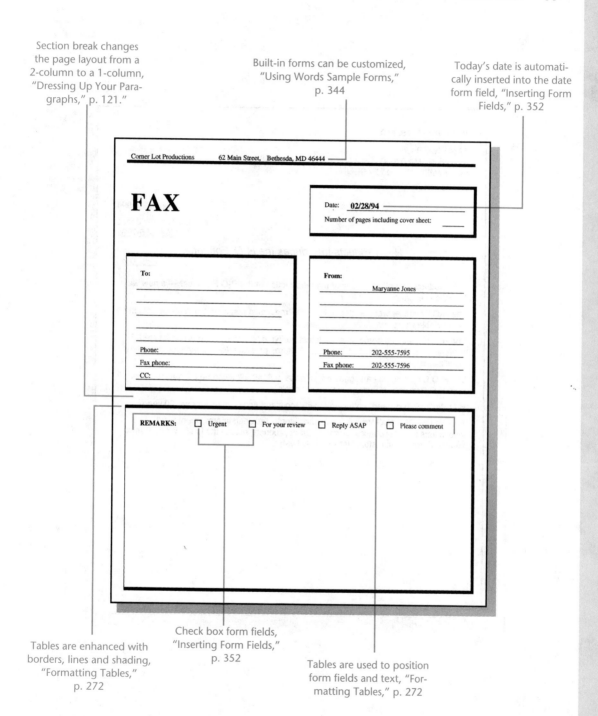

Corner Lot Productions   62 Main Street,   Bethesda, MD 46444

FAX

Date: **02/28/94**
Number of pages including cover sheet:

To:

Phone:
Fax phone:
CC:

From:
                Maryanne Jones

Phone: 202-555-7595
Fax phone: 202-555-7596

REMARKS: ☐ Urgent   ☐ For your review   ☐ Reply ASAP   ☐ Please comment

Tables are enhanced with borders, lines and shading, "Formatting Tables," p. 272

Check box form fields, "Inserting Form Fields," p. 352

Tables are used to position form fields and text, "Formatting Tables," p. 272

Underlined paragraph, "Adding Borders and Shading," p. 139

Today's date, "Inserting the Date and Time," p. 58

H₂O PRODUCTS, INC.

1234 River Road
Lakeshore, MA 02000
FOR IMMEDIATE RELEASE

March 2, 1994
Contact: Maryanne Jones
(202) 555-7595

H₂O Products Introduces the H₂O Enhancer

H₂O Products recently announced the introduction of the H₂O Enhancer — a new way to make your water taste both fresh and clean.

The H₂O Enhancer was developed by H₂O Products in response to customer demand for a reliable way to produce clear water.

The H₂O Enhancer incorporates the latest purifying technology and is constructed entirely of stainless steel. The Enhancer features precision-tooled parts for consistent installation.

The H₂O Enhancer has a suggested list price of $149.99; it can be purchased directly from H₂O Products or through authorized dealers.

H₂O Products has been producing quality tools and accessories for over 30 years.

Founded in 1961, H₂O Products has consistently provided improvements and innovations in water purification tools. Other products include the Laser Water Purifier and the Pyrotechnic Instant Hot Water Activator.

Subscript, "Enhancing the Appearance of Text," p. 104

Different amounts of space between paragraphs, "Controlling Line Spacing," p. 135

Main document created for use in a mail merge, "Creating a Main Document," p. 318

H₂O PRODUCTS, INC.

1234 River Road
Lakeshore, MA 02000

June 7, 1994

«Salutation» «FirstName»
«LastName»
«Title»
«Address1»
«Address2»
«City», «State» «ZipCode»

Dear «Salutation» «LastName»:

Thank you for your past purchases and continuing support of H₂O Products, Inc.. The enclosed price list shows the prices that apply to all purchases effective as of July 5, 1994. As you can see, there have been some price increases.

Because of the current business climate, our costs have increased. We can no longer maintain all of our prices at their past levels and still continue to provide the superior quality and service that you have come to expect from us.

We value you as a customer and hope that these increases will not affect our good relationship with you.

Sincerely,

Stuart Jones

Account Representative

Wide margins leave room for notes, "Setting Margins," p. 158

Header and footer text is aligned and formatted, "Creating Headers and Footers," p. 162

Maryanne Jones   *The Art of Oral Hygiene*   *3/16/94*

The Art of Oral Hygiene

by

Maryanne Jones

Introduction

The first line of each text paragraph is indented, "Indenting Paragraphs," p. 127

Once upon a time, humans did not think about oral hygiene. A mouth was for eating, and maybe for. And then, a mouth was for communication. Exactly when oral hygiene became a concern is unclear. Early cave drawings rarely depict the care of mouths.[1] But with time and civilization came an awareness of fresh breath and clean teeth.

The Purpose of Oral Hygiene

If tThe first goal of oral hygiene wasmay have been sweet-smelling breath, it certainly was not the last. Ibut it soon became understood that holding on to one's teeth could mean the difference between life and deathwas a good thing. OnceWhen humans realized that they could in fact do something to keep theirhis teeth from rotting and falling out, theyhe set out about trying to find out how.out how.

Text lines are double-spaced, "Controlling Line Spacing," p. 135

Rinsing was the first attempt at oral hygieneHumans tried, followed by the eating of fresh-smelling roots and plants.[2] Soon people were rubbing their teeth with cloths and rags. No one is sure who first invented the toothbrush, but it was far from an immediate bestseller. Many people thought it was the work of the devil, and refused to even consider using one. Some who did try the innovative device were jeered at and run out of town.

Revised text is marked, "Customizing Revision Marks," p. 377

---

[1] Alex Daniels, *Cave Art in Northern France*, 1989, Bunion Press.
[2] Karen Patalano, *Medicinal Plants in Prehistoric Times*, 1978, Bunion Press

Page 1

Footnotes, "Adding Footnotes or Endnotes," p. 168

Paragraphs are justified, "Aligning Paragraphs," p. 125

INTEROFFICE MEMO

Date: 03/02/94
To: John Jones
CC: George Jones
From: Maryanne Jones
Subject: Sales Figures

John, I thought you'd be interested in a printout of these preliminary sales figures based on the Excel worksheet Jack's been using...

Expenditures by Site

	Site 1	Site 2	Site 3
TOTAL EXPENDITURES	**$211,325**	**$213,075**	**$215,575**
Salaries	76,700	76,700	76,700
Supplies	19,550	19,300	19,800
Equipment	36,575	36,575	36,575
Lease Pmts	66,850	66,850	66,850
Advertising	11,650	11,650	11,650
Recruiting	0	2,000	4,000

Data is linked from an Excel spreadsheet, "Importing Linked or Embedded Text or Data," p. 406

Let's talk about these numbers when you've had a chance to go over them.

Table is formatted with alignments, borders and different
font styles, "Formatting Tables," p. 272

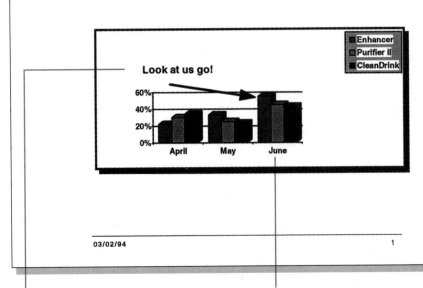

INTEROFFICE MEMO

Date: 03/02/94
To: John Jones
CC: George Jones
From: Maryanne Jones
Subject: Sales Figures

John, thought I'd send along this data re: Enhancer market share vs. the
competition....

	April	May	June
Enhancer	22%	30%	34%
Purifier II	33%	25%	23%
CleanDrink SP	55%	45%	43%

Notice in particular:

List items
are bulleted,
"Formatting
Lists," p. 144

- We keep gaining market share!
- The competition keeps losing market share!
- If this keeps up, we are headed for glory!

Look at us go!

03/02/94   1

Chart is created from table data,
"Creating a Chart from a Word
Table," p. 290

Chart is enhanced with a formatted legend, gridlines,
borders, a shadow, an arrow, and text, "Customizing
a Chart," p. 292

Part I
Creating and Editing Basic Documents

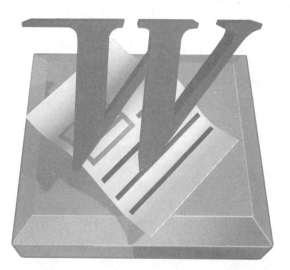

Learning the Basics

Word 6 for Windows is a powerful word processing program that you can use to create many different kinds of documents. This lesson covers the basics of getting started with Word 6 for Windows, including how to start the program, how to use the Word for Windows screen, and how to get help.

In addition, this lesson provides an overview of Word's features, and information on how to use them. Before you begin this lesson, you should already have installed Word 6 on your computer system. If you need information on installing Word, turn to Appendix A.

In this lesson, you learn to do the following:

- Start Word

- Identify the different parts of the Word screen

- Use menus, toolbars, and dialog boxes

- Get Help

- Exit Word

Introducing Word 6 for Windows

Word 6 for Windows is a word processing program you can use to create many different types of documents. With Word 6, you easily can enhance text with underlined, boldface, or italic type and check a document for spelling errors. You also can create complex documents using more sophisticated features such as outlining, annotations, charting, tables, and integrated text and graphics.

Although some of Word's more complicated features are beyond the scope of this book, in the following lessons, you will find information on using most of the tools available in Word 6 for Windows.

The following list explains just some of the Word 6 for Window's features:

- Word is a WYSIWYG (What You See Is What You Get) word processing program, which means it displays documents on-screen the same way it prints them on a page.

- Word comes with templates that you can use to create documents.

- You can automate repetitive tasks by using macros, AutoText, AutoFormat, and Wizards.

- All the tools you need to create and format documents of all types can be displayed on-screen while you work, or remain hidden until you need them. You quickly can access commands using your choice of menus or toolbar buttons.

- Context-sensitive help is available everywhere in the program.

- You can format characters in different fonts and sizes. You also can dress up characters with underlining, boldface, or italic emphasis.

- Word takes advantage of the convenience of a mouse, so that you can select commands and manipulate text and graphics by using simple click and drag techniques.

- Word comes with a spelling checker, a thesaurus, and a grammar checker so that you can ensure that your document meets the highest standards of quality.

- You can add captions, notes, footnotes, and end notes to documents.

- You can generate tables of contents, indexes, and outlines.

- You can create forms to be printed and forms to be completed on-screen.

- You can customize the way documents appear on-screen.

- You can use mail merge to generate form letters, envelopes, and labels.

- You can create professional-looking documents that include newspaper-style columns, tables, charts, pictures, and clip art.

- You can integrate Word for Windows data with data from other Windows applications, including the Microsoft Office series of integrated software application products.

Task: Starting Word for Windows

Word 6 must run in the Windows operating environment.

Note: *During installation, Word 6 for Windows is by default installed in the Microsoft Office program group.*

To start Word from the Windows Program Manager, follow these steps:

1. Double-click the Microsoft Office group icon to open the Microsoft Office program group window.

2. Double-click the Microsoft Word program icon. Word starts and you see the Word screen.

If you have problems... If nothing happens, you may not be double-clicking fast enough. Try again, and be sure to press the mouse button twice, firmly and quickly.

Understanding the Word 6 Screen

When you start Word, the Word screen appears. By default, a Tip of the Day dialog box appears, as well. To remove it from the screen, choose OK.

The Tip of the Day
dialog box provides
information about
using Word 6.

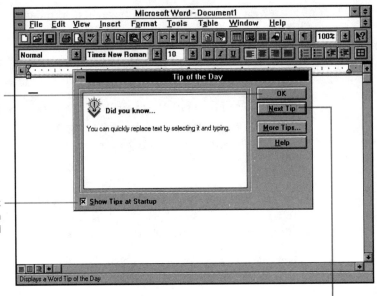

Choose OK to clear the
tip from the screen

Deselect this check box
to *not* display a tip each
time you start Word

Choose to display another tip here

If you have problems...	If you do not want Word to display the Tip of the Day each time you start the program, deselect the **S**how Tips at Startup check box in the Tip of the Day dialog box. You can view the tips at any time by choosing **H**elp, Ti**p** of the Day.

When you close the Tip of the Day dialog box, you see a new, blank
document called Document1 open in the Windows screen. You can
customize the Word screen to display the components you need.

Maximized
Enlarged to fill the
entire screen.

The *title bar* appears at the top of the Word 6 window. It displays the
name of the application—Microsoft Word. If the document is *maximized*,
the title bar also shows the name of the *active document*. If the document
is not maximized, it has its own title bar which shows the document
name.

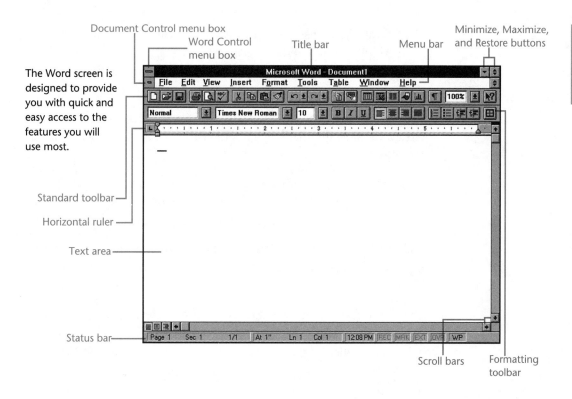

Document Control menu box

Word Control
menu box

Title bar

Menu bar

Minimize, Maximize,
and Restore buttons

1

The Word screen is
designed to provide
you with quick and
easy access to the
features you will
use most.

Standard toolbar

Horizontal ruler

Text area

Status bar

Scroll bars

Formatting
toolbar

There are two *Control menus*: one for Word and one for the document.
The Word Control menu button is at the left end of the title bar, in the
top left corner of the screen. The document Control menu button is at
the left end of the menu bar.

**Active
document**
The document in
which the insertion
point is currently
located.

To display a Control menu, click the Control menu button. You can use
the Control menu commands to control the size of the window, to close
the window, and to switch to another window.

The *menu bar* shows the names of the Word menus. When you choose
a menu name, a menu drops down, displaying a list of commands. If
a command is dimmed, it means it is not available.

The default Word screen displays both the *Standard* toolbar and the *Formatting* toolbar. The Standard toolbar contains buttons you can use to execute Word commands quickly. The Formatting toolbar contains buttons you can use to format characters and paragraphs quickly.

You can customize toolbars, and choose other toolbars to display on-screen. For more information about toolbars, see Lesson 8, "Customizing Word for Windows."

The *horizontal ruler* appears across the top of the text area. You use it to set margins, indents, and column widths. For more information on using the ruler, see Lesson 6, "Dressing Up Your Paragraphs."

The bottom line of the window is the *status bar*. The status bar is divided into sections, all of which display information about the current Word session.

The first section, at the far left, displays information about the current page, action, or toolbar button. The next section displays information about the position of the insertion point within the document. Next, the status bar displays the current time, and last, the status bar displays five buttons:

- ■ REC starts the macro recorder. For more information, see Lesson 9, "Making Your Work Easier."

- ■ MRK turns on revision marks. For more information, see Lesson 16, "Managing Your Documents and Files."

- ■ EXT is used for extending selections. For more information, see Lesson 3, "Revising a Document."

- ■ OVR turns on overtype mode. For more information, see Lesson 2, "Creating a Document."

- ■ WP turns on help messages designed for people who are used to the WordPerfect word processing application.

Task: Choosing Items

In Word you accomplish tasks by choosing items from menus, selecting buttons, and by filling out dialog boxes. With all three, the easiest method of making choices is by using the mouse. Some commands, however, you can execute quickly by using keyboard shortcuts.

Using Menus

To use a menu, point at the menu name and click. To select a command from a menu, point at the command and click. Command names that are dimmed on a menu cannot be selected. Command names that are followed by an ellipsis (...) require additional information in order to execute. When you select an item with an ellipsis, a dialog box appears.

If keyboard shortcuts are available, they are listed on the menu to the right of the command. Press and hold Ctrl and press the letter that is shown, such as Ctrl and F for the Find command.

Dimmed items cannot be selected

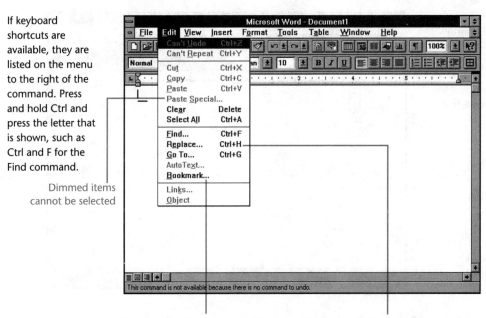

An ellipsis indicates that a dialog box will follow   Keyboard shortcut

To close a menu without making a choice, click outside the menu area, or press Esc.

Using Buttons

In Word, many commands can be executed quickly by choosing *buttons* that appear on-screen. Most buttons appear on toolbars, but some appear at other locations, including the status bar and the scroll bars.

Some buttons provide direct access to a command, while some drop down lists from which you can make a choice. To select a button, point at it and click. If a drop down list appears, point at the item you want and click.

When you point to a button on a toolbar, a *ToolTip* appears displaying the button's name, and a description of the button appears in the status bar.

ToolTip
A small box that displays the name of the button that the mouse pointer is touching.

To find out the name of a button, point at it to display a ToolTip. Look at the status bar to see a description of the button's function.

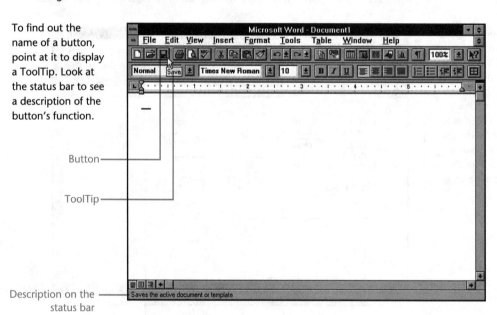

Button

ToolTip

Description on the status bar

Note: *To take advantage of Word's buttons, you must use the mouse. You cannot choose a button from the keyboard.*

Using Dialog Boxes

Many Word commands require additional information before they can be accomplished. You enter that information by using *dialog boxes*.

Each dialog box is different and may contain any or all of the following items:

■ A *list box* displays a list of options from which you select an item.

■ An *option button* is a small round button you use to choose an item from a group of options. A blank dot in an option button indicates that the option is selected.

■ A *check box* is a small square box you use to select an option. An x in the check box indicates that the option is selected.

■ A *text box* is a rectangular box in which you can enter text. Some text boxes have drop-down arrows beside them. Choose the arrow to drop down a list of choices, and then select an item to enter in the text box.

■ A *command button* is a button that executes the command or performs an action. If the name on a command button is followed by an ellipsis (...), that button opens another dialog box.

■ *Selection tabs* appear at the top of the dialog box when there is more than one topic that may require information. Click a tab to display the options for that topic.

■ *Preview boxes* display samples of what your document will look like using the options currently selected in the dialog box.

In dialog boxes, you use many devices to enter information that Word needs to execute commands.

Selection tabs

List box

Drop-down list box

Check boxes

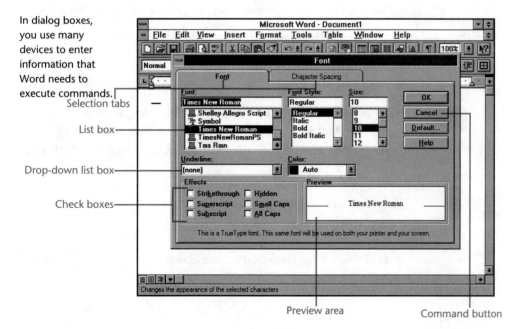

Preview area

Command button

To move among options in a dialog box, use the mouse, or press Tab. To select an option, click it, or press Alt+ the underlined letter. To execute the command, choose OK or press Enter. To clear a dialog box from the screen without executing the command, choose Cancel, or press Esc.

Task: Getting Help

Word comes with extensive on-line, context-sensitive help, which means that you can display help at any time about any topic. In Word, Help actually is a separate program you can access in the following three ways:

- By using general Help to find a Help topic

- By using context-sensitive Help

- By using the Help pointer

The Help menu provides a gateway into the Help program. You can choose one of the commands which starts the Help program and displays a list of topics, or you can choose to view examples and demos, run a short preview about using Word, or display tips.

You also can display help about the current action or screen without going through the Help menu by using one of the following methods:

- To start the Help program and display context-sensitive help information, press F1.

- If a dialog box appears, click the Help command button.

 - To get help before making a choice or executing a command, click the Help button on the Standard toolbar (which changes the pointer shape), and then click the area of the screen for which you want to display help.

To close the Help window, do one of the following:

- Choose File, Exit in the Help window

- Double-click the Help Control menu box

- Choose Close, if a Close button is available

Task: **Finding a Help Topic**

If you need general help about using Word, or if you are not sure exactly what kind of help you need, you can use one of the following methods to locate a specific topic:

- The Help table of contents

- The Help index

- Search

Using the Help Table of Contents

To display the table of contents, choose **H**elp, **C**ontents.

From the Help table of contents, you can select a general subject area which leads to more detailed information.

Choose a general help subject here

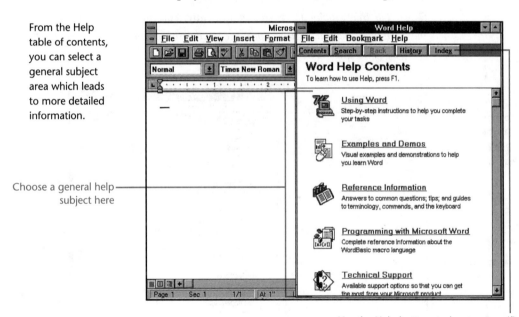

Use the Help buttons to locate a specific topic

Note: *You quickly can display information about any underlined topic simply by pointing at it and clicking. When you point at it, the pointer changes to a hand with an extended index finger, indicating that additional information is available.*

Using the Help Index

If you have an idea about the topic for which you need help, you can use the *Help index*. The index contains listings for every topic on which help is available. Simply locate the topic in the index and choose it to display the Help information.

To use the Help index, follow these steps:

1. Choose **H**elp, **I**ndex.

2. Choose the topic.

3. If necessary, choose a topic from the next window that opens to display the help information.

Note: *The index topics are listed alphabetically. You can use the scroll bars to move through the index listings, or you can click one of the letters at the top of the window to quickly move to that part of the index.*

Click a letter at the top of the Help index to scroll quickly to the topics that begin with that letter.

Choose a topic here

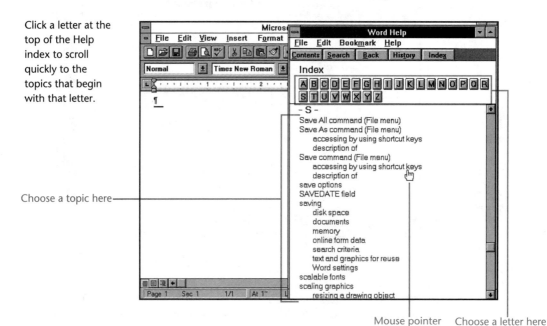

Mouse pointer   Choose a letter here

If you have problems...

Not all of topics in the index lead directly to additional help information. When you point at the topic, if the pointer changes shape to look like a hand, it means that help is available. If the pointer does not change shape, you must choose a different topic.

Searching for a Help Topic

To search for help on a particular topic, follow these steps:

1. Choose **H**elp, **S**earch for Help on.

   Note: *To begin a Help search quickly, double-click the Help button.*

In the Search dialog box, you can find a specific help topic by searching through the index topics.

Choose Close to cancel the search

Enter a general topic here

Select a specific topic here

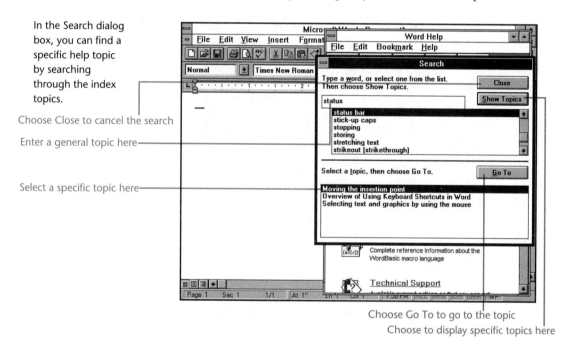

Choose Go To to go to the topic

Choose to display specific topics here

2. Enter a general topic in the text box at the top of the dialog box. You can choose one from the list or type it yourself.

3. Choose **S**how Topics. Word displays a list of specific topics in the bottom half of the dialog box.

4. Choose a specific topic.

5. Choose **G**o To. Word displays the help information.

Note: *You also can begin a search through the Help topics from within the Help program itself. Simply choose the **S**earch button at the top of the Help window to display the Search dialog box.*

Navigating in Help

Once you are in the Help program, you can use many different methods to look up additional topics.

To find additional topics, do one of the following:

- Choose **C**ontents to display the Help table of contents.

- Choose Inde**x** to display the Help index.

- Point at any underlined text (the pointer changes to a pointing hand) and click.

- Choose **S**earch to search for a specific topic.

- Choose His**t**ory to display a list of topics you have accessed.

- Choose **B**ack to display the previous topic you accessed.

Using Help Information

You can keep a Help topic displayed on-screen while you work, you can print a help topic, and you can mark the information so that you can find it quickly in the future.

To print the topic that appears on-screen, choose **F**ile, **P**rint Topic. If a Print button appears at the top of a Help How To window, simply choose it.

Note: *Before printing, make sure that your printer is connected and turned on and that the paper is loaded correctly.*

To mark the current topic for future reference, follow these steps:

1. Choose Book**m**ark, **D**efine.

2. In the **B**ookmark Name text box, enter a name you can use to identify the topic in the future

3. Choose OK.

To quickly display the topic you have marked, choose Bookmark, and then choose the topic name.

To keep a Help topic displayed on your Word screen while you work, choose the On Top button that appears at the top of the Help How To window.

Task: Exiting Word

To exit Word 6 for Windows, choose **F**ile, **E**xit.

If you have made changes to a document, a message box appears asking if you want to save the changes. Choose **Y**es to save the changes and exit. Choose **N**o to exit without saving the changes. Choose Cancel to continue working in Word.

Summary

To	Do This
Start Word	Choose the Microsoft Word program icon from the Microsoft Office program group.
Open a Word menu	Point at the menu name and click.
Choose a Word command	Point at the command name and click.
Use a button	Point at the button icon and click.
Find a Help topic	Choose **H**elp, **I**ndex and then choose a topic.
Get context-sensitive Help	Press F1.
Turn on the Help pointer	Choose the Help button.
Exit Word	Choose **F**ile, **E**xit.

On Your Own

Estimated time: 10 minutes

1. Start Word.

2. Display Help on using menus.

3. Print the Help information.

4. Search for help on exiting Word.

5. Mark the Help topic.

6. Return to the Word screen.

7. Use the Help pointer to display information about the status bar.

8. Go to the Help topic you marked.

9. Exit Word.

Lesson 2

Creating a Document

With Word, you can create many different types of documents, from simple memos to long, complex reports. In this lesson, you learn to create a new document by choosing a template and typing text. You also learn how to change the way the document appears on your screen, how to save the document for future use, to print it, and to close it.

In this lesson, you learn how to perform the following tasks:

- Open a new document

- Type text in the document

- Change the document display

- Save the document

- Print the document

- Close the document

Understanding Templates

In Lesson 1, "Learning the Basics," you learned that when you start Word, a blank document titled Document1 appears on-screen.

If you plan to create a simple document with no particular formatting requirements, you can begin typing in Document1 right away. If you know that you are creating a business letter, a memo, a FAX, or other

Document template
An existing file that contains predefined settings for such formatting features as fonts, margins, tabs, and line spacing, as well as text that will be included in all documents created using the template.

kind of document clearly defined by page layout, however, use the File, New command to open a new document based on a specific *document template.*

Word comes with many templates you can use to create common documents. By using a template to create a new document, you do not need to spend time setting up page layout, formatting characters and paragraphs, or typing standard text.

Note: *You also can use automated templates, called* Wizards, *to create documents. To learn how to use Wizards, see Lesson 9, "Making Your Work Easier."*

When you open a new document, you select the template closest to the type of document you want to create. This selection makes formatting even sophisticated documents easy.

Style
A collection of settings you can apply to text or paragraphs for quick formatting.

When you select a document template, Word applies automatically the predefined page layout settings, such as margins and tab stops. As you type into the document, you easily can select from the template's built-in *styles* to embellish your text with different fonts, font sizes, alignment, and spacing.

Each Word document is based on a template. When you start Word, Document1 is based on the NORMAL template.

The NORMAL template provides basic page layout settings and styles you can use for a variety of simple documents.

Heading 1
Heading 2
Normal text
Heading 3

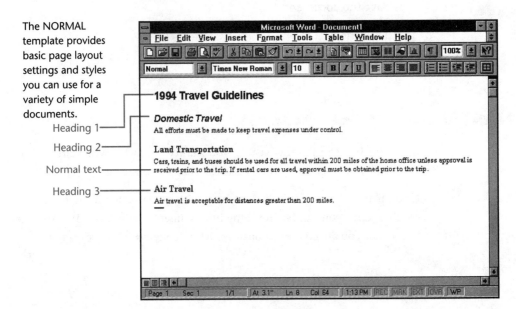

In addition to formatting settings, many templates include text. Some of the text, such as the date, or a salutation, is supposed to remain in the document. Some of the text tells you the information you should enter in a particular place; you type your own text over it.

Note: *You can change the predefined settings and text in a template, or create a new template to suit your own requirements. For more information, see Lesson 8, "Customizing Word for Windows."*

Task: Opening a New Document

Word always starts with Document1 open on-screen. If you want to create a document that uses a template other than NORMAL, or if you typed in Document1 and want to start a new document, you must choose the **F**ile, **N**ew command. To open a new document, follow these steps:

1. Choose **F**ile, **N**ew. The New dialog box appears.

If you have problems...

If you choose the New file button on the Standard toolbar, the New dialog box does not appear. Word automatically creates a new document using the current default template, NORMAL. To create a document using a different template, choose **F**ile, **N**ew to display the New dialog box.

In the New dialog box, choose a template to use for opening a new document.

Select a template here

View a description of the template here

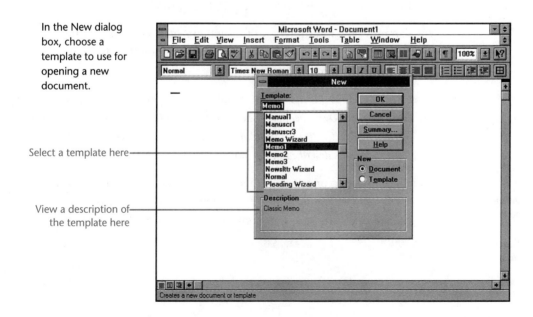

2. From the list of templates, choose the one you want to use. Here, a template for creating a memo is selected.

   Note: *Do not choose a Wizard at this time. To learn how to use Wizards, see Lesson 9, "Making Your Work Easier."*

3. In the New area, choose **D**ocument to create a new document. To learn about creating a new template, see Lesson 8, "Customizing Word for Windows."

4. Choose OK to open a new document based on the highlighted template. The document opens on-screen.

Note: *If you type in Document1, and then open a new document, Word names the new document Document2. Each new document is numbered sequentially. The number of documents you can open is limited only by the amount of memory in your computer.*

Task: Typing in the Document

Insertion Point
A flashing bar in the document window that indicates where text will appear when you type.

When you type, characters appear to the left of a flashing bar, called the *insertion point.* They are formatted according to the styles associated with the document template. To see the name of the current style, look in the Style box on the Formatting toolbar. For information on changing styles, see the section "Selecting Styles," later in this lesson.

You can move the insertion point throughout the document by using the keyboard or the mouse. This way, you can position the insertion point where you want to edit or enter text.

Note: *If you selected a template that includes text, the text appears on-screen. Use Backspace and Overtype mode—explained later in this section—to replace the instructional text with your own information. Move the insertion point using the techniques described in the following section.*

Word Wrap
The way text moves down to the beginning of the next line when the current line is filled.

You do not need to press Enter when you reach the end of a line. Word has *word wrap*, which means text is automatically moved to the beginning of the next line. Press Enter only when you are ready to start a new paragraph.

If you notice a mistake such as a typing error, press Backspace to delete the character to the left of the insertion point. Press Backspace until you delete the mistake, and then type the correct text. (Other ways to correct mistakes are covered in Lesson 3, "Revising a Document.")

Text appears to the left of the insertion point. On the Formatting toolbar, the names of the current style, font, and font size, appear from left to right.

Style name

Font name

Font size

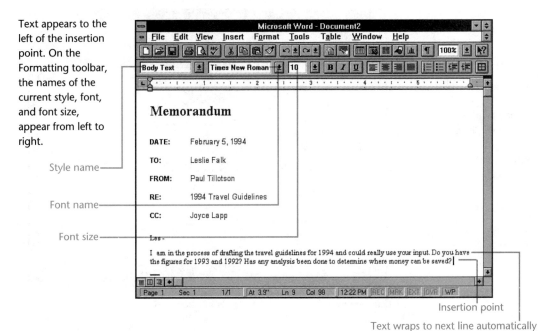

Insertion point

Text wraps to next line automatically

If you have problems...

If characters appear in uppercase when you want them in lowercase, and in lowercase when you want them in uppercase, you pressed the Caps Lock key on your keyboard. Press the key again to turn off the Caps Lock indicator and resume typing.

Moving the Insertion Point with the Mouse

To move the insertion point with the mouse, position the mouse pointer where you want to place the insertion point and click.

To position the insertion point in a part of the document that does not appear on the current screen:

1. Click the scroll arrows on the scroll bars until the part of the document you want appears.

2. Position the mouse pointer where you want to place the insertion point.

3. Click to move the insertion point.

You must click the mouse button at the new location to move the insertion point. Here, the mouse pointer is at the new location, but the insertion point is not. If you start typing, text appears back at the insertion point.

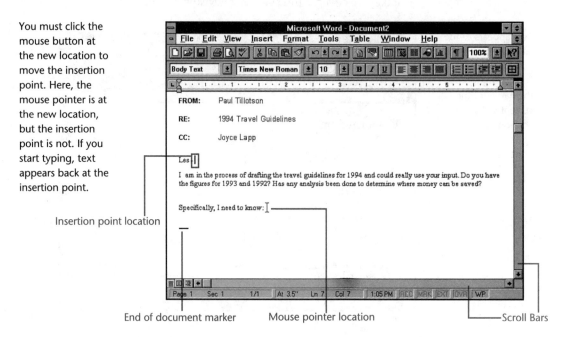

Insertion point location

End of document marker   Mouse pointer location   Scroll Bars

Note: *You cannot move the insertion point into the screen area past the end of the document. The end of the document is marked by a short horizontal bar.*

Moving the Insertion Point with the Keyboard

To move the insertion point with the keyboard, use the direction keys. To move left, for example, press ←; to move right, press the →. To move quickly, use the keystrokes described in Table 2.1.

Table 2.1 Common Keystrokes for Moving the Insertion Point	
Key or Key Combination	**Effect**
Ctrl+←	Moves one word to the left
Ctrl+→	Moves one word to the right
Home	Moves to the beginning of the line
End	Moves to the end of the line

Key or Key Combination	Effect
PgUp	Moves up one screen
PgDn	Moves down one screen
Ctrl+Home	Moves to the beginning of the document
Ctrl+End	Moves to the end of the document

2

Note: *To return quickly to one of the three most recent insertion point locations, press Shift+F5 once, twice, or three times.*

If you have problems...

If the cursor does not move the way it is supposed to—for example, if you press Ctrl+Home and a Go To dialog box opens on your screen—you may have Help for WordPerfect Users turned on. To turn it off, choose **H**elp, **W**ordPerfect Help. Choose **O**ptions, and deselect both the Help for **W**ordPerfect Users and the **N**avigation keys for WordPerfect users check boxes.

Inserting and Typing Over Text

Insert mode
A setting that tells Word to insert new text to the left of the insertion point, pushing existing text to the right.

By default, Word enters text in *Insert mode*, which means that text is inserted in the document to the left of the insertion point. If the insertion point is in the middle of a sentence, text is inserted in the middle of the sentence. The existing text moves to the right.

If you change to *Overtype mode*, the text you type replaces text to the right of the insertion point.

Overtype mode
A setting that tells Word to replace existing text as you type.

You use Insert mode when you want to add text in the middle of existing text. Also, when you type in Insert mode, you cannot accidentally type over text you want to keep. Overtype mode is used when you want to replace existing text with new text.

Look at the status bar to see if you are typing in Insert mode or Overtype mode. If OVR is dimmed, Word is in Insert mode. If OVR is black, Word is in Overtype mode. To change from one mode to the other, press Insert on your keyboard, or double-click OVR on the status bar.

If the letters OVR are black, you are in Overtype mode.

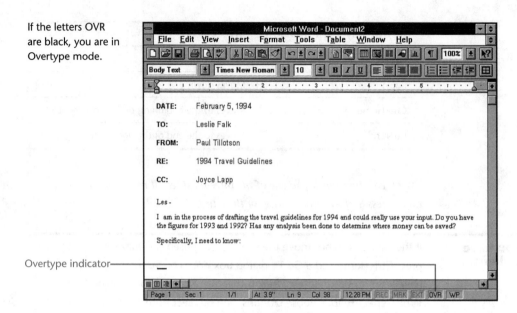

Overtype indicator

Task: Selecting Styles

Style Sheet
A collection of associated styles stored with a document template.

As you learned earlier in this lesson, you use styles to quickly apply formatting settings to text and paragraphs. Each template comes with a *style sheet* that includes the styles typically used to create the type of document associated with the template. Most templates, for example, come with styles that can be used to format different levels of headings, and different types of lists. All templates come with a Body Text style to use for entering basic text paragraphs.

When you want text or paragraphs to have a different look, you can select a different style to use for typing new text.

To select a style, you use the Style list.

Style box

Style list

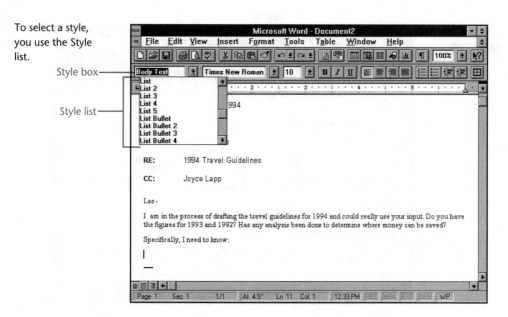

To select a style, follow these steps:

1. Position the insertion point where you want the text in the new style to begin. If necessary, press Enter to begin a new paragraph.

2. Click the drop-down arrow next to the Style box on the Formatting toolbar to display the Style list.

3. Click the style name in the Style list.

When you type, the characters appear formatted according to the selected style—in this case, the List Bullet style.

Message Head style

Body Text style

List Bullet style

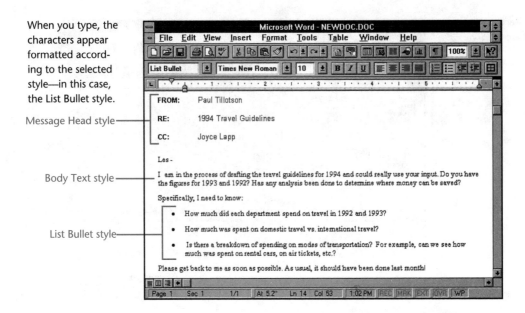

Note: *In documents you create using a template that includes text, the text already is assigned styles. To see the paragraph's style, position the insertion point within the paragraph, and look at the Style box on the Formatting toolbar. Text you insert within that paragraph appears formatted according to the current style. To enter text in a different style, choose the style you want from the Style list.*

Task: Saving the Document

Word has three commands for saving a document. You use File, Save to save any document; you use File, Save As to save a document with a new name; you use File, Save All to save all open documents.

Note: *To save a new document, you can use any of the Save commands. If the document has never been saved, Word displays the Save As dialog box.*

Saving a New Document or a Document with a New Name

With the File, Save As command, you not only save the document to disk, you also give the file a name and specify the drive and directory path where you want to store the document. Use File, Save As to save a new document or to save a copy of an existing document with a different name or path.

To save a new document, follow these steps:

1. Choose **F**ile, Save **A**s. The Save As dialog box appears on-screen.

In the Save As dialog box, you give a document a name and specify where on disk you want the document stored.

Type the file name here

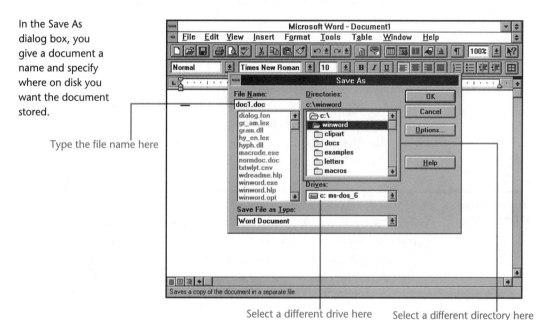

Select a different drive here   Select a different directory here

2. In the File **N**ame text box, type a name for the document, following DOS naming conventions. The name can be up to eight characters; Word assigns the extension .DOC when the document is saved.

Note: *If the document already has a name, it appears in the File **N**ame text box. If you are saving an unnamed document for the first time, Word enters a name based on the number in the title bar. If you are saving Document1, for example, DOC1.DOC appears. To type over the existing text, just type. To insert text to the left of or within the existing text, position the insertion point before you type.*

3. Make the changes you want to the directory or drive in which the file will be saved. If you make no changes, the file is saved in the default document location directory, usually \WINWORD on drive C:.

Note: *To avoid cluttering your \WINWORD directory, you should not store documents there. Create a subdirectory where you can store all Word documents, such as \WINWORD\WINDOCS. You then can choose it in the Directories list in the Save As dialog box, or you modify the location of the default document directory by using the **T**ools, **Op**tions, File Locations command. For information on changing the default document directory, see Lesson 8, "Customizing Word for Windows."*

4. Choose OK. Word saves the file in the specified drive and directory. The document remains on-screen so that you can continue working. Notice that the document name now appears in the Title Bar at the top of the screen.

If you have problems...   If Word displays a message asking whether you want to replace the existing file, it means that a file saved with the name you entered in the File Name text box already exists. Choose **Y**es, to save the new file over the old file— you cannot recover the old file! Choose **N**o to return to Save As dialog box. Type a different name in the File **N**ame text box, and then choose OK.

Saving a Document Again

After you save a document once, you quickly can save this document over and over with the same name, directory, format and other specifications without going through the Save As dialog box each time.

 To save the file again if you don't want to change anything in the Save As dialog box choose **F**ile, **S**ave.

The file you save overwrites the old version on the disk so any changes you made since the last time you saved replaces the previous version of the stored file. The document still appears on-screen so you can continue to edit.

Note: Save a document often! Until you save, your work is stored only in memory. If you lose power, you lose work. Develop the habit of saving at regular intervals, or use Word's automatic saving option to save files. Automatic Save is covered in Lesson 8, "Customizing Word for Windows."

2

If you have problems...

You want to save the document with the same name and file specifications, but you accidentally selected **F**ile, Save **A**s and the Save As dialog box appears. Just choose Cancel to remove the dialog box, and then choose **F**ile, **S**ave.

Saving All Open Documents

When you have more than one document open at a time, choose **F**ile, Save All to quickly save them all.

Words saves all of the files that have been saved before using the same file name and directory location. If a file has not been saved before, Word displays the Save As dialog box, so that you can enter a file name and directory location.

Task: Viewing the Document Before Printing

By default, Word displays a document on-screen in Normal view. You can see character and paragraph formatting, but you cannot see exactly the way the page will look when it is printed. To see how a document will look when it is printed, you can change to Print Preview.

 To change to Print Preview, choose **F**ile, Print Pre**v**iew.

Print Preview toolbar   Zoom Control text box.

In Print Preview, Word displays the document as it will print. You can print the document, or edit the document before printing.

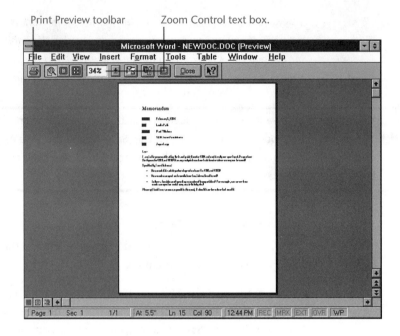

In Print Preview, Word adjusts the image so that complete pages can fit on-screen. You might not be able to see individual characters, but you can see the overall layout and positioning of the components of the document.

You can adjust the way the document appears in Print Preview by changing the magnification percentage or by using the buttons on the Print Preview toolbar. To adjust the magnification, click the drop-down arrow next to the Zoom Control text box, and choose a different magnification percentage. Choose Page Width, for example, to automatically adjust the magnification percentage to display the complete width of the page.

Table 2.2 describes the Print Preview buttons and their functions.

Table 2.2 Print Preview Toolbar Buttons	
Button	**Effect**
	Prints the current document.
	Toggles the mouse pointer to a magnifying glass, which you can use to display any part of the document on-screen at 100% magnification.
	Displays only the page on which the insertion point is located.
	Enables you to drag the mouse pointer to select the number of pages you want displayed.
	Displays the horizontal and vertical rulers on-screen.
	Reduces the amount of space between characters and lines so that the document fits on one less page.
	Expands the view to fill the full screen.
Close	Returns to Normal view.
	Toggles the mouse pointer to the Help pointer.

To exit Print Preview, choose **C**lose.

In Lesson 7, "Setting Up Your Pages," you will learn about other ways to change the document display.

Task: Printing Your Document

After you create a document, you can print it. Before printing, make sure that your printer is connected to the computer, turned on, and loaded with paper.

To print the document displayed on-screen, follow these steps:

1. Choose **F**ile, **P**rint. The Print dialog box appears.

In the Print dialog box, you specify print options such as how many copies and which pages you want to print.

Specify a page range here ———

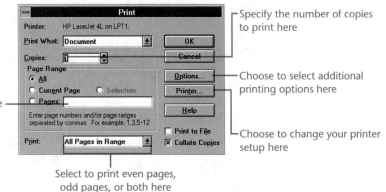

Specify the number of copies to print here

Choose to select additional printing options here

Choose to change your printer setup here

Select to print even pages, odd pages, or both here

2. Make all needed changes to the number of copies, what range to print, and which pages to include. Choose the **O**ptions button to select additional printing options, or the Prin**t**er button to select printer options.

3. Choose OK to print the document. Word prints the document.

If you have problems...   If the document doesn't print, make sure that the printer is loaded with paper and correctly connected to the computer. Then try printing again.

Task: Closing Your Document

Closing a document clears it from both the screen and the computer's memory. If too many documents are open simultaneously, you may notice Word runs more slowly. Too many documents also may leave you with insufficient memory to open another document, so saving and closing files you aren't working on is a good idea.

To close the current document, choose **F**ile, **C**lose.

If you haven't saved the document, or if you made changes to the document since the last time you saved it, Word displays a message box asking if you want to save the changes now. Take one of the following actions:

- Choose **Y**es to save the document and clear it from the screen. If the document is new, the Save As dialog box appears.

- Choose **N**o to clear the document from the screen without saving the changes.

- Choose Cancel to continue working with the document.

When Word closes the current document, it displays another open document. If no other documents are open, Word displays a blank application screen.

To close all open documents, exit Word. For each document you have not yet saved, a message box appears that prompts you to save the changes.

Summary

To	Do This
Open a new document	Choose **F**ile, **N**ew. In the New dialog box, choose a template. Choose OK.
Change from Insert to Overtype mode	Press Insert or click the Overtype indicator on the status bar.
Move the insertion point with the mouse	Position the mouse pointer and click.
Move the insertion with the keyboard	Press the arrow keys or Page Up and Page Down. Use the Ctrl key combinations.
Select a Style	Open the Style list and choose the style.
Save a new document	Choose **F**ile, Save **A**s. In the Save As dialog box, enter a document name, and then choose OK.
View the document before printing	Choose **F**ile, Print Preview.

To	Do This
Print your document	Choose **File**, **P**rint. In the Print dialog box, choose OK.
Close your document	Choose **File**, **C**lose.

On Your Own
Estimated time: 25 minutes

Create a document.

1. Start Word if it is not already running.

2. Create a new document, using the MEMO1 template.

Enter and save the document.

1. Replace the template text with the memo information.

2. In the body of the memo, type a paragraph in a different style.

3. Change back to the Body Text style and type a closing paragraph.

4. Save the document.

Print and close the document.

1. Change the view to see how the document will look when printed.

2. Print the document.

3. Close the document.

Lesson 3

Revising a Document

One advantage to creating a document with a word processor rather than on a typewriter is that you can make changes without retyping everything. In this lesson you learn how to use Word to open and revise a document you have already created and saved.

Specifically, you learn to do the following:

- Open an existing document

- Start a new line

- Insert today's date

- Select, move, and copy text

- Change the style of existing text

- Correct mistakes

- Work with more than one document at a time

Task: Opening an Existing Document

To revise a document that has been closed, you must first open it on-screen.

To open an existing document, follow these steps:

 1. Choose **F**ile, **O**pen.

In the Open dialog box, the File Name list shows all files in the current directory that have names with the .DOC extension.

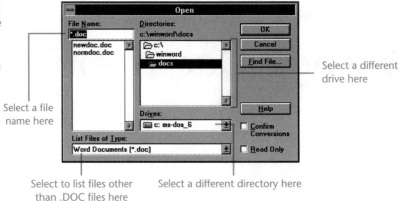

Select a file name here

Select a different drive here

Select to list files other than .DOC files here

Select a different directory here

2. In the File **N**ame text box, type the name of the document you want to open, or select the document name from the File **N**ame list.

3. Choose OK.

Note: *To open the document quickly, double-click the document name in the File* **N***ame list.*

If you have problems...

If the document you want to open is not in the File **N**ame list, it might be stored in a different directory, on a different drive, or it might not have a .DOC extension. See the following section for information on opening a document from a different drive or directory. See Lesson 17, "Working with Other Windows Applications," for information on opening files of a different type.

If you do not know where the file you want to open is stored, or even what name it has, you can use **F**ind File to locate it. For information on finding files, see Lesson 16, "Managing Your Documents and Files."

Opening a Document from a Different Drive or Directory

To open a file from a different drive or directory, follow these steps:

1. Choose **F**ile, **O**pen. The Open dialog box appears.

2. From the Dri**v**es drop-down list, select the drive in which your file is stored.

3. In the **D**irectories list box, double-click the directory that contains the file you want to open.

4. In the File **N**ame list box, double-click the name of the file you want to open.

If you have problems...

If the document you want to open does not appear in the File **N**ames list box, you may have opened the correct directory, but not the correct subdirectory. Try double-clicking the directory name to display a list of subdirectories. Then, choose the subdirectory name.

If Word displays a message telling you that the selected disk drive is not valid, you probably forgot to insert a disk. Insert a non-write protected disk and choose **R**etry.

Opening a Document from the File Menu

Word keeps track of the last four documents you open, and lists them at the bottom of the **F**ile menu. To open one of these documents, simply choose **F**ile, and then choose the document name.

To open a document from the **F**ile menu, just click the document name.

File names

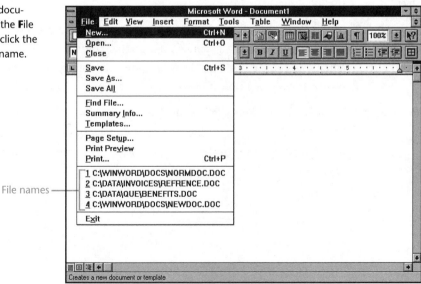

Task: Starting a New Line

In Lesson 2, "Creating a Document," you learned that Word wraps text from one line to the next as you type. Sometimes, however, you will want to start a new line. You can start a new line in the following two ways:

Line break
Starting a new line without starting a new paragraph. In Word, a line break is sometimes called a *soft return*.

- Start a new paragraph

- Insert a *line break* within a paragraph

To start a new paragraph, simply press Enter. Word inserts a *paragraph mark*, and moves the insertion point to the beginning of the next line.

Note: *To see paragraph marks on-screen, choose **T**ools, **O**ptions. Click the View tab to display the View options, and then choose Paragraph **M**arks in the Nonprinting characters area. Choose OK to return to the document. For more information about paragraph marks, see Lesson 6, "Dressing Up Your Paragraphs."*

Paragraph mark
A non-printing symbol Word inserts each time you start a new paragraph by pressing Enter. Paragraph marks contain information about the current paragraph style.

When you press Enter to start a new line, the amount of blank space left between two paragraphs is determined by the current paragraph formatting or style.

In the NORMAL template, for example, the Normal style is set to leave no space above or below paragraphs, so that there is no blank space left when you press Enter. The Heading 3 style, however, is set to leave 12 *points* above and 3 points below each paragraph.

Point
A unit of measurement commonly used in publishing. 72 points equal one inch.

If you are typing in the Normal style in a document created with the NORMAL template, you must press Enter twice to leave blank space between paragraphs; in the Heading 3 style, you only need to press Enter once.

The paragraph marks indicate that to leave blank space between lines in a Normal style paragraph, Enter was pressed twice. In the Heading 3 style paragraph, Enter was pressed only once.

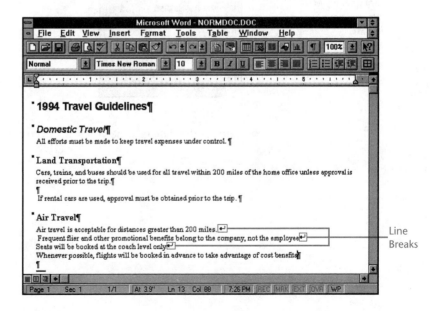

Line breaks are used to start a new line without starting a new paragraph. To insert a line break, follow these steps:

1. Position the insertion point at the end of the previous line.

2. Press Shift+Enter. Word inserts a line break rather than a paragraph mark.

With a line break, the insertion point jumps to the beginning of the next line, but Word does not start a new paragraph. No blank space is left between the lines.

Note: To quickly insert a blank line before the current paragraph, press Ctrl+0. Word inserts the blank line without inserting a paragraph mark. To remove the blank line, press Ctrl+0 again. For more information about line spacing, see Lesson 6, "Dressing Up Your Paragraphs."

Task: Inserting the Date and Time

Word keeps track of the current date and time by using your computer system clock and calendar. You automatically can insert the date or time into your document, in a variety of formats. This is useful for keeping track of when you make certain changes, or just to avoid typing the date over and over.

To insert the date or time into your document, follow these steps:

1. Position the insertion point where you want the information to appear. If necessary, use one of the preceding methods to start a new line.

2. Choose **I**nsert, Date and **T**ime.

In the Date and Time dialog box, you can choose from a variety of date and time formats.

Date and Time

Available Formats:

2/8/94
Tuesday, February 08, 19
8 February, 1994
February 8, 1994
8-Feb-94
February, 94
Feb-94
02/08/94 7:27 PM
02/08/94 7:27:13 PM
7:27 PM
7:27:13 PM
19:27
19:27:13

☐ Insert as Field

OK
Cancel
Help

Choose the format here

3. Choose the date or time you want from the **A**vailable Formats list.

4. Choose OK.

Word inserts the date at the insertion point location.

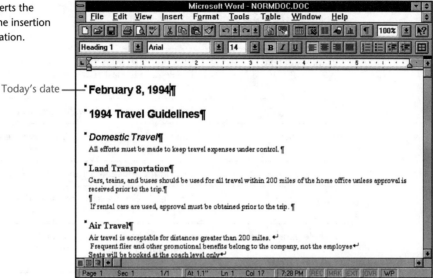

Today's date

If you have problems...

Word inserts the information in the style of the paragraph in which the insertion point was located. If you do not like the style, you can change it. See the section "Changing Styles," later in this lesson for more information.

Task: Selecting Text

Select

Highlight the text you want to change or manipulate.

Selection bar

The area between the left edge of the screen and the left margin.

In Word, you must *select* the text you want to change *before* you can change it. You can select text by using the mouse or the keyboard.

When you select text with the mouse, you often use the *selection bar*. The selection bar is not marked in any way on-screen, but within it, the mouse pointer changes to an arrow pointing up and slightly to the right.

Table 3.1 lists techniques for selecting text with the mouse. To cancel, or deselect, selected text, click anywhere with the mouse.

Table 3.1 Select Text with the Mouse	
To select	**Use the mouse to**
Any block of text	Click and drag from the first character you want to select, to the last character you want to select.
One word	Double-click anywhere within the word.
One sentence	Press and hold Ctrl as you click anywhere within the sentence.
One line	Click in the selection bar to the left of the line.
One paragraph	Double-click in the selection bar to the left of the paragraph.
Multiple paragraphs	Click in the selection bar to left of the first paragraph, and then drag through the selection bar to the last paragraph.
A document	Triple-click in the selection bar.

Selected text always appears highlighted on-screen.

Selection bar

Selected text

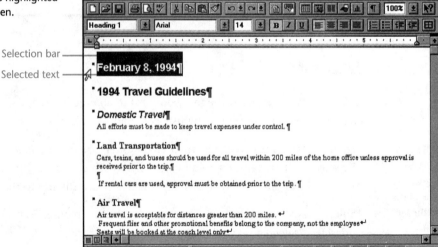

Task: Changing the Style of Existing Text

In Lesson 2 you learned to select a different style before typing text. You also can change the style after the text has been typed.

To change the style of a paragraph, follow these steps:

Caution
No matter whether you select text with the keyboard or the mouse, if you press *any* letter key once text is selected, Word replaces the selected text with the letter you type.

1. Position the insertion point within the existing paragraph.

2. Click the drop-down arrow beside the Style box to display the Style list.

3. Choose the new style. Word changes the paragraph to the selected style.

Note: *To change the style of selected text, select the text before you choose the style.*

3

Task: Correcting Mistakes

We all make mistakes. With Word, it is easy to fix them. Word provides numerous methods for going back and undoing incorrect actions, and then redoing them correctly. Word even gives you the opportunity to correct spelling mistakes before they occur!

Deleting Text

One simple method of correcting mistakes is to erase them. In Lesson 2, "Creating a Document," you learned to press Backspace to delete the characters to the left of the insertion point. Word also offers many other ways to delete text.

Following is a list of some common methods of removing unwanted text:

- To delete the character to the right of the insertion point, press Delete.

- To delete selected text, select the text, and then press Delete.

If you have problems...	If you press Delete to delete the selected text, and Word displays a message in the status bar asking you to confirm the deletion, it means you have Help for WordPerfect Users turned on. Use one of the other methods to delete the text, or do the following to turn off Word Perfect Help. Choose **H**elp, **W**ord-Perfect Help. Choose **O**ptions, and then deselect the Help for **W**ordPerfect Users and **N**avigation Keys for WordPerfect Users check boxes.

    ■ To replace selected text with new text, select the text, and then type the new text.

If you have problems...	If Word does not replace selected text with the characters you type, you may need to change your Editing Options. Choose T**o**ols, **O**ptions, and click the Edit tab to display the Edit Options. Choose the **T**yping Replaces Selection check box, and then choose OK.

Cut
To delete selected data from a document and place it in the Clipboard.

If you are not sure whether deleting the text is the right thing to do, you can *cut* the text to the *Windows Clipboard*. If you cut an item to the Clipboard, you have the option of pasting it back into the document.

To delete an item using the Clipboard, follow these steps:

Windows Clipboard
A storage area that Windows uses to temporarily hold one selection at a time.

1. Select the text.

2. Choose **E**dit, Cu**t**. Word deletes the selection from the document and places it in the Clipboard.

Paste
To copy data from the Clipboard into a document.

Note: *The Clipboard can only hold one item at a time. As soon as you place another selection in the Clipboard, the previous selection is removed.*

Undoing Mistakes

Undo
To cancel the most recent action or series of actions performed with Word.

Word 6 makes it easy for you to change your mind. It remembers the most recent actions you perform, and, if you don't like the results, you can *undo* them in sequence.

To undo the most recent action, choose **E**dit, **U**ndo.

**If you have
problems...**

If you see the words Can't Undo on the menu, it means the last action you
performed cannot be undone.

To undo a series of actions, choose **E**dit, **U**ndo again, until you have
canceled all actions in reverse sequence.

Alternatively, follow these steps:

1. Click the drop-down arrow beside the Undo button on the Standard toolbar. Word displays a list of the most recent actions that
can be undone, in reverse order.

From the Undo
drop-down list, you
can select to undo
one action, or a
series of actions.

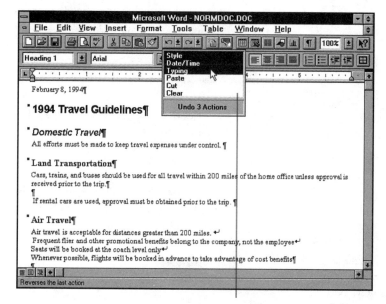

Choose the actions to undo here

2. Drag the mouse down the list until all of the actions you want to
undo are highlighted.

3. Release the mouse button. Word undoes the selected actions, in
reverse order.

Note: You can choose to undo one action from the drop-down list, or a series of actions that does not begin with the most recent action in the list. Remember, however, that one of the actions you undo may effect the remaining actions, causing unexpected results.

Redo
To replace the most recently undone action, or series of actions, performed with Word.

Redoing the Mistakes You Undo

If immediately after you undo an action you decide you were right in the first place, you can *redo* the actions you just undid!

To redo the most recently undone action, choose **E**dit, **R**edo.

If you have problems...

If **R**edo does not appear on the Edit menu, you have not just undone an action. **R**edo is only available *immediately* after you use **U**ndo. If you perform any other action after choosing **U**ndo, you cannot redo the undone action. If **R**edo is not available, **R**epeat appears on the **E**dit menu. You can choose to repeat the last action.

To undo a series of actions, choose **E**dit, **R**edo again, until you have redone all actions in reverse sequence.

Alternatively, follow these steps:

1. Click the drop-down arrow next to the Redo button on the Standard toolbar. Word displays a list of the most recent actions that can be redone, in reverse order.

From the Redo drop-down list, you can select to redo actions that you have undone.

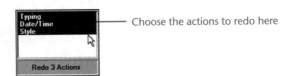 Choose the actions to redo here

2. Drag the mouse down the list until all of the actions you want to redo are highlighted.

3. Release the mouse button. Word redoes the selected actions, in reverse order.

Note: You can choose to redo one action from the drop-down list, or a series of actions that does not begin with the most recent action in the list. Remember, however, that one of the actions you redo may affect the remaining actions, causing unexpected results.

Preventing Spelling Mistakes

You can set Word to automatically detect and correct common spelling mistakes as you type. For example, typing *adn* when you mean to type *and*, or typing *teh* when you mean to type *the*, are very common typos. You can set Word to fix these, and others, automatically!

Word's AutoCorrect feature comes preset to correct some common typing errors, such as those mentioned in the previous paragraph. You can add your own particular typos to the AutoCorrect list.

To add to the AutoCorrect list of words, follow these steps:

3

1. Choose **T**ools, **A**utoCorrect.

In the AutoCorrect dialog box, you can set options and add to the list of words to correct as you type.

Choose options here

Enter incorrectly spelled word here

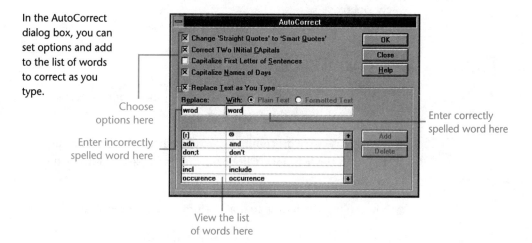

Enter correctly spelled word here

View the list of words here

2. In the **R**eplace text box, type the word spelled incorrectly.

3. In the **W**ith text box, type the word spelled correctly.

4. Choose **A**dd.

Use the other AutoCorrect options as follows:

- ■ To delete a word in the AutoCorrect dialog box, choose it, and then choose **D**elete.

- ■ To edit a word in the AutoCorrect dialog box, choose it, make the changes in the **R**eplace and **W**ith text boxes, and then choose **A**dd.

- To automatically change plain quotation marks to typesetters' quotation marks, choose the Change Straight Quotes to Smart **Q**uotes check box.

- To automatically correct words typed with two initial capital letters, choose the Correct TWo INitial **C**Apitals check box.

- To automatically capitalize the first letter in every sentence, choose the Capitalize First Letter of **S**entence check box.

- To capitalize the names of days automatically, choose the Capitalize **N**ames of Days check box.

- To turn off AutoCorrect, deselect the Replace **T**ext as You Type check box.

Task: Moving Text

With Word, you can move text from its current location to a new location by using one of the three following methods:

- You can use the Edit commands to cut it from its current location, store it in the Windows Clipboard, and then paste it into its new location.

- You can use the mouse to drag it from it current location to its new location.

Moving Text by Using Edit Commands

To move text with the Edit commands, follow these steps:

1. Select the text you want to move.

2. Choose **E**dit, Cu**t**. Word cuts the selected text from the document and places it in the Clipboard.

3. Position the insertion point where you want the text to appear. Remember to click the left mouse button to move the insertion point from its previous location!

4. Choose **E**dit, **P**aste. Word inserts the text at the new location.

Note: *The Clipboard can only hold one selection at a time; when you cut or copy a new selection, the old selection is replaced.*

Moving Text with the Mouse

There are two ways to move text with the mouse: drag and drop editing and the right mouse-button shortcut.

To move text by using drag and drop editing, follow these steps:

1. Select the text you want to move.

2. Position the mouse pointer anywhere within the selected text. The pointer changes to an arrow.

3. Click and hold the left mouse button.

4. Drag the mouse pointer to the new location.

3

As you drag, a small box appears at the bottom of the pointer arrow. A non-flashing dotted gray line indicates the insertion point location.

New text location

Mouse pointer   Selected text

5. Release the mouse button. Word moves the text to the new location.

An alternative method of drag-and-drop editing is the right mouse button shortcut. To use this shortcut, follow these steps:

1. Select the text you want to move.

2. Position the mouse pointer at the new location. *Do not click to move the insertion point!*

3. Press and hold Ctrl and click the right mouse button. Word moves the text to the new location.

Task: Copying Text

Copy
To duplicate selected text.

In Word, you can *copy* text from one location to another location by using the Edit command or the mouse.

Copying Text by Using Commands

To copy text by using commands, follow these steps:

1. Select the text you want to copy.

2. Choose **E**dit, **C**opy. Word copies the selected text from the document to the Clipboard.

   Note: *When you choose Copy from the Edit menu, the selected text does not disappear. It is copied into the Clipboard, but it remains in its original location as well.*

3. Position the insertion point where you want the copied text to appear. Remember to click the left mouse button to move the insertion point from its previous location!

   Note: *When you move the insertion point, the text you selected to copy is no longer highlighted. Don't worry! It is safe in the Clipboard until you cut or copy another selection.*

4. Choose **E**dit, **P**aste. Word copies the text in the new location.

Note: *After you copy text to the Clipboard, you can copy it into your document as many times as you want. Simply continue to reposition the insertion point, and then paste the text at each new location.*

Copying Text with the Mouse

To copy text by using drag-and-drop editing, follow these steps:

1. Select the text you want to copy.

2. Position the mouse pointer anywhere within the selected text. The mouse pointer changes to an arrow.

3. Press and hold Ctrl, and then press and hold the left mouse button.

4. Drag the mouse pointer to the new location.

5. Release the mouse button. Word copies the selected text at the new location.

3

As you drag, a small box appears at the end of the arrow, and a plus sign appears beside the arrow. A non-flashing dotted gray line indicates the insertion point location.

New text location

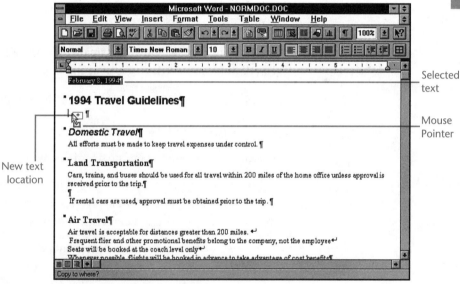

Selected text

Mouse Pointer

To use the right mouse button shortcut, follow these steps:

1. Select the text you want to copy.

2. Position the mouse pointer at the new location. *Do not click* to move the insertion point!

3. Press and hold Ctrl+Shift and click the right mouse button. Word copies the text to the new location.

Task: Working with More than One Document Window

Document window
A rectangular area on-screen where a Word 6 for Windows document appears.

In Word, you can open more than one document at the same time, each in its own document window. Opening multiple documents makes it easy to copy or move text from one to another, or to refer to information in one document while working in another.

Some of the ways you can use multiple document windows include the following:

- You can work with different documents in different full-sized windows.

- You can work with copies of the same document in different full-sized windows.

Pane
A portion of a window.

- You can split one window into smaller parts—called *panes*—that can both be displayed on screen at the same time.

- You can move or copy text from one window or pane to another.

To open more than one document window at a time, follow these steps:

1. Choose **F**ile, **O**pen to open the first document.

2. Without closing the first document, choose **F**ile, **O**pen again to open another document, or **F**ile, **N**ew to create a new document. Word opens the second document window *on top* of the first.

3. Continue opening or creating documents until you have as many open documents as you need, or until you run out of memory.

To close a window, choose **C**lose from the Control menu, or double-click the Control menu box.

Active window
The window in which the insertion point is currently located.

No matter how many windows are open, you can only work in one at a time—the *active window*. By default, the active window is *maximized* to fill the entire screen—all other open windows are hidden behind it.

Maximized
Enlarged to fill the entire screen.

To arrange open windows on screen so that they are not all hidden behind the active window, choose **W**indow, **A**rrange All. Word arranges each open window to fit equally on-screen.

If you have problems...

If you choose **W**indow, **A**rrange All when you have many open documents, each window will be very small. Because it is difficult to work in a very small window, only use **A**rrange All when you have two or three open documents.

Choose **W**indow, **A**rrange All to display all open windows on-screen at the same time.

The active window —

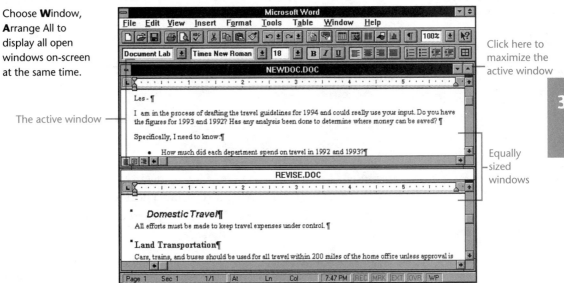

Click here to maximize the active window

Equally sized windows

3

To make a window active, click in it. If you cannot see a portion of the window on-screen, follow these steps:

1. Open the **W**indow menu.

All open documents are listed at the bottom of the Window menu. A check mark appears beside the active window.

Active document —

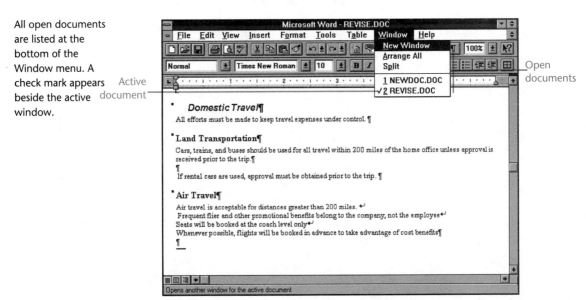

Open documents

2. Choose the document you want to make active. Word makes the selected document active and maximizes it to fill the screen.

If you have problems...   If you have more than one window displayed on-screen, and you close one window, the other windows do not enlarge to fill the empty space. Choose **W**indow, **A**rrange All to automatically adjust the size of the remaining open windows to fill the entire screen.

Task: Copying or Moving Text Between Document Windows

The procedures for copying and moving text between documents are the same as for copying and moving text within a document. You can use the Edit commands and the Clipboard, or you can use drag and drop editing.

To use Edit commands to move or copy text between documents, follow these steps:

1. Open the document that contains the text you want to move or copy (the *source* document).

2. Open the document to which you want to copy or move the text (the *destination* document).

3. Make the source document active.

4. Select the text.

5. Do one of the following:

   ■ To move the text, choose **E**dit, Cu**t**.

   ■ To copy the text, choose **E**dit, **C**opy.

6. Make the destination document active and position the insertion point where you want the text to appear.

7. Choose **E**dit, **P**aste. Word inserts the text into the destination document.

To use drag and drop editing to copy or move text from one document window to another, follow these steps:

1. Open the document which contains the text you want to copy or move (the source document).

2. Open the document to which you want to copy or move the text (the destination document).

3. Choose **W**indow, **A**rrange All to display both documents on-screen.

4. Make the source document active and select the text.

5. Do one of the following:

   ■ To move the selected text, position the insertion point anywhere within the selection, and then click and drag the mouse pointer to the new location in the destination document window.

   ■ To copy the selected text, position the insertion point anywhere within the selection, press and hold Ctrl, and then click and drag the mouse pointer to the new location in the destination document window.

Task: Working with One Document in Two Panes

Although you cannot work in more than one document at a time, you can split the active document into two panes. With the active document split, you can work in different parts of the same document. This is useful for moving or copying text from one place in a long document to another.

To split the active document into two panes, follow these steps:

1. Choose **W**indow, S**p**lit. A vertical bar appears in the document window.

2. Drag the bar up or down until the panes are the size you want.

3. Click the mouse button.

To view or edit two parts of the same document, split the document window into panes.

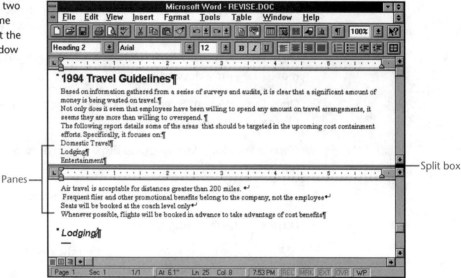

To make a pane active, click it, or press F6.

To restore the window to a single pane, choose **W**indow, Remove S**p**lit.

Split box

A black rectangular box that appears at the top of the vertical scroll bar, or between two panes, used to split and unsplit the active window into panes.

With a mouse, you can split the active document into panes by using the *split box*.

To use the split box, use the following actions:

■ Double-click the split box to divide the text area into two equal panes.

■ Drag the split box to divide the text area into unequal panes. Release the mouse button when the panes are sized the way you want.

■ To change the size of the panes, drag the split box up or down.

■ To restore the window to a single pane, double-click the split box again.

Task: **Working with One Document in More than One Window**

If you need to see two parts of the same document, but the amount of text you want to view does not fit within a pane, you can display the active document in two windows. Edits that you make in one window are also made in the other window, but movement within each window is independent.

To open a document in more than one window, follow these steps.

1. Open the document. If it is not active, click in it, or choose it from the Window menu to make it active.

2. Choose **W**indow, **N**ew Window.

Word opens the document in another window. To differentiate the two, Word adds a number to the document name in the title bar. In the first document, it adds a colon and the number 1. In the second document, it adds a colon and the number 2, and so on.

You can use the same techniques for editing one document in two windows as you use to edit different documents in two windows.

Choose **W**indow, **A**rrange All to arrange two windows with the same document to appear on screen at the same time.

The second copy of the document

The original document

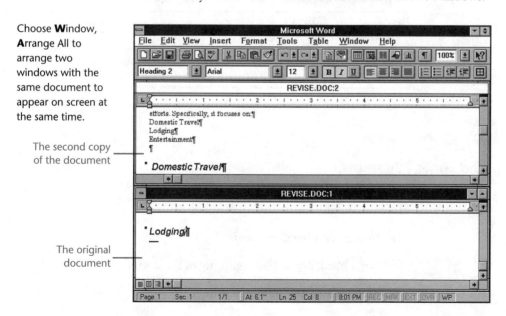

To return to working in one window, close the other window.

Summary

To	Do This
Open an existing document	Choose **F**ile, **O**pen. Choose the name in the File Name list, and then choose OK.
Start a new line	Press Enter.
Insert the time or date	Choose Insert, Date and **T**ime. Choose the format, and then choose OK.
Select text	Drag from the first character to the last character.
Change styles	Position the insertion point within the paragraph, or select the specific text. Select the new style from the Style list.
Undo the last action	Choose **E**dit, **U**ndo.
Redo the last undone action	Choose **E**dit, **R**edo,
Move Selected text	Choose **E**dit, Cu**t**. Reposition the insertion point. Choose **E**dit, **P**aste.
Copy selected text	**C**hoose **E**dit, **C**opy. Reposition the insertion point. Choose **E**dit, **P**aste.
Open multiple windows	Choose **F**ile, **O**pen.
Open multiple copies of the active document	Choose **W**indow, **N**ew Window.
Split the active window into panes	Choose **W**indow, S**p**lit.

On Your Own

Estimated time: 20 minutes

Use basic editing.

1. Start Word.

2. Open an existing document.

3. Start a blank line at the beginning of the document.

4. Insert today's date on the new line.

Select and revise text.

1. Select the paragraph containing the date.

2. Change it to a different style.

3. Move the date to the last line of the document.

4. Copy the date to the first line of the document.

5. Change the style of the date on the last line.

Correct mistakes.

1. Delete the date on the last line of the document.

2. Undo the last action.

3. Redo the last action.

4. Try to spell *The Teh*.

5. Add a word that you commonly misspell to AutoCorrect's list of words.

Use multiple windows.

1. Open a new document.

2. Arrange the open windows on-screen so you can see them both.

3. Copy some text from the original document to the new document.

4. Maximize the new document.

5. Split the new document into two panes.

6. Change the size of the panes.

7. Move text from one pane to the other.

8. Close all open documents.

Checking Your Document

In this lesson, you learn about some of the features of Word that help you improve the quality of your work. You learn how to search for specific text, characters, or formatting in a document, and how to replace them, if necessary. You also learn to use Word's three proofreading tools: Spelling Checker, Thesaurus, and Grammar Checker. Finally, you learn how to set Word to use correct hyphenation throughout a document.

Specifically in this lesson, you learn to do the following:

- Find and replace information in a document

- Check and correct spelling in a document

- Check and correct grammar in a document

- Use the Thesaurus to choose synonyms and alternative wording

Finding and Replacing Information in a Document

With Word, you can search through a document to locate specific information. This is useful if you have a very long document, and you do not want to read through it to find a particular phrase. You also can replace automatically the information you find with something else. This is useful if you realize you made the same mistake consistently throughout a document. If you realize that you used the word *affect* when you meant *effect*, for example, you can set Word to find all occurrences of *affect*, and then replace them with *effect*.

In addition, you can use find and replace to locate nonprinting characters, such as paragraph marks, and formatted text, such as a word that appears in italics. Using all of these tools, you easily can find text you need to edit, replace a word, phrase or character string with another, delete a word everywhere it appears in the document, and replace one format with another.

Task: Finding Text

To search through a document to find specific text, follow these steps:

1. Choose **E**dit, **F**ind.

In the Find dialog box, specify the information you want Word to find.

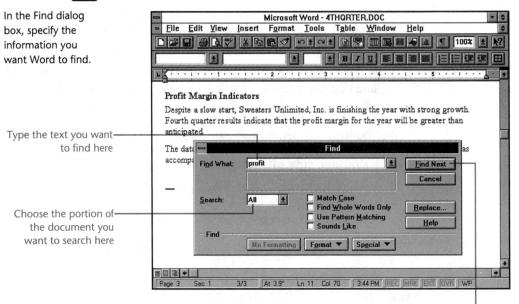

Type the text you want to find here

Choose the portion of the document you want to search here

Choose to begin the search here

2. In the Fi**n**d What text box, type the text that you want Word to find.

3. From the **S**earch drop-down list, choose whether you want Word to search all of the document, up from the insertion point, or down from the insertion point.

4. Choose **F**ind Next. Word begins the search and highlights the first occurrence of the specified text.

5. Choose **F**ind Next again to find the next occurrence of the word or word group.

6. When the search is complete, Word displays a message box indicating that it has finished searching the document. Choose OK to return to the Find dialog box.

7. Choose Cancel to return to the document.

4

If you have problems...	If Word displays a message telling you that the search item cannot be found, and you are sure the text appears somewhere, there are two likely solutions: check your spelling to be sure you entered the text correctly in the Find What text box—Word only searches for the information you enter. Also, be sure that you selected All from the **S**earch drop down list. If Word is searching from the insertion point up or down, it may not search the part of the document that contains the text you want to find.

Narrowing the Search

You can take several actions to limit, or narrow the search. Narrowing the search helps Word to find exactly the information you want, in the quickest possible way.

To narrow the search, choose **E**dit, **F**ind, and then perform one or more of the following:

Note: *To search only part of a document, select the part before you choose* **Edit, F**ind.

■ To find only text that appears in the exact pattern of uppercase and lowercase letters entered in the Fi**n**d What text box, choose the Match **C**ase check box.

- To match the specified text only if it is preceded and followed by spaces or punctuation, choose the Find **W**hole Words Only check box.

Wildcard character

Characters you can use to represent one or more other characters.

- To search using *wild card characters*, such as *?* (for the character in a specific place) and * (for a character and all characters that follow it), entered in the Fi**n**d What text box, choose the Use Pattern **M**atching check box.

- To find homophones for the word entered in the Fi**n**d What text box, choose the Sounds **L**ike check box. If you enter *red* and choose the Sounds **L**ike check box, for example, Word stops at the word *read*, as well.

Task: Finding Special Characters

With Word, you can find nonprinting and other special characters such as paragraph marks, em dashes, and line breaks.

To find special characters, follow these steps:

1. Choose **E**dit, **F**ind.

2. In the Find dialog box, choose Sp**e**cial. Word displays a list of special characters.

When you select a special character from the list, Word inserts it in the Fi**n**d What text box. Here, the symbol for a paragraph mark appears.

Choose a special character here

Paragraph mark symbol

Choose to display the list of characters here

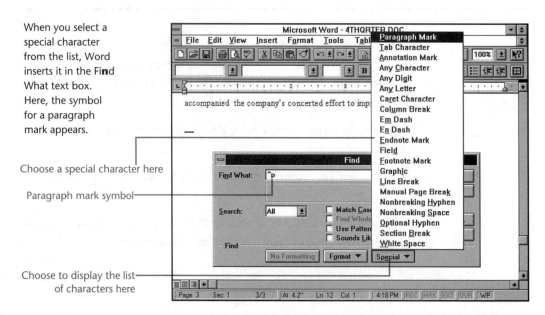

3. Choose the character you want to find.

4. Choose **F**ind Next. Word highlights the first occurrence of the character in your document.

5. Choose **F**ind Next again to continue the search. Choose Cancel to return to the document.

6. When the search is complete, Word displays a message box. Choose OK to return to the Find dialog box.

Note: *If nonprinting characters do not appear in your document, Word highlights the space in the document where they would appear.*

Finding Text with Specific Formats

Word usually does not care how the text you want to find is formatted. It searches for characters only. If you want to find text that has been formatted, you can set Word to search for characters that appear in a specific format.

To find text with specific formats, follow these steps:

1. Choose **E**dit, **F**ind.

2. In the Fi**n**d What text box, enter the text you want to find.

3. Choose F**o**rmat. Word displays a list of format options.

You can use the
Find dialog box to
search for text with
specific formatting.

Enter the text to find here

Select the type of formatting
to find here

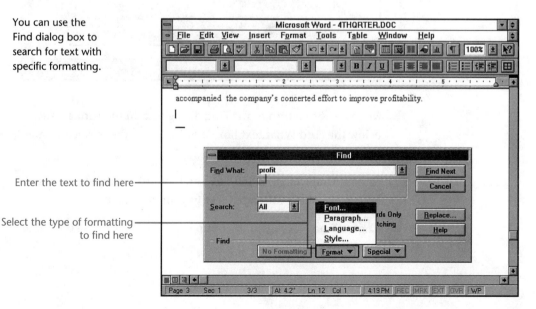

4. Choose one of the following from the list of formatting types:

   ■ Choose **F**ont to find a particular font, or character attribute, such as italics.

   ■ Choose **P**aragraph to find a particular paragraph format, such as center-aligned, or indented.

   ■ Choose **L**anguage to find text in a particular language.

   ■ Choose **S**tyle to find text formatted with a particular style.

5. In the dialog box that appears, choose the formatting options that you want to find.

Specify the font and font style in the Find Font dialog box. In this case, Word will find the word "profit" only if it appears in bold, 10 point Times New Roman.

View a sample of the formatted text here

6. Choose OK to return to the Find dialog box. In the Format: area, below the Fi**n**d What text box, Word specifies the selected formatting.

7. Choose **F**ind Next to begin the search. Word highlights the first occurrence of the formatted text in your document.

8. Choose **F**ind Next again to continue the search. Choose Cancel to return to the document.

9. When the search is complete, Word displays a message box. Choose OK to return to the Find dialog box.

Task: **Replacing Information**

With Word, you can replace information throughout a document in two ways:

- Choose **E**dit, **F**ind to find the information, and then choose **R**eplace.

- Choose **E**dit, **R**eplace, to find and replace the information all in one step.

Either way, when you choose **R**eplace, Word displays the Replace dialog box.

In the Replace dialog box, specify the information you want to find, and the replacement information. You can specify text, formatting, or special characters.

Enter the information to find here

Enter the replacement information here

Choose to specify formatting here

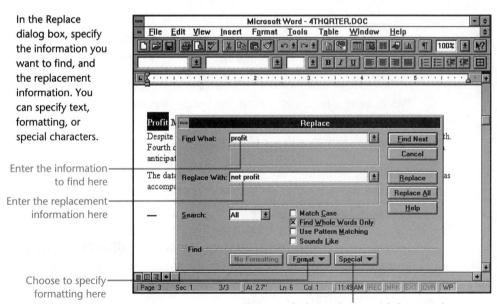

Choose to find or replace special characters here

To find and replace information in a document, follow these steps:

1. Choose **E**dit, **R**eplace.

2. In the Fi**n**d What text box, enter the information to find, as described in the previous sections.

3. In the Replace With text box, enter the replacement information.

4. With the insertion point in the Replace With text box, specify any formatting you want to apply to the replacement text. Use the same methods described in the previous section for specifying formatting in the Find dialog box.

5. Choose one of the following:

   ■ **F**ind Next to instruct Word find and highlight the first occurrence of the information in the Find What text box. Word waits for you to decide whether or not you want to replace the highlighted text.

   ■ **R**eplace if the Find What text is already highlighted. Word replaces it with the information in the Replace With text box, and then highlights the next occurrence of the Find What information.

   ■ Replace **A**ll if you want Word to go ahead and automatically replace all occurrences of the Find What information with the Replace With information.

Note: *Use Replace **A**ll with care. If you forget to select the Find Whole Words Only check box, you accidentally might replace parts of words. If you choose to replace all occurrences of the word cat with the word dog, for example, you may inadvertently end up with word like:* dogastrophe, *or* dogatonic.

Task: Checking the Spelling in a Document

Main dictionary
A built-in list of words which Spelling Checker uses to check your spelling and to provide suggestions for alternative words.

You can use Word's Spelling Checker to check the spelling of individual words, all words in a selected portion of a document, or all words in an entire document.

Spelling Checker checks your spelling against the spelling in its extensive *main dictionary*. In addition, you can create *custom dictionaries* which Word can use. Custom dictionaries are useful for listing names and other proper nouns, industry-related words, and other less common terminology that Word may not be familiar with.

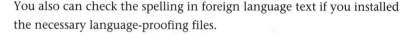

You also can check the spelling in foreign language text if you installed the necessary language-proofing files.

Detecting and Correcting Misspelled Words

To begin checking the spelling in a document, choose **T**ools, **S**pelling. To check a portion of the document, first select the portion. To check just one word, select that word first.

Word immediately begins checking the document. When it finds a word that it does not recognize, it highlights it, and displays the Spelling dialog box.

Spelling Checker highlights words that it does not find in its main dictionary or any available custom dictionaries.

Unrecognized word—

Suggested replacement—

Choose another—
word here

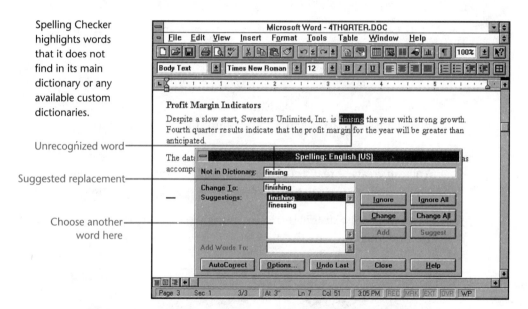

You can choose to replace the highlighted word with the word in the Change **T**o text box, you can enter a different word in the Change **T**o text box, or you can ignore the highlighted word and continue the spell check.

Do one or more of the following actions:

■ Choose a word in the Suggestions list box to insert it into the Change **T**o text box.

■ Type another word into the Change **T**o text box.

- Choose **I**gnore to leave the highlighted word unchanged.

- Choose **Ig**nore All to leave all occurrences of this word unchanged.

- Choose **C**hange to replace the highlighted word with the word in the Change **T**o text box.

- Choose Change A**ll** to replace all occurrences of this word in the rest of the document with the word in the Change **T**o text box.

- Choose AutoCo**rr**ect to replace the word, and add it to the AutoCorrect list of words. For information on AutoCo**rr**ect, see Lesson 3, "Revising a Document."

- Choose **U**ndo Last to undo the last replacement you made with Spelling Checker.

- Choose Close to stop checking the spelling.

When Spelling Checker is finished checking the document, Word displays a message box. Choose OK to return to the document.

Working with Custom Dictionaries

You can create as many custom dictionaries as you want, and then select one or more to use any time you check the spelling in a document.

You can create a custom dictionary during a spell check, or before a spell check. Either way, you use the Spelling Options dialog box.

You use the
Spelling Options
dialog box to
create custom
dictionaries and
to set options for
conducting a spell
check.

Choose spell check
options here

Create custom
dictionaries here

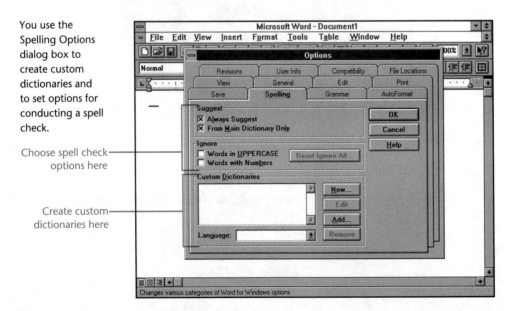

In the Spelling options dialog box, you can do the following:

- Create custom dictionaries

- Choose the dictionaries to use during a spell check

- Set Word to automatically make suggestions when it finds an unrecognized word

- Set Word to ignore words in uppercase letters

- Set Word to ignore words that include numbers

To create a custom dictionary, follow these steps:

1. Choose **T**ools, **O**ptions.

2. In the Options dialog box, click the Spelling tab to display the Spelling options.

3. Choose **N**ew.

In the Create
Custom Dictionary
dialog box, name
your dictionary file.

Enter a file name here

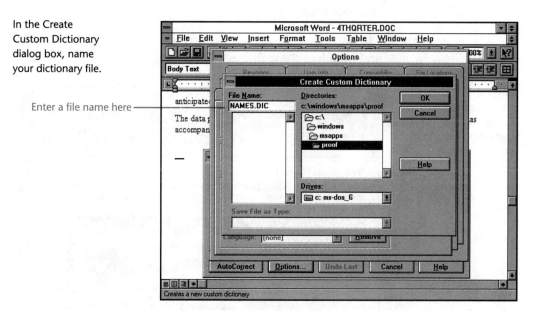

4. In the Create Custom Dictionary dialog box, enter an eight letter name for your custom dictionary in the File **N**ame text box. Word automatically assigns the file a .DIC extension.

5. Choose OK to return to the Spelling Options dialog box.

6. To use the dictionary in all spell checks, select the check box next to it in the Custom **D**ictionaries list.

7. Choose OK to return to the document or to the Spelling dialog box.

Spell Checker gives you the option of adding any word it does not recognize to one of the custom dictionaries in use during a spell check.

To add a word to a custom dictionary, follow these steps:

1. In the Spelling Options dialog box, be sure that the check box beside the custom dictionary you want to use is selected so that Word uses it during the spell check.

2. Choose **T**ools, **S**pelling to begin the spell check.

3. When Spell Checker highlights the word you want to add to the custom dictionary, choose the dictionary in the Add **W**ords To drop down list.

4. Choose **A**dd. Spell Checker adds the word to the selected dictionary and continues the spell check.

During a spell check, you can add words to any custom dictionary in use.

Choose to add the unrecognized word here

Choose a custom dictionary here

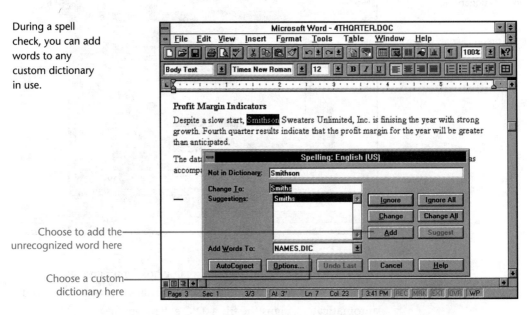

Task: **Checking Your Grammar**

With Word's Grammar Checker, you can identify sentences that do not conform to generally accepted rules of grammar, style, usage, and punctuation. Grammar Checker points out sentences it believes are incorrect, and sometimes makes suggestions for correcting them.

You can check the grammar in a single sentence, in a selected portion of a document, or in an entire document.

Readability statistics
An evaluation designed to determine how much education a person needs to read and understand your document.

By default, Grammar Checker uses grammar and style rules for business writing. It also checks your spelling, and displays *readability statistics* when it is finished checking the grammar.

To begin checking the grammar in a document, choose **T**ools, **G**rammar. To check a portion of the document, select the portion first. To check just one sentence, select that sentence first.

4

Word immediately begins checking the document. When it finds a sentence with questionable grammatical structure or style, it highlights it and displays the Grammar dialog box.

Grammar Checker highlights sentences that it believes use faulty grammar, and suggests a correction.

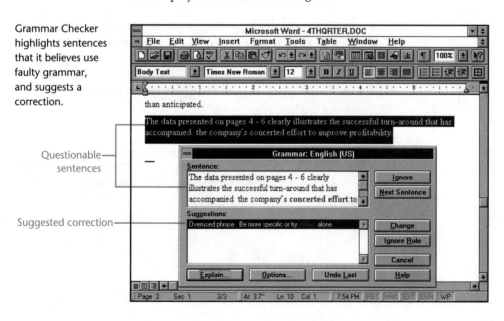

Questionable sentences

Suggested correction

You can choose to change the highlighted sentence based on the sentence in the Suggestions text box, you can edit the document yourself, or you can ignore the suggestion and continue the grammar check.

In the Grammar dialog box you can choose one of the following:

- Choose a suggestion from the Suggestions list box, and then choose **C**hange to make the correction.

- Click anywhere within the document window to edit the document yourself. Choose **S**tart to begin the grammar check again.

- Choose **I**gnore to ignore Word's suggestion and continue checking the document. If Grammar Checker finds another problem in the same sentence, it highlights it in the **S**entence text box.

- Choose **N**ext Sentence to ignore the current problem and all problems in the highlighted sentence and move right on to the next sentence.

- Choose Ignore **R**ule to skip all occurrences of the grammatical problem throughout the document.

- Choose **E**xplain to display an explanation of the current grammatical problem. Double-click the control menu box to clear the explanation from your screen.

- Choose Undo **L**ast to undo the last correction you made with Grammar Checker.

- Choose Close to stop checking the grammar.

Note: *If Grammar Checker is checking spelling as well as grammar, it displays the Spelling dialog box when it finds a mistake. For information on using the Spelling dialog box, see the preceding section.*

When Grammar Checker is finished checking the document, it displays the readability statistics. Choose OK to clear the dialog box from your screen.

The readability statistics are intended to give you an idea of how easy it is to read and understand your writing style.

Check the number of words, characters, paragraphs and sentences here

Check the education level required to understand the document here

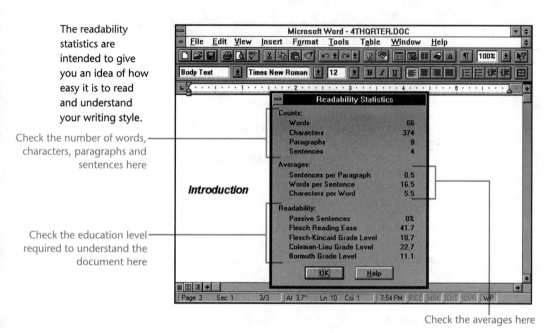

Check the averages here

Task: **Finding Alternative Words**

Antonym
A word meaning the opposite of the selected word.

Synonym
A word with the same meaning as the selected word.

Word includes a thesaurus to help you find *antonyms, synonyms,* and related words for words you use in a document

To use the Thesaurus, follow these steps:

1. Position the insertion point within the word you want to look up.

2. Choose **T**ools, **T**hesaurus.

Word highlights the word and looks it up in the Thesaurus.

In the Thesaurus dialog box, Word displays the selected word, a list of synonyms and a list of meanings.

Selected word

Choose another word to look up here

Choose to display a list of antonyms here

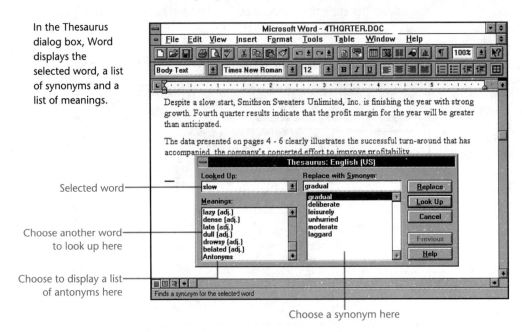

Choose a synonym here

In the Thesaurus dialog box, you can do any of the following:

- Replace the selected word. Choose a word in the Replace with **Syn**onym list, and then choose **R**eplace.

- Look for additional synonyms. Choose a word in the Replace with **S**ynonym list, and then choose **L**ook Up. Word displays the meanings and synonyms for the new word.

- Look for even more synonyms. Choose a word in the **M**eanings text box, and then choose **L**ook Up. Word displays the meanings and synonyms for the new word.

- If *Antonyms* appears in the Meanings list, choose it to display a list of antonyms.

- If *Related Words* appears in the Meanings list, choose it to display a list of related words.

- Choose Cancel to return to the document.

Summary

To	Do This
Find information	Choose **E**dit, **F**ind.
Replace information	Choose **E**dit, **R**eplace.
Check spelling	Choose **T**ools, **S**pelling.
Correct spelling	Choose **R**eplace in the Spelling dialog box.
Create a custom dictionary	Choose **T**ools, **O**ptions, Spelling. Choose **N**ew. Enter a File **N**ame. Choose OK.
Check grammar	Choose **T**ools, **G**rammar.
Fix grammar	Choose **C**hange in the Grammar dialog box.
Find a synonym or antonym	Choose the word. Choose **T**ools, **T**hesaurus.

4

On Your Own
Estimated time: 25 minutes

Find and replace text.

1. Open an existing document.

2. Use **F**ind to locate a specific word in the document.

3. Use **R**eplace to change the word to something else.

Check the spelling.

1. Open an existing document.

2. Check the spelling in the document.

3. Correct the spelling in the document.

4. Add a common spelling error to AutoCorrect.

5. Create a custom dictionary for proper names.

6. Add names to the dictionary.

Check the grammar.

1. Open an existing document.

2. Check the grammar in the document.

3. Read Word's explanation of the problem.

4. Correct the grammar in the document.

Use the Thesaurus.

1. Open an existing document.

2. Use the Thesaurus to find synonyms for any word.

3. Look up additional synonyms.

4. If available, look up antonyms.

5. Replace the original word with a synonym.

Part II
Formatting for a Professional Look

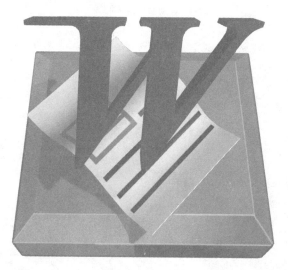

Lesson 5
Dressing Up Your Text

Character formatting
The process of enhancing the appearance of text characters.

With Word, you easily can make your documents attractive. By using *character formatting*, you can change the appearance or emphasis of the letters, numbers, punctuation marks, and symbols that make up the body of your text.

You use character formatting to change the font, font size, style, color, and placement of characters. You also can format text so that it appears in a document, but does not print.

In this lesson you learn to do the following:

- Choose fonts, font sizes, and font colors
- Apply character styles, such as boldface, italics, and underline
- Copy character formatting
- Insert special characters in a document
- Change character spacing
- Use dropped capital letters
- Use Word Art

Understanding Fonts and Font Sizes

Font
A set of characters in a distinctive typeface available in a variety of sizes and styles. Some common fonts are Times New Roman, Courier, and Helvetica.

One of the easiest ways to change the appearance of text in a document is to change the text *font*.

Each font has a distinctive look. Because Word supports WYSIWYG editing, the characters that you see on-screen closely resemble the characters that are printed on paper. Whether the text prints the way it looks on-screen, however, depends on the fonts available in your system, and on the kind of printer you use.

The TrueType fonts supplied with Windows and Word look the same on-screen as they do on a printed page, but you cannot print these fonts unless your printer supports them.

Note: *For more information about screen fonts and printer fonts, consult Que's* Using Windows 3.1, *Special Edition.*

Point
A unit used to measure the size of typographic characters.

Font sizes are measured in *points*. There are 72 points in an inch, which means that if you use a 12-point font, you get six lines of text in an inch. Some fonts, such as the TrueType fonts, can be *scaled*.

Scale
To change the size of something, such as a font, a frame, or an object.

Most typed documents use 12-point fonts for body text; books and magazines usually use 9- or 10-point fonts. Larger font sizes are good for titles, headings, and other text that you want to stand out.

You already have used different fonts and font sizes in the styles you used to create documents. In the NORMAL.DOT template, for example, the default Normal style font is 10-point Times New Roman.

Note: *After you change a font, font size, style, effect, or character spacing, you can make the new choice the default setting. To make a new setting the default setting for the current document template, simply choose* **D***efault in the Font dialog box. Choose* **Y***es to confirm the change. For more information on changing defaults, see Lesson 8, "Customizing Word for Windows."*

You can dress up your text by using different fonts and font sizes. To see which font and font size you are currently using, look at the Formatting toolbar on your Word screen.

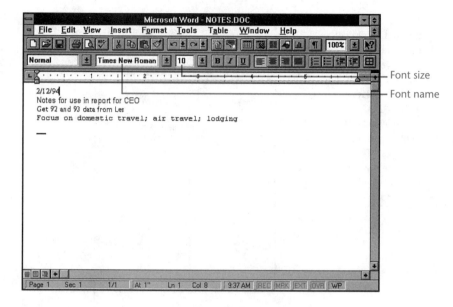

Font size

Font name

Task: Choosing Fonts and Font Sizes

5

You can choose fonts and font sizes by using the Formatting toolbar or the Format menu commands. You can choose a font before you type the text, or you can change the font of existing text. To change the font of existing text, select the text first.

To choose a font with the Formatting toolbar, follow these steps:

1. Position the insertion point where you want to start typing in the new font, or select the characters you want to appear in the new font.

2. Choose the drop-down arrow to the right of the Font text box. Word displays the Font list.

3. Choose the font from the Font list.

If you have problems...

If the Formatting toolbar is not on-screen, choose View, Toolbars, and then choose the check box next to Formatting in the Toolbars option list. Choose OK to close the dialog box and display the Formatting toolbar on-screen.

The top section of the Font list displays the names of fonts you have used recently. The bottom section displays an alphabetical list of all available fonts. The double-T symbol indicates a TrueType font; the computer icon indicates a screen font.

Choose the new font here

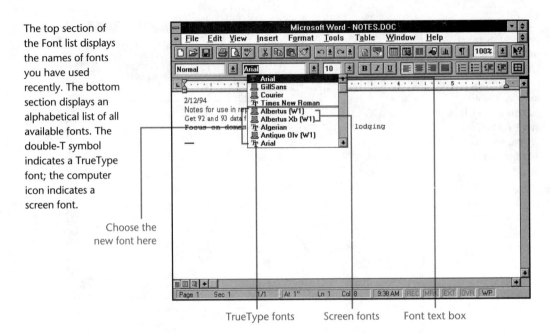

TrueType fonts   Screen fonts   Font text box

When you type, text appears in the selected font. If you selected text first, the text changes to the new font.

Note: *The font list is quite long. To quickly scroll to the font you want, type the first character of the font name. Word scrolls the list to display the fonts that begin with the letter you type.*

To change the font size using the Formatting toolbar, follow these steps:

1. Position the insertion point where you want to begin typing in a different font size, or select the characters you want to change.

2. Click the drop-down arrow to the right of the Font Size text box. Word displays the Font Size list.

If you have problems...

If you want to use a font size that does not appear in the Font Size list, you can type the font size directly into the Font Size text box.

Choose the font size
from the Font Size
list.

Font Size
text box

Choose the new
font size here

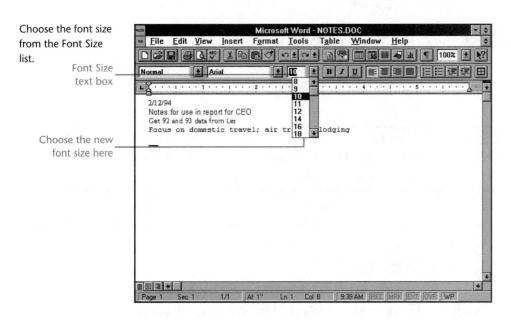

To choose a font and font size using the Format menu commands, follow
these steps:

1. Position the insertion point where you want to begin typing in the
new font or font size, or select the characters you want to change.

2. Choose Format, Font.

Choose to display character spacing options here   Choose the font size here

In the Font dialog
box you can choose
Font effects and
styles, or adjust
character spacing.

Choose font
styles here

Choose the
font here

Choose font
effects here

Preview the
font here

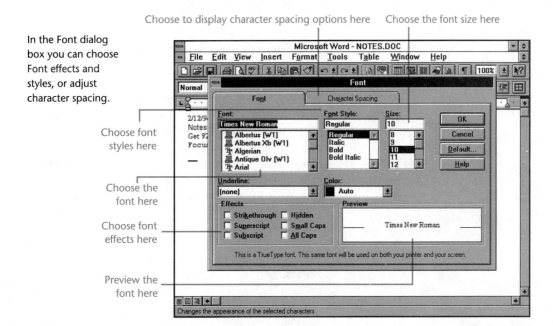

3. Choose a font from the **F**ont list in the Font dialog box.

4. Choose a font size from the **S**ize list in the Font dialog box.

5. Choose OK.

If you have problems...   If you do not see the **F**ont and **S**ize lists in the Font dialog box, the Character Spacing options probably are displayed. Click the **F**ont tab at the top of the dialog box to display the Font options.

Note: *To quickly display the Font dialog box, point anywhere within the document text area and click the right mouse button. From the shortcut menu, choose Font.*

Task: Enhancing the Appearance of Text

Font styles
A particular variation of the appearance of characters in a font. Italics, boldface, and bold italics are examples of font styles.

In addition to fonts and font sizes, you can enhance the appearance of text by applying *font styles* and *character effects*.

Bold, italics, and underlines are the most common character styles and effects; however, Word provides a whole dialog box full of alternatives. You can apply more than one style or effect to a character. You can, for example, apply boldface and italics to a word; for even more emphasis, you can underline it as well.

Character Effects
Modifications added to characters to enhance or otherwise change their appearance. Underlines, color, and strikethrough are examples of character effects.

You can choose character styles and effects before typing, or you can apply them to selected text.

To choose character styles and effects before you type text, simply choose the options in the Font dialog box. To apply character styles and effects to existing text, select the text before you choose the options.

Note: *Word displays buttons for Bold, Italics, and Underline on the Formatting toolbar. To apply these effects with buttons, you do not have to open the Font dialog box—simply click the button. To remove these effects, click the button again.*

By applying character styles and effects, you can make your words stand out on the page. Too many attributes on one page, however, can be overwhelming.

Word underline ⎯

Dotted underline ⎯
All caps ⎯
Subscript ⎯

Strikethrough ⎯

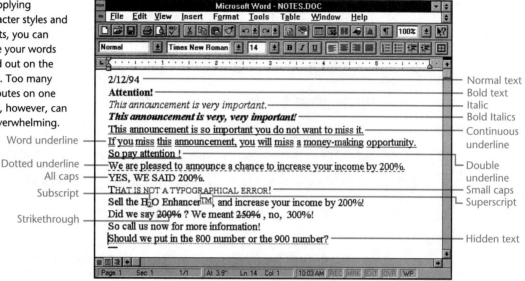

```
                    Microsoft Word - NOTES.DOC
  File  Edit  View  Insert  Format  Tools  Table  Window  Help
```

Normal   Times New Roman   14   B I U

2/12/94 ⎯⎯⎯⎯⎯⎯⎯⎯⎯⎯⎯⎯⎯⎯⎯⎯⎯⎯⎯⎯ Normal text
Attention! ⎯⎯⎯⎯⎯⎯⎯⎯⎯⎯⎯⎯⎯⎯⎯ Bold text
This announcement is very important. ⎯⎯⎯⎯ Italic
This announcement is very, very important! ⎯ Bold Italics
This announcement is so important you do not want to miss it. ⎯ Continuous underline
If you miss this announcement, you will miss a money-making opportunity.
So pay attention ! ⎯⎯⎯⎯⎯⎯⎯⎯⎯⎯⎯⎯ Double underline
We are pleased to announce a chance to increase your income by 200%.
YES, WE SAID 200%.
THAT IS NOT A TYPOGRAPHICAL ERROR! ⎯⎯⎯ Small caps
Sell the H$_2$O Enhancer™, and increase your income by 200%! ⎯ Superscript
Did we say ~~200%~~ ? We meant ~~250%~~ , no, 300%!
So call us now for more information!
Should we put in the 800 number or the 900 number? ⎯ Hidden text

Page 1   Sec 1   1/1   At 3.9"   Ln 14   Col 1   10:03 AM REC MRK EXT OVR WP

Note: *When applying character attributes, keyboard shortcuts may save time. To use keyboard shortcuts, you do not have to open the Font dialog box—simply press the appropriate keys. To remove the effects, press the keys again.*

5

If you have problems...

If you try to use a keyboard shortcut and a letter appears in your document at the insertion point, you did not hold down the Ctrl key. Delete the character that appeared—probably *B, N, I, U,* or *W*—and try again, this time holding down the Ctrl key while pressing the other key.

To apply character styles, follow these steps:

1. Choose Fo**r**mat, **F**ont.

2. From the Font Style list, choose one of the following options:

   ■ To apply boldface, choose Bold. If you like using keyboard shortcuts, press Ctrl+B.

   ■ To apply italics, choose Italic or press Ctrl+I.

- To apply bold and italics, choose Bold Italic.

- To revert to the default style formatting, choose Regular.

3. Choose OK.

To apply underline effects, follow these steps:

1. Choose Format, Font.

2. Choose the drop-down arrow to the right of the **U**nderline text box.

3. From the Underline drop-down list, choose one of the following:

- To underline words and spaces continuously, choose Single or press Ctrl+U.

- To underline words only, choose Words Only or press Ctrl+Shift+W.

- To apply a continuous double underline, choose Double, or press Ctrl+Shift+D.

- To apply a continuous dotted underline, choose Dotted.

- To remove all underlines, choose (none).

4. Choose OK.

To apply other effects, follow these steps:

1. Choose Format, Font.

2. In the Effects area, choose the check boxes of any of the following:

- To strikethrough text, choose Strikethrough.

- To raise characters slightly above the main text, choose Superscript.

- To drop characters slightly below the main text, choose Subscript.

- To enter text that can be displayed in the document but not printed, choose Hidden, or press Ctrl+Shift+H.

- To display text in small-sized capital letters, choose Small Caps, or press Ctrl+Shift+K.

■ To display text in all capital letters, choose **A**ll Caps, or press Ctrl+Shift+A.

■ To remove the effects, deselect the check box, or press Ctrl+spacebar.

3. Choose OK.

To change the color of text, follow these steps:

1. Choose F**o**rmat, **F**ont.

2. Choose the drop-down arrow to the right of the **C**olor text box.

3. Choose the color you want to use. Choose Auto to use the default foreground text color.

4. Choose OK.

> **Note:** *To display hidden text in a document, choose **T**ools, **O**ptions, View, and select the Hidden Text check box in the Nonprinting Characters area. When you choose OK, hidden text appears in the document, indicated by a dotted underline. The text does not print unless you select to include Hidden Text in the Print options dialog box.*

If you have problems...	If you are not happy with the style or effect you selected, choose **E**dit, **U**ndo or press Ctrl+Z.

> **Note:** *You can use Word shortcut keys to change the case of selected text. Press Shift+F3 to toggle the selected text between initial characters in uppercase, all uppercase, and all lowercase characters.*

Task: Changing Character Spacing

You can adjust the amount of space between characters by changing the character spacing settings in the Font dialog box. Adjusting the character spacing can be useful for improving the document's appearance or for fitting text into a certain amount of space.

Expand
Increase the distance between characters.

Condense
Decrease the distance between characters.

In the Font dialog box, you can change the distance between characters by choosing to *expand* or *condense* the text, and then setting the spacing. You also can set characters to appear either above or below the normal line of text, and you can set Word to automatically adjust the character spacing to improve the appearance of a document.

To adjust character spacing, choose F**o**rmat, **F**ont, and then click the Cha**r**acter Spacing tab.

Use the Character Spacing settings to adjust the amount of space between characters and to adjust the position of characters in relation to the line of text.

Set spacing here

Set position here

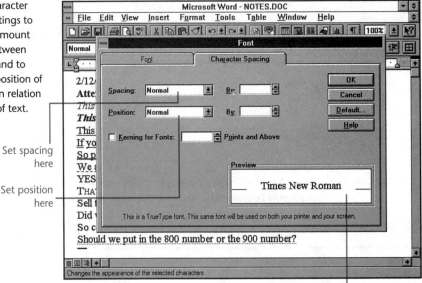

Preview the character spacing here

If you have problems...

If you do not see the character spacing options in the Font dialog box, you forgot to click the Cha**r**acter Spacing tab.

Note: *You can change the spacing of characters before you type, or you can change the spacing of existing characters by selecting the characters first.*

To expand or condense character spacing, follow these steps:

1. Choose F**o**rmat, **F**ont.

2. Click the Cha**r**acter Spacing tab at the top of the Font dialog box.

3. Choose the drop-down arrow to the right of the **S**pacing text box.

4. Choose one of the following:

   ■ Expanded to increase the distance between the characters.

   ■ Condensed to decrease the distance between the characters.

   ■ Normal to adjust the distance to the normal font spacing.

5. In the **By** text box to the right of the **S**pacing text box, enter the width of the spacing. Use the up and down arrows to adjust the spacing in one-tenth-point increments.

6. Choose OK.

To raise or lower characters in relation to the normal text line, follow these steps:

1. Choose F**o**rmat, **F**ont.

2. Click the Character Spacing tab at the top of the Font dialog box.

3. Choose the drop-down arrow to the right of the **P**osition text box.

4. Choose one of the following:

   ■ Raised to display characters above the normal line of text.

   ■ Lowered to display characters below the normal line of text.

   ■ Normal to display characters on the normal line of text.

5. In the B**y** text box to the right of the Position text box, enter the distance you want to raise or lower the characters. Use the up and down arrows to adjust the spacing in one-tenth-point increments.

6. Choose OK.

Kerning

Changing the space between selected pairs of characters.

To automatically adjust character spacing to improve the appearance of a document, choose the **K**erning for Fonts check box. By default, Word automatically adjust the spacing for fonts that are 10 points or larger. To change the minimum font size for *kerning*, enter the size in the P**o**ints and Above text box.

5

Task: **Copying Character Formatting**

After you format the text exactly the way you want it, you can copy that formatting to other text, without having to select each setting again.

To copy character formatting, follow these steps:

1. Position the insertion point anywhere within the formatted text.

2. Click the Format Painter button on the Standard toolbar.

3. Click and drag the mouse pointer from the first character you want to change to the last character you want to change. Word highlights the selected text.

When you click the Format Painter button, the mouse pointer changes to a paintbrush.

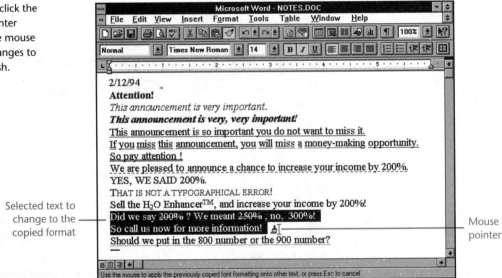

Selected text to change to the copied format

Mouse pointer

4. Release the mouse button to copy the formatting. Word automatically turns off the Format Painter.

If you have problems...

If you want to copy the same format to more than one block of text, but Word keeps turning off the Format Painter as soon as you copy the formatting one time, try this: Double-click the Format Painter button to turn it on. Word leaves the Format Painter on until you click the button again to turn it off.

Task: **Inserting Special Characters in a Document**

Most characters you need for creating a document are available directly from the keyboard. All you have to do is type. Sometimes, however, you may need to insert special characters or symbols that are not available from the keyboard. With Word, you easily can choose symbols, such as foreign language characters and astrological signs, or special characters, such as ellipses, dashes, and hyphens.

Many fonts come with their own set of symbols. Word provides an extensive list of fonts from which you can choose a set of symbols.

To insert a special character or symbol into a document, follow these steps:

1. Position the insertion point where you want the character to appear.

2. Choose **I**nsert, **S**ymbol.

The Symbol dialog box displays a complete set of characters from which you can choose.

Choose to display special characters here

Choose to display symbols associated with a different font here

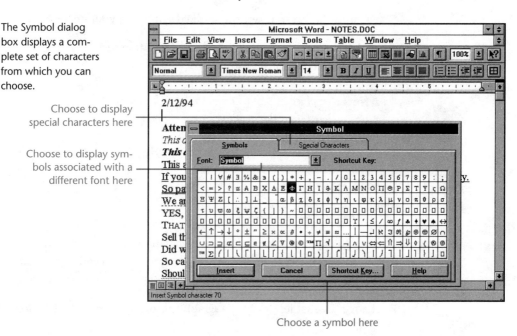

Choose a symbol here

3. From the **F**ont drop-down list, choose a font. Word displays the character set associated with that font.

4. Choose a symbol; an enlarged version of the symbol appears.

Here, the Windings font character set is displayed, and a happy face symbol is selected.

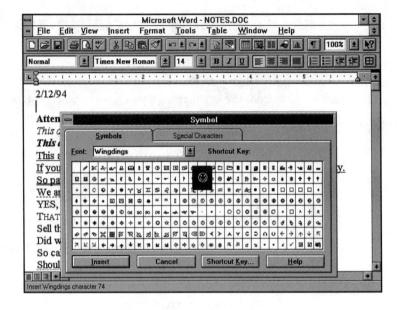

5. Choose **I**nsert to insert the selected symbol in your document.

6. Choose another symbol, or choose Close to return to your document.

    Note: *To place a special character into your document, click the S**p**ecial Characters tab at the top of the Symbol dialog box. Choose the character you want, and then choose **I**nsert.*

Task: Emphasizing Text with Dropped Capital Letters

One way to distinguish an important paragraph from the rest of the document is to start it with a dropped capital letter. Dropped caps can enhance the appeal of your document by creating a striking and professional look.

To change the first letter of a paragraph to a dropped capital letter, follow these steps:

1. Position the insertion point within the paragraph.

2. Choose F**o**rmat, **D**rop Cap.

Starting a paragraph with a dropped capital letters makes your document look more professional.

Choose the position of the dropped cap here

Choose the font here

Enter how many lines you want the character to drop here

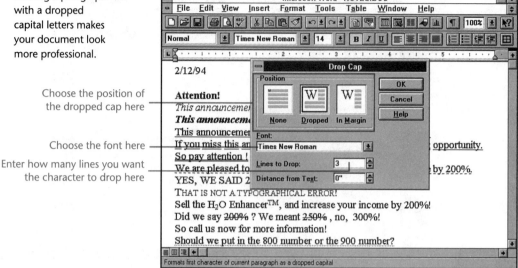

3. Choose one of the following:

   ■ **D**ropped: Drops the capital within the main body of text

   ■ In **M**argin: Positions the dropped cap in the left margin

4. Choose OK. Word changes the first letter in the paragraph to a dropped capital.

   Note: *If you are not in Page Layout view, you cannot see the way the dropped capital really looks in your document. Word prompts you to change to Page Layout view so you can see the way the dropped capital looks in your document. Choose **Y**es to change to Page Layout view. Choose **N**o to continue editing your document in Normal view.*

If you have problems...

If you choose to display the document in Page Layout view, and then want to return to Normal view, choose **V**iew, **N**ormal. If you choose to continue editing in Normal view, and then want to see the way the dropped capital looks, choose **V**iew, **P**age Layout. For more information on changing the document view, see Lesson 7, "Setting Up Your Pages."

5

In Print Preview, you can see the way the dropped capital looks in position on the page.

Dropped capital————

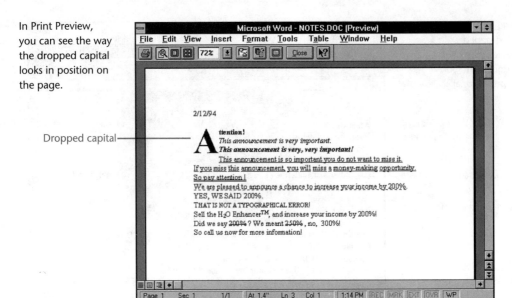

Task: Using WordArt

When you really want to enhance your text, you can use *WordArt*. WordArt is a program built into Word that enables you to turn your text and characters into works of art.

With WordArt, you can choose from fonts that may not be available in the Font dialog box, you can position your text into different shapes, and you can enhance your text with borders, lines, and shading. WordArt is especially useful for creating titles and headings.

To start WordArt, follow these steps:

1. Position the insertion point in the document where you want the text created with WordArt to appear.

2. Choose **I**nsert, **O**bject.

In the Object dialog box, choose the **C**reate New tab, then choose to create a WordArt object.

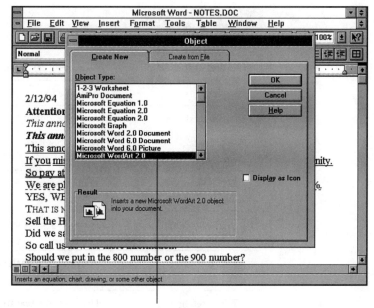

Choose WordArt here

3. From the **O**bject Type list box, choose Microsoft WordArt 2.0.

4. Choose OK.

If you have problems...

If you do not see the Object Type list box, click the **C**reate New tab in the Object dialog box.

When WordArt starts, you see on-screen a text-entry box and a preview frame, as well as the WordArt menu and toolbars. You use the buttons on the WordArt toolbar to format the WordArt text. Table 5.1 describes the buttons and their effects.

Table 5.1 WordArt Toolbar Options

Option	Effect
Line and Shape text box	Aligns your text in the chosen shape
Font text box	Applies a font
Font size text box	Applies a font size
B Bold	Applies boldface
I Italic	Applies italics
Ee Even height	Makes all characters the same height
Flip	Turns each character onto its side
Stretch	Elongates the text to the edges of the frame
Alignment	Displays a choice of alignments
Character Spacing	Adjusts the spacing between characters
Special Effects	Displays a choice of effects such as letter height and rotation
Shading	Enables you to choose shading to apply to text
Shadow	Enables you to choose shadows to apply to text
Border	Enables you to add borders to the text

Note: *For more information on adding borders, shading, and shadows, see Lesson 6, "Dressing Up Your Paragraphs."*

WordArt replaces temporarily the Word menu and toolbars with its own menu and toolbar.

WordArt menu

Preview your text here

Type your text here

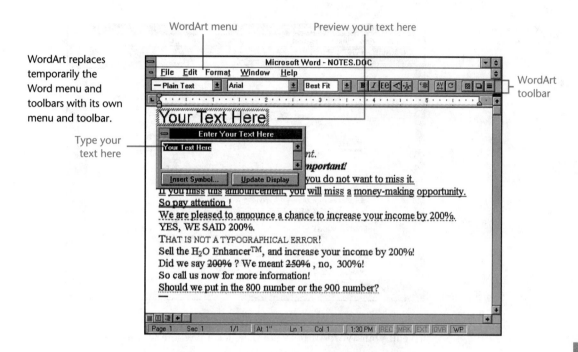

WordArt toolbar

5

To create text with WordArt, follow these steps:

1. In the WordArt text entry box, where it says Enter Your Text Here, type the text you want to appear in the document.

2. Use the options on the WordArt toolbar to format the text.

3. Choose **U**pdate Display to see how your text will look formatted.

4. Click anywhere in the Word document window to insert your text into the document.

Frame
A nonprinting box that contains pictures, drawings, or other objects.

WordArt inserts the text into your document in a *frame*. To select the frame, click it. To change its size, drag one of the black boxes you see around its edges. For more information about frames see Lesson 10, "Working with Frames."

With WordArt, you can turn your text into a work of art.

To edit your WordArt text, double-click anywhere within the text. To delete the WordArt title, click it to display the frame, and then press Delete.

Summary

To	Do This
Change fonts	Choose Format, Font. Choose a font.
Change font size	Choose Format, Font. Choose a font size.
Select a character style	Choose Format, Font. Choose a font style.
Select a character effect	Choose Format, Font. Choose the effects.
Copy character formatting	Position the insertion point within the format. Choose the Format Painter button. Select the text to format.
Insert a symbol	Choose Insert, Symbol. Choose the Symbol. Choose Insert.
Drop a Capital	Position the insertion point within the paragraph. Choose Format, Drop Cap. Choose Dropped or In Margin.
Start WordArt	Choose Insert, Object, Microsoft WordArt 2.0. Choose OK.

On Your Own

Estimated time: 25 minutes

Choose fonts and font sizes.

1. Create a document.

2. Type each line in a different font.

3. Change each line in a different font size.

4. Change the entire document to the same font.

5. Change the entire document to the same font sizes.

Apply character styles and effects.

1. Enhance some of the existing text by using bold, italics, and bold italics.

2. Underline one line.

3. Add a double-underline to a line.

4. Change the text color.

5. Type a note to yourself that you do not want to print with the document.

6. Change a line to all capital letters.

7. Start the document with a dropped capital

Change character spacing.

1. Condense a line of text.

2. Expand another line of text.

3. Position one word higher than the normal line of text.

4. Position one word lower than the normal line of text.

Copy character formatting.

1. Type a new line.

2. Format the new line by copying the format of another line.

Insert symbols and special characters.

1. Insert a trademark symbol into your document.

2. Open the Wingdings character set, and insert an astrological sign into your document.

Use WordArt.

1. Start WordArt

2. Create a title for your document.

3. Choose to make the title curved.

4. Elongate the title to fill the frame.

5. Place the title in your document.

Dressing Up Your Paragraphs

Paragraph formatting
The process of specifying the appearance of paragraphs.

In Word, a paragraph is any amount of text or graphics followed by a paragraph mark. So far, you have formatted paragraphs by using the styles built into Word's document templates. In this lesson, you learn how to use *paragraph formatting* to override the style settings to change the way paragraphs look.

With paragraph formatting you can change the appearance of some of the paragraphs in a document without changing the entire document.

In this lesson, you learn to do the following:

- Understand paragraph formatting
- Use rulers
- Align paragraphs
- Indent paragraphs
- Set tabs
- Set line and paragraph spacing
- Add borders and shading to paragraphs
- Create lists

Understanding Paragraph Formatting

With Word, you use paragraph formatting to control the alignment, indentations, tabs, and spacing of text in a paragraph. You also can enhance the paragraph by adding numbers, bullets, borders, and shading.

Note: *You can choose paragraph formatting options before you type text, or you can apply it to existing text.*

Word stores paragraph formatting settings in the *paragraph mark* at the end of each paragraph.

Task: **Displaying Paragraph Marks**

Paragraph mark
A non-printing character that Word inserts whenever you press Enter. Word uses paragraph marks to store paragraph formatting settings.

If you delete a paragraph mark, you delete all of the paragraph formatting information it contains. When that happens, the paragraph that preceded the deleted paragraph mark takes on the formatting settings of the next paragraph. Likewise, if you move a paragraph mark, the paragraph formatting may change.

To avoid accidentally deleting or moving a paragraph mark, you should keep paragraph marks displayed on-screen when you are editing.

To display paragraph marks on-screen, follow these steps:

1. Choose **T**ools, **O**ptions.

2. Click the View tab.

In the View Options dialog box, you can select to display non-printing characters on-screen while you work.

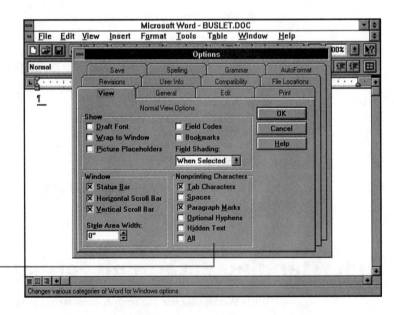

Choose to display nonprinting characters here

3. In the Nonprinting Characters area, choose Paragraph **M**arks.

4. Choose OK.

If you have problems...

When you click the Show/Hide Marks button, you display all nonprinting characters, not just paragraph marks. You learn more about some of the other marks later in this lesson.

Understanding Rulers

Ruler

A measuring device that you can display on-screen to use for showing and setting certain formatting options.

Many of Word's paragraph formatting options are controlled by using a *ruler*. Word has two rulers: the horizontal ruler, which appears across the top of your screen, and the vertical ruler, which appears along the left side of your screen in Page Layout view. For paragraph formatting, you use the horizontal ruler.

If you have problems...

If you do not see the horizontal ruler on-screen, choose **V**iew, **R**uler.

The horizontal ruler measures the width of your document, starting at the left margin. You use it to see where your text is positioned, and to change settings.

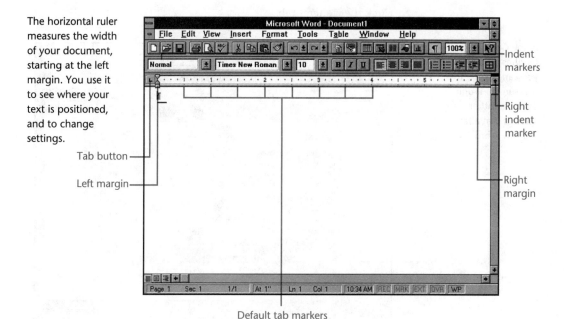

Default tab markers

Current paragraph
The paragraph in which the insertion point is currently positioned.

In Word, each paragraph can have different paragraph formatting settings. With the horizontal ruler displayed on-screen, you see the indentation and tab settings for the *current paragraph* while you work.

Word starts measuring at the left margin, not the left edge of the page. The 0 at the left end of the ruler, therefore, is the left margin.

Note: *Word uses the ruler to measure from the margins to the edges of the page as well as from the left margin to the right margin. If you see the number* 1 *twice near the left of the ruler, you are seeing measurements from the left margin to the left edge of the page (this probably appears gray, not white), and the measurements from the left margin toward the right margin.*

Task: Changing the Ruler Measurement Unit

Pica
A unit of measurement used in the printing industry. One pica is equal to 12 points; one point is equal to 1/72 of an inch.

By default, Word uses inches as the unit of measure. You can change the unit of measure to centimeters, points, or *picas*.

To change the unit of measure, follow these steps:

1. Choose **T**ools, **O**ptions.

2. Click the General tab.

In the General Options dialog box, you can change the measurement unit as well as other settings that affect the way Word runs.

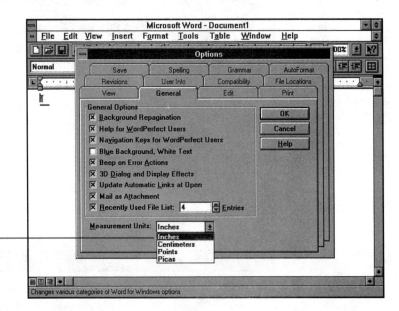

Choose to change the measurement unit, here

3. Choose the drop down arrow to the right of the **M**easurement Units text box to display a list of unit choices.

4. Choose the unit you want to use.

5. Choose OK.

Task: Aligning Paragraphs

Alignment
The way text is arranged in relation to the margins.

One of the ways you can change paragraph formatting is to change the *alignment*.

Word provides four alignment settings:

- *Flush left*: All lines in the paragraph are flush against the left margin and the right margin is left uneven or ragged.

- *Centered*: Text is evenly positioned around the center of the page, leaving both the left and right margins uneven or ragged.

- *Flush right*: All lines in the paragraph are flush against the right margin, leaving the left margin uneven.

- *Justified*: Text is spaced across each line so that both the left and right margins are even.

By changing alignment, you can single out paragraphs for attention or customize the format of a document. Titles, for example, look good when they are centered on a page. In formal business letters, the return address often is placed flush right. Justified text has a neat, orderly appearance.

You can choose an alignment before you type the paragraph text, or you can change the alignment of an existing paragraph.

To change the alignment of one existing paragraph, position the insertion point anywhere within the paragraph. (You do not need to select the whole paragraph.) To change the alignment of two or more existing paragraphs, select the paragraphs first.

To align a paragraph, follow these steps:

1. Position the insertion point where you want to begin the paragraph, or position it within the existing paragraph.

6

2. Choose Format, Paragraph. The Paragraph dialog box appears.

In the Paragraph dialog box, you can choose paragraph formatting options such as alignment.

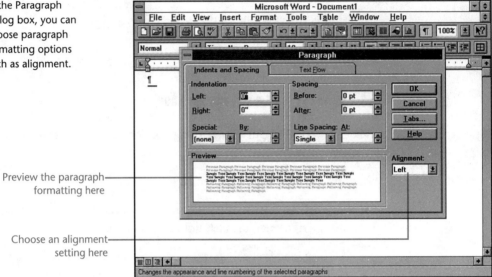

Preview the paragraph formatting here

Choose an alignment setting here

3. In the Paragraph dialog box, click the Indents and Spacing tab, and then choose the drop-down arrow next to the Alignment text box to display a list of alignment choices.

4. Choose one of the following options:

- To align flush left, choose Left or press Ctrl+L.
- To center, choose Centered or press Ctrl+E.
- To align flush right, choose Right or press Ctrl+R.
- To justify, choose Justify or press Ctrl+J.

If you have problems...

If you do not see the Alignment text box in the Paragraph dialog box, you forgot to click the Indents and Spacing tab. Try again.

In this document, different alignments are used to format the paragraphs.

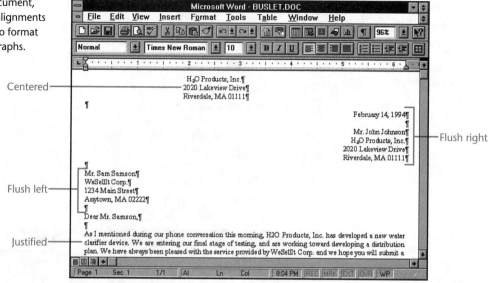

Centered ────

Flush left ────

Justified ────

Flush right

Task: Indenting Paragraphs

Indent

To adjust the distance between the left or right margin and the paragraph text.

With Word, you can use *indents* to change the position of paragraphs on a page.

Word provides three indentation options:

- *First Line Indent*: Controls the distance between the first character in the first line of the paragraph and the left margin.

- *Left Indent*: Controls the distance between all lines in the paragraph *except the first line* and the left margin.

- *Right Indent*: Controls the distance between the last character in all lines in the paragraph and the right margin.

By using one or more of the indentation options, you can create the following effects:

- For a traditional look, you can indent the first line of every paragraph from the left margin.

- For a callout, you can indent all lines in the paragraph from both the left and right margins.

Hanging indent
To leave the first line in a paragraph hanging out to the left while all other lines are indented.

■ For a list, you can create a *hanging indent* by indenting all but the first line of a paragraph from the left margin.

Word provides many options for setting indents:

■ Click the Increase Indent button on the Formatting toolbar to quickly indent all lines in a paragraph right to the next set tab stop.

■ Click the Decrease Indent button on the Formatting toolbar to quickly move all lines left to the previous tab stop.

■ Drag the indent markers on the horizontal ruler to see the location of the indents on-screen as you work.

To adjust indents using the ruler, drag the indent markers to the desired position.

Indent box

Left indent marker

First line indent marker

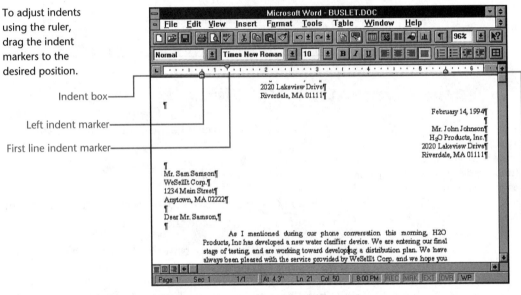

Right indent marker

■ Set precise indent measurements in the Paragraph dialog box.

To change the indentation of one existing paragraph, position the insertion point anywhere within the paragraph. (You do not need to select the whole paragraph.) To change the indentation of two or more existing paragraphs, select the paragraphs first.

If you have problems...

If you select more than one paragraph, and the indent markers on the horizontal ruler dim, it means that the paragraphs do not have the same indentation settings. The new settings you choose will affect all the selected paragraphs.

To indent a paragraph by using the horizontal ruler, follow these steps:

1. Position the insertion point where you want to begin the paragraph, or position it within the existing paragraph.

2. Choose from the following:

   - To indent all lines from the right, drag the right indent marker from the right end of the horizontal ruler to the indented position.

   - To indent the first line from the left, drag the first line indent marker from the top left of the horizontal ruler to the indented position.

   - To indent all but the first line from the left, drag the lower indent marker from the bottom left of the horizontal ruler to the indented position.

   - To indent all lines from the left, drag the indent box from the bottom left of the horizontal ruler to the intended position.

To indent a paragraph precisely, follow these steps:

1. Position the insertion point where you want to begin the paragraph, or position it within the existing paragraph.

2. Choose Format, Paragraph.

6

In the Paragraph
dialog box, you can
set precise indent
measurements.

Enter left indentation
settings here

Enter right indentation
settings here

Enter first line or hanging
indentation settings here

Preview the paragraph
formatting here

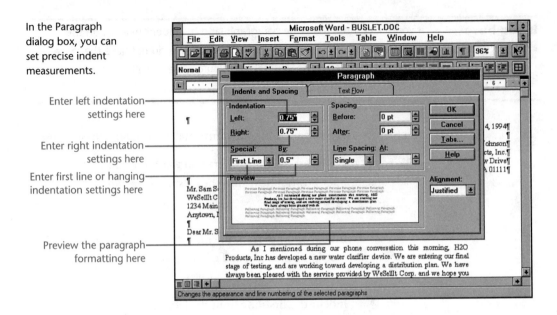

3. In the Paragraph dialog box, click the **I**ndents and Spacing tab.

4. In the Indentation area, enter the distance to indent all lines from
   the left margin in the **L**eft text box, and the distance to indent all
   lines from the right margin the **R**ight text box.

**If you have
problems...**

If you do not see the Indentation text boxes in the Paragraph dialog box, you
forgot to click the **I**ndents and Spacing tab. Try again.

---

5. To set a first line or hanging indent, choose the drop down arrow
   next to **S**pecial text box and choose either First Line or Hanging.
   Then, enter the distance to indent in the B**y** text box.

6. Choose OK. Word positions the indent markers on the horizontal
   ruler at the indent positions.

Note: *Enter positive numbers to indent toward the center of the document.
Enter negative numbers to indent toward—or even into—the margins.*

If you have problems...

You set the first line indent at .9" but it appears to be indented nearly 1.5 inches! When you adjust indentations using the Paragraph dialog box, Word sets the first line indent position by adding the measurement you enter in the First Line **B**y text box to the measurement you enter in the **L**eft text box. You probably set the left indent at .6", and the First Line indent at .9", so you ended up with a first line indent of 1.5 inches!

Here, paragraphs are formatted with different indentations. Some use both indents and alignments to achieve a customized look.

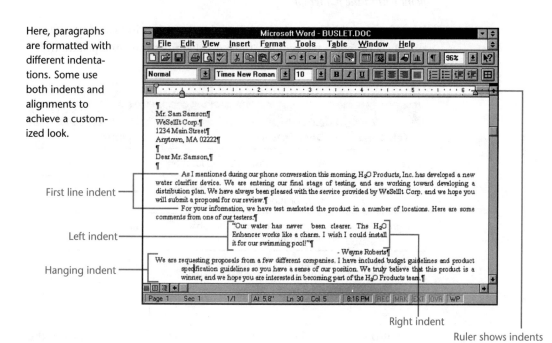

First line indent

Left indent

Hanging indent

Right indent

Ruler shows indents for the hanging indent paragraph

6

Task: Setting Tabs

In Word, you use tabs and tab stops to align text at different locations along one line. When you press the Tab key, the insertion point moves forward until it reaches a set tab-stop location.

By default, whenever you start a new document, Word sets tab stops at 1/2-inch intervals across the width of the page. The tab stops are indicated along the bottom of the horizontal ruler by dim gray dots.

To change the tab stop settings for individual paragraphs, you set custom tab stops. You can place a custom tab stop anywhere across the page; when you set a custom tab stop, Word removes all default tabs stops to the left of it.

Note: *To change the tab settings for existing paragraph, you must select the paragraph before setting the tabs. You cannot simply position the insertion point within the paragraph.*

Word has four kinds of tab stops. Each kind of tab is indicated on the ruler by a different tab symbol. Table 6.1 describes the tab type and the tab symbol.

Table 6.1 Tab Types and Symbols		
Tab Type	**Description**	**Symbol**
Left	Aligns text at the tab stop location	**L**
Center	Aligns text evenly around the tab stop location	**⊥**
Right	Aligns text to end at the tab stop location	**⌐**
Decimal	Aligns decimal points or periods within the text at the tab stop location	**⊥.**

Tab leader
A series of characters used to fill the space to the left of text typed at a tab stop location.

In addition, you can choose to fill the space between the tab text and the location where you pressed the Tab key with a dotted, dashed, or solid line *tab leader.*

Note: *Word marks the location in the document where you press the Tab key with a nonprinting tab mark—an arrow pointing right. To see the tab marks on screen, click the Show/Hide marks button on the Standard toolbar, or choose* **T***ools,* **O***ptions, View, and select the Tab Characters check box.*

To set tabs by using the ruler, follow these steps:

1. Position the insertion point where you want to start a paragraph with custom tab settings, or select the paragraphs to which you want to add custom tabs.

2. Click the Tab button at the far left end of the horizontal ruler until it displays the symbol for the tab you want to set.

3. Click the insertion point on the ruler at the location where you want to set the tab stop. Word places a tab stop symbol at the location, and deletes all default tab stops to the left.

To move a custom tab stop, drag it to the new location. To remove a custom tab stop, drag it down off of the ruler.

In this document, you can see the different tab stops in use.

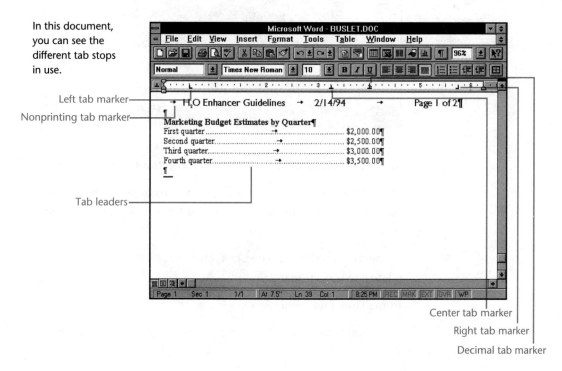

Left tab marker

Nonprinting tab marker

Tab leaders

Center tab marker

Right tab marker

Decimal tab marker

6

To set tab stops at precise locations, follow these steps:

1. Position the insertion point where you want to start a paragraph with custom tab settings, or select the paragraphs to which you want to add custom tabs.

2. Choose Format, Tabs.

In the Tabs dialog
box, you can set tab
stops at precise
locations, and
choose tab leaders.

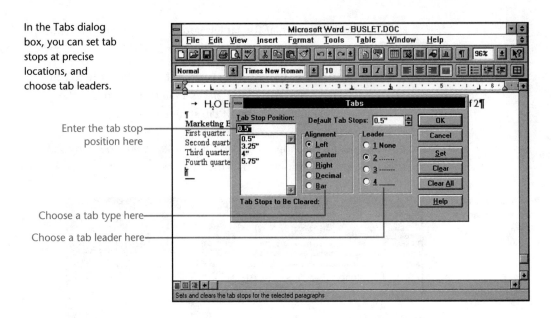

Enter the tab stop position here

Choose a tab type here

Choose a tab leader here

3. In the Tabs dialog box, choose a tab type in the Alignment area.

   Note: *Choose **B**ar in the Alignment area to insert a vertical bar through the paragraph at the tab stop location. The bar appears on the horizontal ruler.*

4. In the **T**ab Stop Position text box, enter its position on the page, relative to the left margin.

5. In the Leader area, choose a tab leader.

6. Choose **S**et to set the tab. The tab appears in the **T**ab Stop Position list box.

7. Repeat steps 3 through 6 to set additional tabs.

8. Choose OK to accept all tab settings and return to the document. The appropriate tab symbols appear on the horizontal ruler at the tab stop locations.

   To remove a tab stop, choose it in the Tab Stop position list box, and then choose Cl**e**ar. To remove all tabs, choose Clear **A**ll.

Note: *To open the Tabs dialog box quickly, double-click anywhere within the horizontal ruler.*

Controlling Line Spacing

With Word, you control the amount of blank space left between lines and paragraphs by adjusting the line spacing.

By default, spacing is determined by the current paragraph style. By using the Paragraph dialog box, you can change the line spacing within a paragraph, and you can change the spacing between paragraphs.

Note: *You can set spacing before you type, or you can change the spacing of existing text. To change the spacing of more than one paragraph, select the paragraphs, first.*

Changing the space between lines and paragraphs can help you fit more text on a page, or spread text out to fill a page.

Single-spaced lines

Double-spaced lines

1 1/2-spaced lines

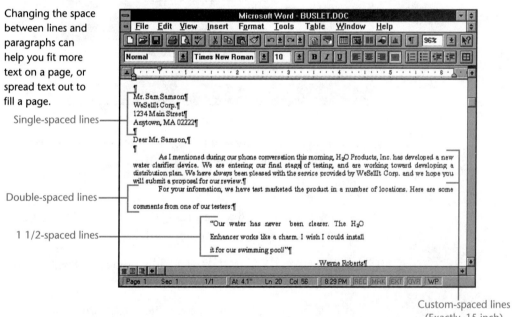

Custom-spaced lines
(Exactly .15 inch)

Task: Setting Line Spacing within a Paragraph

Within a paragraph, you can specify spacing in terms of lines, or in terms of specific measurements. If you specify spacing in terms of lines, the spacing is determined by the size of the characters in the line.

To set line spacing within paragraphs, follow these steps:

1. Position the insertion point where you want to begin the paragraph, or position it within the paragraph you want to change.

2. Choose F**o**rmat, **P**aragraph.

In the Paragraph
dialog box, open
the Line Spacing
drop-down list to
select the line
spacing setting
you want.

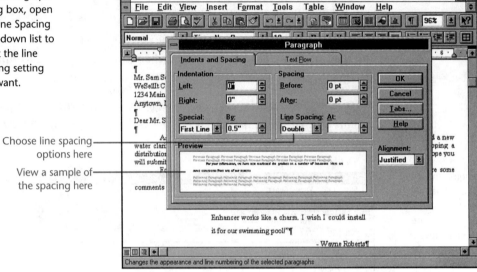

Choose line spacing
options here

View a sample of
the spacing here

3. Click the drop down arrow to the right of the Li**n**e Spacing text
box to display the list of line spacing settings.

4. Choose one of the following:

- *Single*: Spaces the lines according to the height of the largest
characters in each line, or press Ctrl+1.

- *1.5*: Spaces the lines at one-and-a-half times the height of the
largest character in each line, or press Ctrl+5.

- *Double*: Spaces the lines at twice the height of the largest
characters in each line, or press Ctrl+2.

- *At Least*: Spaces the lines at the distance entered in the **At**
text box, or more if required to accommodate larger characters.

- *Exactly*: Spaces the lines at the exact distance entered in the
At text box, even if some of the characters are too large to fit
in this space.

■ *Multiple*: Spaces the lines at the distance equal to the height of the largest character in the line multiplied by the number entered in the **A**t text box.

5. If you choose At Least, Exactly, or Multiple, enter the appropriate value in the **A**t text box. By default Word uses points as the unit of measurement. To use a different unit of measurement, enter the abbreviation for that measurement after the value in the box. Use *cm* for centimeters, *in* for inches, or *pi* for picas.

6. Choose OK.

Task: Setting Spacing Between Paragraphs

To set line spacing between paragraphs, follow these steps:

1. Position the insertion point where you want to begin the paragraph, or position it within the paragraph you want to change.

2. Choose **F**ormat, **P**aragraph.

In the Paragraph dialog box, set the amount of space you want to leave before and after a paragraph.

Enter the amount of space to leave before the paragraph here

View a sample of the spacing here

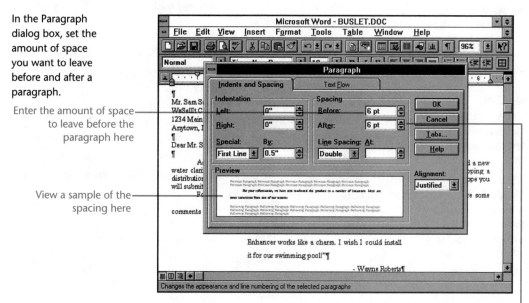

Enter the amount of space to leave after the paragraph here

3. In the **B**efore text box, enter the amount of space to leave before the paragraph. By default, Word measures the spacing in points. To specify a different unit of measurement, enter the abbreviation after the value in the text box.

4. In the Aft**er** text box, enter the amount of space to leave after the paragraph. By default, Word measures the spacing in points. To specify a different unit of measurement, enter the abbreviation after the value in the text box.

5. Choose OK.

Note: *To quickly add a 12-point space before a paragraph, press Ctrl+0. To remove the space, press Ctrl+0 again. To add a 12-point space between all paragraphs in a document, select the entire document, and then press Ctrl+0.*

Adding Borders and Shading

Borders
Lines placed above, below, beside, or around a paragraph.

Shading
A dotted pattern that appears over text to create the effect of a highlight.

Shadow
A box you can add to a border to give a three-dimensional effect.

You can give your paragraphs a customized look by dressing them up with *borders* and *shading*.

Borders can be drawn in various line styles, thicknesses, and colors, and can include a *shadow*. Shading is controlled by the fill pattern or percentage of gray you select.

Before you spend time shading paragraphs throughout a document, it is a good idea to shade a typical paragraph, and then print it to see how it looks. Usually, a very low percentage or gray is all that is necessary to create a shading effect. If you use too much gray, it becomes difficult to read the text.

Add borders and
shading to
paragraphs to give
your document a
professional look.

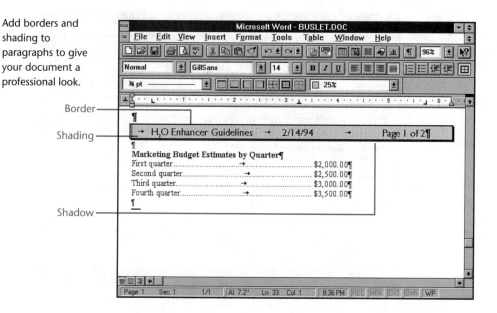

Border

Shading

Shadow

Task: Adding Simple Borders and Shading

If you want to add simple borders and shading to a paragraph, you can
use the Borders toolbar.

To display the Borders toolbar, follow these steps:

1. Choose **V**iew, **T**oolbars, and then select the Borders toolbar check
   box and choose OK. Word displays the Borders toolbar on-screen
   between the Formatting toolbar and the horizontal ruler.

6

Add simple borders
and shading to
paragraphs by using
the Borders toolbar.

Choose a line style here ———

Choose a line
position here ———

Choose the shading here ———

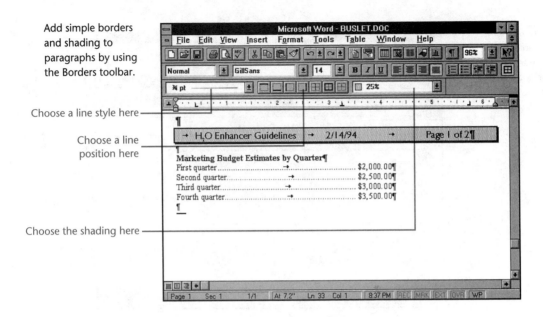

To use the Borders toolbar, choose any of the following options:

- *Line Style drop-down list*: Displays a list of line widths and styles for borders.

- *Top Border*: Applies a border above the selected paragraph.

- *Bottom Border*: Applies a border below the selected paragraph.

- *Left Border*: Applies a border along the left side of the selected paragraph

- *Right Border*: Applies a border along the right side of the selected paragraph

- *Inside Border*: Applies a border between adjacent, selected paragraphs.

- *Outside Border*: Applies a border around the selected paragraph.

- *No Border*: Removes all existing borders.

- *Shading drop-down list box*: Displays a list of patterns and gray scales for shading.

Note: *To remove the Borders toolbar from the screen, choose* **V***iew,* **T***oolbars, and then deselect the Borders check box and choose OK.*

Task: Customizing Border Options

You also can set precise border placement, add shadows to borders, and change the border color.

To customize border and shading options, follow these steps:

1. Position the insertion point within the paragraph you want to change.

2. Choose Format, Borders and Shading.

You can set the position and line style of a border in the Paragraph Borders and Shading dialog box.

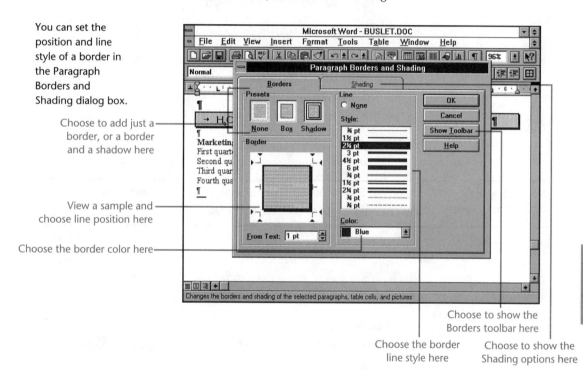

Choose to add just a border, or a border and a shadow here

View a sample and choose line position here

Choose the border color here

Choose to show the Borders toolbar here

Choose the border line style here

Choose to show the Shading options here

6

3. To set border options, choose the **B**orders tab at the top of the Paragraph Borders and Shading dialog box.

4. In the Presets area, choose one of the following:

   ■ **N**one: Removes all existing borders and shadows.

   ■ Bo**x**: Adds just a border.

   ■ Sh**a**dow: Adds a border and a shadow.

5. From the Style list, choose the thickness or style of the border line.

6. In the Border area, click the lines around the sample paragraph to select the position of the border. Do any of the following:

   ■ To apply a box around the paragraph, leave as is.

   ■ To remove any line, click the location where it should appear.

   ■ To restore a line, click it again. Click any border line to remove that line from the border.

7. From the Color drop-down list, select the color of the border.

8. In the From Text box, enter how far from the text you want Word to place the border. By default, Word measures in points. To use a different measurement, type the abbreviation after the value in the text box.

9. Choose OK.

If you have problems... If you do not see the Borders options in the Paragraph Borders and Shading dialog box, you forgot to click the **B**orders tab. Try again.

Note: *Word extends borders across the width of the line. To adjust the shading so that it extends only as far as the text, try adjusting the left and right indent markers.*

Task: Customizing Shading Options

You can change shading colors, and select customized shading patterns and gray scales.

Note: *By default, Word creates shading and patterns with the foreground color set to black and the background color set to white. If you have a color printer, you can change the colors.*

To customize shading options, follow these steps:

1. Position the insertion point within the paragraph you want to change.

2. Choose Format, Borders and Shading.

You can customize
the shading options
in the Paragraph
Borders and
Shading dialog box.

Choose to show the
Borders options here

Choose the percentage
of gray or the fill
pattern here

Choose the Foreground color here

Choose the Background color here

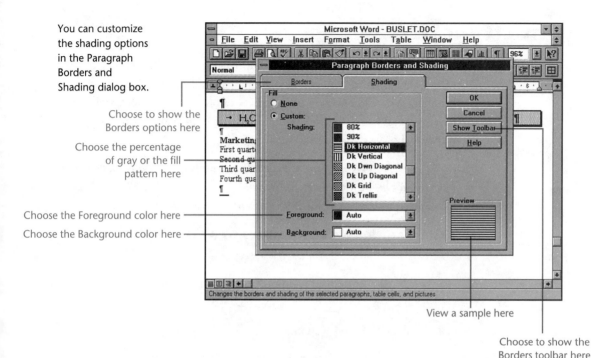

View a sample here

Choose to show the
Borders toolbar here

3. To set shading options, click the **S**hading tab at the top of the
   Paragraph Borders and Shading dialog box.

4. In the Fill area, choose one of the following:

   ■ **N**one to remove all existing shading

   ■ **C**ustom to select a Sha**d**ing percentage of gray or pattern.

5. From the **F**oreground drop-down list, choose a foreground color.

6. From the Background drop-down list, choose a background color.

7. Choose OK.

**If you have
problems...**

If you do not see the Shading options in the Paragraph Borders and Shading
dialog box, you forgot to click the **S**hading tab. Try again.

Formatting Lists

Lists are effective tools for detailing information in a precise, easy-to-read format. With Word, you can identify items in a list by adding bullets or numbers. You can choose from a variety of bullet and number styles, and you even can have Word sort the list into alphabetical, chronological, or numerical order.

Note: *By default, Word formats bulleted and numbered list with a hanging indent. That means that the bullet or number is flush left, but all other lines in the paragraph are indented to line up with an even left margin.*

Task: Add Bullets or Numbers to a List

To create a bulleted list, follow these steps:

1. Enter the list items. Press Enter after each item to insert a paragraph mark.

2. Select all of the list items.

3. Click the Bullets button on the Formatting toolbar.

With Word, it is simple to create bulleted or numbered lists.

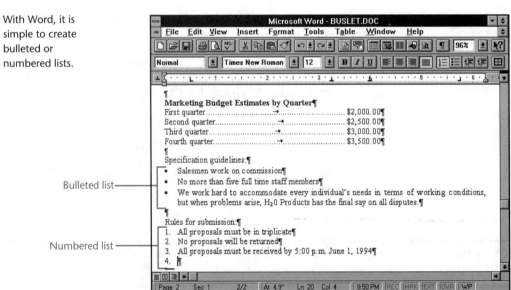

Bulleted list

Numbered list

To create a numbered list, follow these steps:

1. Enter the list items. Press Enter after each item to insert a paragraph mark.

2. Select all of the list items.

 3. Click the Numbering button on the Formatting toolbar.

If you have problems...

If the insertion point is positioned at the end of an item in a numbered or bulleted list, and you press Enter, Word assumes you want to add another item to the list. It automatically places a bullet or number at the beginning of the new line. To change back to regular text, simple click the Bullets or Numbers button again.

Task: Customizing Bullets and Numbers

By default, Word uses a small, solid, round bullet and numbers followed by periods for creating lists. You can customize the appearance of the bullets and numbers, and you can create multileveled lists.

To customize bullets and numbers, follow these steps:

1. Choose Format, Bullets and Numbering.

You can choose from a variety of bullet and numbering styles and schemes

Choose the bullet options here

Choose the numbering options here

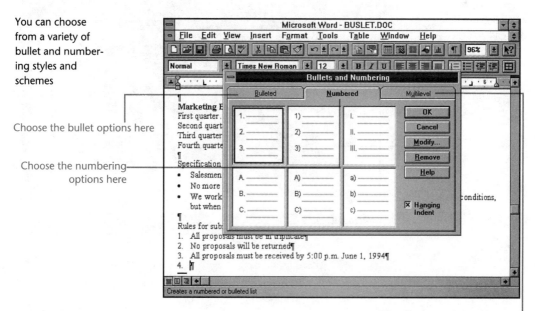

Choose to set multilevel list options here

2. Do any of the following:

■ To select a different bullet, click the **B**ulleted tab, and choose the style you want to use.

■ To select a different number, click the **N**umbered tab, and choose the style you want to use.

■ To set multilevel options, click the M**u**ltilevel tab, and choose the style you want to use.

3. Choose OK.

Task: Sorting Lists

As long as you press Enter to insert a paragraph mark between each item, you can sort the list by number, by initial letter, or by date.

To sort a list, follow these steps:

1. Choose the items in the list that you want to sort.

2. Choose T**a**ble, Sor**t** Text.

Word can sort alphabetically, numerically, or chronologically; in ascending order or descending order.

Choose to sort numbers, letters, or dates here

Choose to leave the first line unsorted here

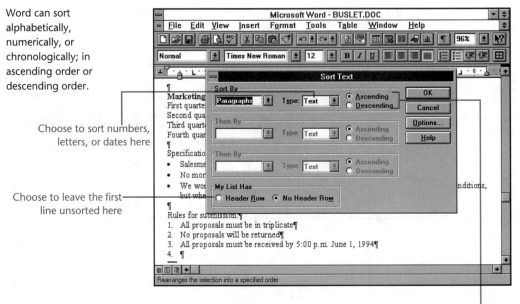

Choose the sort order here

3. From the **S**ort By drop-down list, choose Paragraphs.

4. From the Sort By T**y**pe drop-down list, choose one of the following:

   ■ *Text* if you are sorting alphabetical characters.

   ■ *Number* if you are sorting numerical characters.

   ■ *Date* if you are sorting dates

5. Choose either **A**scending, to sort the list from A to Z or from 1 up to the highest number, or **D**escending to sort the list from Z to A or from the highest number down to 1.

6. If you want to leave the first row unsorted for a title or header, choose Header **R**ow in the My List Has area.

7. Choose OK.

| If you have problems... | If you forget to select the items you want to sort, Word tries to sort your entire document. If this happens, it may take Word a while to complete the sort. When the sort is finished, choose **E**dit **U**ndo immediately. Try again, but this time remember to select the items in the list, first. |

Summary

6

To	Do This
Choose an alignment	Choose F**o**rmat **P**aragraph. Click the **I**ndents and Spacing tab. From the Ali**g**nment drop-down list, choose the alignment option.
Indent a paragraph	Drag the indent markers on the horizontal ruler.
Set tabs	Choose a tab type by clicking the tab button on the ruler. Click at the tab stop position on the horizontal ruler.
Set line spacing	Choose F**o**rmat, **P**aragraph. From the Line Spacing drop-down list, choose the line spacing setting.

(continues)

To	Do This
Set paragraph spacing	Choose Format, Paragraph. In the Before text box, enter the amount of space to leave before the paragraph. In the After text box, enter the amount of space to leave after the paragraph.
Add borders and shading	Display the Borders toolbar. Choose the line style. Choose the border position. Choose the fill pattern or gray scale.
Create a bulleted	Select the items in the list.
or numbered list	Click the Bullets button or the Numbers button.
Sort a list	Select the items in the list. Choose Table Sort Text. Choose the sort type and the sort order.

On Your Own

Estimated time: 15 minutes

1. Open a document.

2. Align the first paragraph flush right.

3. Align the second paragraph flush left.

4. Align the third paragraph in the center.

5. Justify the fourth paragraph.

6. Indent the first paragraph .5 inches from both the left and the right margins.

7. Indent the first line of the second paragraph .5 inches from the left.

8. Type a paragraph using a hanging indent.

9. On the top line of the document, use tabs to type a line of text with a company name flush left, a date in the center, and a page number flush right.

10. Type a row of numbers using a decimal tab stop.

11. Give each paragraph a different line spacing setting.

12. Put 6 points of space before and 3 points of space after each paragraph.

13. Put a border with a shadow around the first line of the document.

14. Put a border along the left edge of the whole page.

15. Add a pale gray shading pattern to the first line of the document.

16. Create a bulleted list.

17. Create a numbered list.

18. Sort the numbered list alphabetically in ascending order.

19. Resort the numbered list alphabetically in descending order.

6

Setting Up Your Pages

Page setup
The process of specifying the appearance and layout of a document page or section.

The overall look of a document, in large, partly depends on the way you arrange text and graphics on each page. With Word's *page setup* features, you can customize a page layout to suit a particular document.

Components of a page layout include margins, headers, footers, columns, footnotes, and endnotes. You also can choose a page size and orientation, number pages, and divide a document into sections.

Note: *Unlike character and paragraph formatting, page setup options affect an entire document or section.*

In this lesson, you learn to do the following:

- View a document in different ways
- Choose a page size and orientation
- Set margins
- Number pages
- Create headers and footers
- Create footnotes and endnotes
- Create sections
- Use columns
- Control breaks

Displaying a Document in Different Views

View
One of six different ways Word can display a document on-screen.

Word can display different *views* of the same document. Views determine the size of the characters displayed on-screen by adjusting the amount of magnification, and the amount of formatting shown on-screen.

Word offers six views. Selecting a different view can make seeing how a page will look when printed or make editing a particular section easier.

■ *Normal view*: Enables you to see character and paragraph formatting, alignment, tab positions, and line, section, and page breaks. You do not see headers, footers, footnotes, or side-by-side columns.

Normal view is the default view. Editing in Normal view is quicker than in some of the other views. To change to Normal view, choose **V**iew **N**ormal.

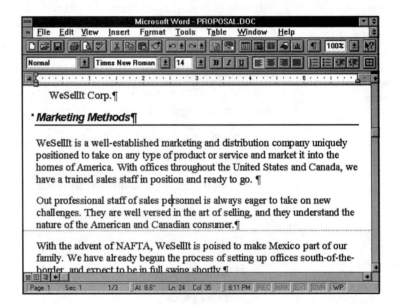

■ *Outline view*: Enables you to create and edit document outlines. To learn more about outlining see Lesson 16, "Managing Your Documents and Files."

In Outline view, you create and manipulate levels of headings to organize your document. To change to Outline view, choose **V**iew, **O**utline.

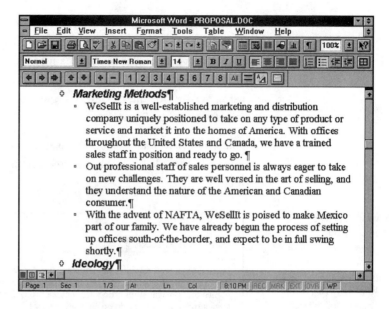

 ■ *Page Layout view*: Enables you to see all document formatting. All parts of a document appear in the correct positions.

In Page Layout view, you can see exactly how your document is set up. Editing in Page Layout view is slower than in other views, but it is the most effective view to use for certain features, such as positioning frames. To change to page layout view, choose **V**iew, **P**age Layout.

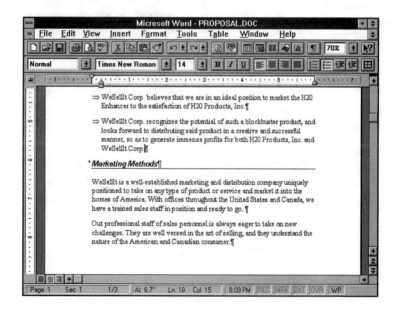

7

■ *Master Document view*: Enables you to manage large, multifile projects. It displays all files in the master document, and enables you to move among them. To change to Master Document view, choose **View** **M**aster Document. For more information about using Master Document view, see Que's *Using Word Version 6 for Windows*, Special Edition.

■ *Full Screen view*: Enables you to see as much of the document on-screen as possible by hiding all screen elements except the document text area.

Even though the menus are not displayed, you can edit and use commands in Full Screen view. To change to Full Screen view, choose **V**iew, **F**ull Screen. To change back to the previous view, click the Full Screen icon that appears on-screen.

> WeSellIt Corp.¶
>
> **Marketing Methods¶**
>
> WeSellIt is a well-established marketing and distribution company uniquely positioned to take on any type of product or service and market it into the homes of America. With offices throughout the United States and Canada, we have a trained sales staff in position and ready to go. ¶
>
> Out professional staff of sales personnel is always eager to take on new challenges. They are well versed in the art of selling, and they understand the nature of the American and Canadian consumer.¶
>
> With the advent of NAFTA, WeSellIt is poised to make Mexico part of our family. We have already begun the process of setting up offices south-of-the-border, and expect to be in full swing shortly.¶
>
> **Ideology¶**
>
> At WeSellIt, we only take on products that we believe in. We know the potential of every item we sell, and we are eager to share this knowledge with consumers everywhere.¶
>
> Proposal¶

■ *Print Preview*: Enables you to see a miniature version of how your document will look when printed. Print Preview is discussed in Lesson 2, "Creating a Document."

In Print Preview, Word scales the document image so that you can see a complete page or many pages. To change to print preview, choose **F**ile, Print Pre**v**iew.

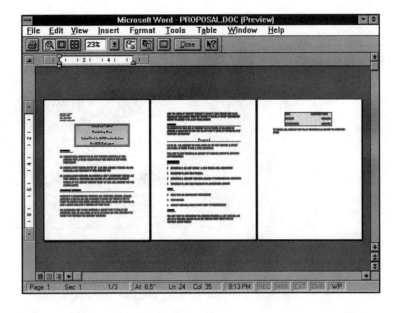

If you have problems...

If you are not sure what view you are in, choose **V**iew to look at the View menu. A bullet appears next to the current view.

Task: Enlarging and Reducing the Document Display

You can control the document display by increasing or decreasing the magnification of any of the document views. Increasing the magnification enlarges the view so that you can work closely in a particular area of the document. Decreasing the magnification reduces the view so that you can see more of the document on-screen, or get the overall effect of a page layout.

7

To change the magnification, follow these steps:

You can control the document view by increasing or decreasing the magnification.

1. Choose **V**iew, **Z**oom.

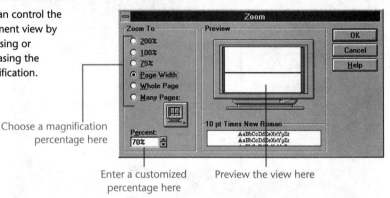

Choose a magnification percentage here

Enter a customized percentage here

Preview the view here

2. In the Zoom To area, choose one of the following:

   ■ **2**00% to display the document at twice its actual size.

   ■ **1**00% to display the document at its actual size.

   ■ **7**5% to display the document at 2/3rds of its actual size.

   ■ **P**age Width to automatically adjust the magnification percentage so that the whole width of the page fits on-screen.

   ■ **W**hole Page to display a complete page.

   ■ **M**any Pages to choose how many pages to display.

3. Choose OK.

   Note: *You also can choose a magnification from the Zoom drop-down list on the Standard toolbar.*

If you have problems...

Not all views support all magnification options. If some of the magnification options are dimmed, it is because the view you are currently using does not support them. Change to another view, such as **P**age Layout view, and try again.

Task: **Choosing a Page Size and Orientation**

Portrait Orientation

In portrait orientation, text is printed horizontally across the page. You use portrait orientation for most letters, reports, and business documents.

Perhaps the most basic page layout setting is the page size. In Word, the default page size is a standard business letter—8-1/2 x 11-inches. You easily can change the page size if the document you are creating is larger or smaller. By default, Word prints in *portrait orientation*, but you can select to print in *landscape orientation* if you want your document to print across a wide page.

To change the page size or orientation, follow these steps:

1. Choose **F**ile Page Set**u**p.

2. In the Page Setup dialog box, click the Paper **S**ize tab to display the page size and orientation options.

Word offers a list of standard American and European page and envelope sizes, or you can enter a custom size.

Choose a standard paper size here

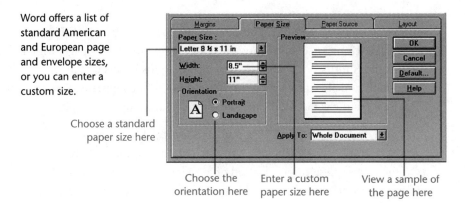

Choose the orientation here

Enter a custom paper size here

View a sample of the page here

Landscape Orientation

In landscape orientation, text is printed vertically across the page. You often use landscape orientation for brochures, forms, and other wide documents that make use of graphics, charts, or tables.

3. From the Pape**r** Size drop down list, choose a paper or envelope size.

4. If you choose Custom Size in step 3, enter the dimensions in the **W**idth and H**e**ight text boxes. If you did not choose Custom Size, skip this step.

5. In the Orientation area, choose either Portra**i**t or Lands**c**ape.

7

*Note: To save the settings as defaults to use for all new documents based on the current document template, choose **D**efault. Word asks you if you are sure you want to change the page setup default settinos. Choose **Y**es to change the defaults, or **N**o to return to the Page Setup dialog box.*

If you have problems...   If you changed the paper size and orientation, but the document is not printing correctly, check to be sure that your printer can print the page settings you selected. Some printers, for example, require special fonts for landscape printing, and some can only accommodate certain paper sizes.

Setting Margins

Margins
The space between the edge of the paper and the edge of the text.

Every page in a Word document has four *margins*: top, bottom, left, and right.

By changing margin widths, you can change the amount of text that fits on a page. Using smaller margins causes more text to fit on a page, which results in a shorter document. Using larger margins results in a longer document and also leaves room for margin notes or comments. You also can increase the *gutter* width, to leave room for binding.

Gutter
The inside edge between two facing pages or between two columns.

In Word, the margin area is differentiated from the text area by color. The text area generally is white, and the margin area generally is gray. On the rulers, these colors are used on either side of the *margin markers* to indicate where the margin ends and the text area begins.

Margin markers
Solid lines on each ruler that separate the gray margin area from the white text area.

Each of the margins is sized independently, which means they do not need to be the same width. The quickest method of sizing margins is to drag the margin markers on the horizontal and vertical rulers in Print Preview or Page Layout view. To set precise margin widths, you use the Page Setup dialog box.

If you have problems...   In Normal view, you cannot see the margins on-screen, nor can you drag the margin markers. To see the margins, change to **P**age Layout or Print Preview. In these views, you can display both rulers on-screen, and drag the margin markers, as well.

Task: Setting Margins Quickly

To quickly change the margins by using the rulers, drag the margin markers to the correct location. You know you are pointing at the margin marker when the pointer changes to a double-headed arrow.

If you have problems...	If the pointer doesn't change to a double-headed arrow, and you can't drag the margin markers, you are not in Print Preview or Page Layout view. Change views, and try again.

Use the horizontal ruler to do the following:

- Drag the left margin marker to adjust the width of the left margin.

- Drag the right margin marker to adjust the width of the right margin.

Use the vertical ruler to do the following:

- Drag the top margin marker to adjust the width of the top margin.

- Drag the bottom margin marker to adjust the width of the bottom margin.

You easily can adjust the widths of all four margins by dragging the margin markers on the rulers.

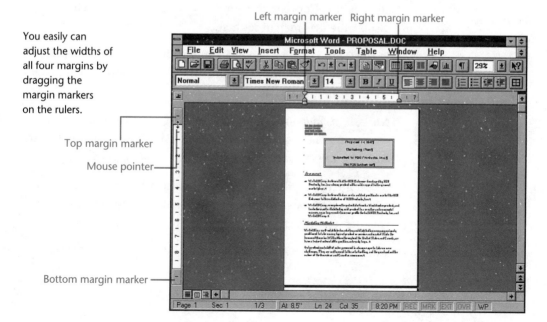

Left margin marker   Right margin marker

Top margin marker

Mouse pointer

Bottom margin marker

7

If you have problems...   If you do not see the rulers on screen, choose **V**iew **R**uler. If you still do not see the rulers on-screen, change to Print Preview or **P**age Layout view.

Task: Setting Precise Margins

To set precise margin widths, follow these steps:

1. Choose **F**ile, Page Set**u**p.

2. Click the **M**argins tab at the top of the Page Setup dialog box.

You can set precise margin widths for all four margins.

Enter the margin widths here

Enter a gutter width here

Preview the page setup here

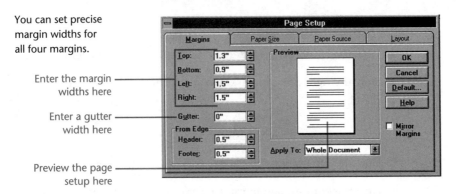

3. In the **M**argins area, enter the size of each margin in the appropriate text box. Notice that the preview of the page layout changes to display the new margin settings.

4. In the **Gu**tter text box, enter a gutter width. Word adds this value to the right margin width of left-hand pages, and to the left margin width of right-hand pages.

   Note: *By default, margins are measured in inches. To use a different measurement unit, type the unit's abbreviation after the value in the text box. Type **cm** for centimeters, **pt** for points, or **pi** for picas.*

5. If you intend to print on both sides of the page, select the **M**irror Margins check box. You then set inside and outside margins rather than left and right margins.

6. Choose OK.

Note: *To save the settings as defaults to use for all new documents based on the current document template, choose* **D***efault. Word asks you if you are sure you want to change the page setup default settings. Choose* **Y***es to change the defaults, or* **N***o to return to the Page Setup dialog box.*

Task: Numbering Pages

Word automatically keeps track of the number of pages in a document. You can see the current page number on the status bar. To print page numbers, however, you must insert them into the document.

You can choose to place page numbers at the top or bottom of a document, and you can choose to align them flush right, flush left, or centered. You also can select from a variety of formats, including roman numerals and letters of the alphabet. You can even include the current chapter number, separated from the page number by a hyphen.

To insert page numbers, follow these steps:

1. Position the insertion point on the page where you want numbering to begin.

2. Choose **I**nsert, Page N**u**mbers.

Choose page number position here

Choose to set page number format here

You can select a placement and an alignment for page numbers in the Page Numbers dialog box.

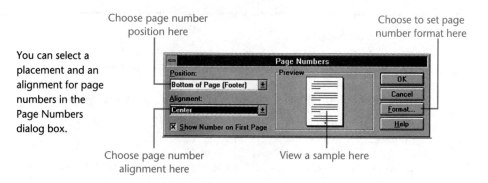

Choose page number alignment here

View a sample here

7

3. From the **P**osition drop-down list, choose to place the page numbers at the top of the page or at the bottom of the page.

4. From the **A**lignment drop-down list, choose to place the page numbers flush left, flush right, or centered.

5. Choose **F**ormat.

You can choose from a variety of page number formats in the Page Number Format dialog box.

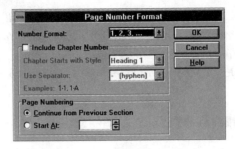

6. From the Number **F**ormat drop-down list, choose the format you want to use.

7. To start with any number other than the correct page number, enter that number in the Start **A**t text box.

8. Choose OK to return to the Page Numbers dialog box.

9. Choose OK to insert the page numbers into the document.

   Note: *You also can place page numbers into headers or footers. That process is discussed in the next section.*

If you have problems...   To see the page numbers on-screen, you must change to Print Pre**v**iew or **P**age Layout view.

Task: Creating Headers and Footers

Header
The area between the top edge of the page and the top edge of the text.

Footer
The area between the bottom edge of the page and the bottom edge of the text.

With Word, you can place a *header* and a *footer* on every page of a document. Within the header or footer, you can enter and format text and graphics.

Headers and footers are useful for placing information such as page numbers, dates, and author names in an obvious, yet out-of-the-way location.

You can create headers or footers that appear the same on each page, or you can alternate pages—one header or footer on odd-numbered pages and a different header or footer on even-numbered pages.

You can add headers and footers to an existing document, or you can create headers and footers in a new document.

To create a header or footer, follow these steps:

1. Choose **V**iew, **H**eader and Footer. Word displays the Header area on-screen surrounded by a dashed line, and the Header and Footer toolbar.

You enter headers and footers in page layout view, using the buttons on the Header and Footer toolbar. The document text appears dimmed.

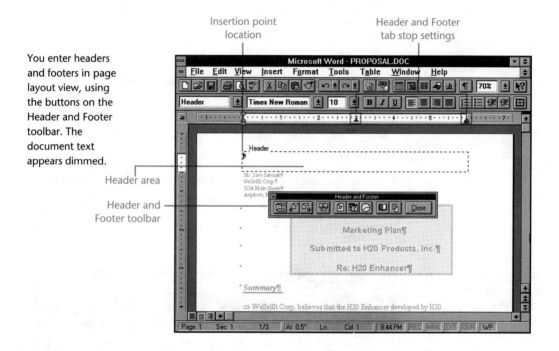

Insertion point location

Header and Footer tab stop settings

Header area

Header and Footer toolbar

2. Type the text you want to appear in the header. Use the tab stops to position text in the center or flush right. Use character formatting to format the text.

3. You can click the Header and Footer toolbar buttons to complete the header, as follows:

■ Switch from header area to footer area.

■ Move back to a previous section of the document that has different headers or footers.

■ Move forward to the next section of the document that has different headers or footers.

■ Copy the headers or footers from the previous section to the current section.

7

■ Insert page numbers into the header or footer.

■ Insert the date into the header or footer.

■ Insert the time into the header or footer.

■ Open the Page Setup dialog box to modify the header or footer settings.

■ Show or hide the current document text.

■ Close the header or footer display and return to the document view.

4. Click the Switch from Header to Footer button to move to the footer area.

5. Enter and format the footer text using the same methods you used for the header.

6. Choose Close to return to the document view.

Here, you can see the header and footer displayed on two pages of a document.

Headers

Microsoft Word - PROPOSAL.DOC [Preview]

Footers

You can change the way headers and footers appear by adjusting the space left between the header or footer and the edge of the page. You also can change the way headers and footers appear by placing different headers and footers on different pages.

To place different headers or footers on different pages, follow these steps:

1. Choose **F**ile, Page Set**u**p.

2. Click the **L**ayout tab at the top of the Page Setup dialog box.

You can set Word to display different headers and footers on different pages.

Choose header and footer page options here

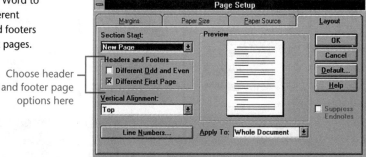

3. Do any of the following:

   ■ To put different Headers and Footers on odd and even pages, choose the check box next to Different **O**dd and Even.

   ■ To put a different header or footer on the first page than on the rest of the document, choose the check box next to Different **F**irst Page.

4. Choose OK.

5. Choose **V**iew, **H**eader and Footer to display the header area.

   The title of the header area has changed to indicate that different headers and footers will appear on different pages. If you selected to display a different header or footer on the first page, the area is now called the *First Page Header*. If you selected to display a different header or footer on odd and even pages, the header area is now called the *Odd Page Header* or the *Even Page Header*.

7

6. Enter the header or footer information as described earlier in this section. Use the scroll bars to page forward or back to be sure to enter headers for the different pages you selected.

Here, you see that the first page header and footer are different from the header and footer on the other pages.

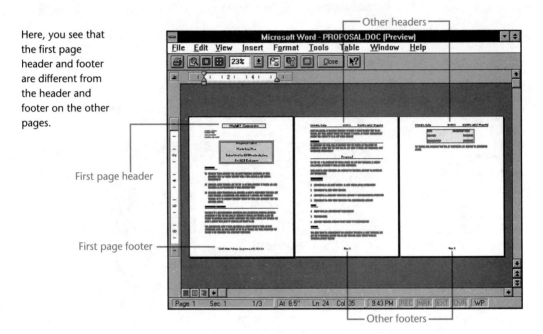

First page header

First page footer

Task: Dividing a Document into Sections

In Word, page setup settings affect an entire document. If you need to change the page setup settings for any part of a document, you must divide the document into sections. You can have as many sections as you want within a document.

To set up a section differently than the rest of the document, position the insertion point anywhere within the section before you choose the setup commands.

To divide a document into sections, follow these steps:

1. Position the insertion point where you want to start a new section.

2. Choose **I**nsert, **B**reak.

In the Break dialog box, you can choose to start the new section at one of four different locations in the document.

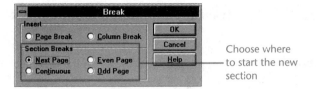

Choose where to start the new section

3. In the Section Breaks area, choose one of the following:

   ■ **N**ext Page to move the text immediately following the insertion point, starting the new section at the top of the next page.

   ■ **Con**tinuous to leave the text immediately following the insertion point in its current location, starting the new section on the current page.

   ■ **E**ven Page to move the text immediately following the insertion point, starting the new section at the top of the next even-numbered page.

   ■ **O**dd Page to move the text immediately following the insertion point, starting the new section at the top of the next odd-numbered page.

4. Choose OK. Word starts a new section at the insertion point location.

In Normal view, a nonprinting double line appears across the screen, with the words End of Section in it, indicating where one section ends and the next begins. To delete a section break, position the insertion point on the double line and press Delete. The text preceding the insertion point takes on the formatting of the text following the insertion point.

7

Task: Adding Footnotes or Endnotes

Footnote
Reference text that appears at the bottom of the page containing the reference mark.

Endnote
Reference text that appears at the end of a document or at the end of a section, regardless of what page contains the reference mark.

You use *footnotes* or *endnotes* to reference information in a document. When you insert a footnote or endnote, Word inserts a reference number in superscript at the insertion point location. You type the footnote or endnote text at the bottom of the page.

Word automatically numbers footnotes and endnotes, and adjusts the length of text on each page to allow space for the notes.

To add a footnote or an endnote to a document, follow these steps:

1. Choose **V**iew, **N**ormal to change to Normal view.

2. Position the insertion point in the document where you want the reference mark to appear.

3. Choose **I**nsert, Foot**n**ote.

In the Footnote and Endnote dialog box choose the type of note to insert and the numbering scheme.

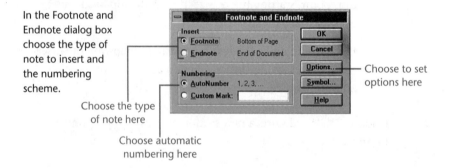

Choose the type of note here

Choose automatic numbering here

Choose to set options here

4. In the Insert area, choose either Footnote or Endnote.

5. In the Numbering area, choose **A**utoNumber to use standard, automatic numbering with AutoNumber, or choose **C**ustom Mark. If you choose Custom Mark, you can choose **S**ymbol to insert a symbol or a special character. See Lesson 5, "Dressing Up Your Text," for more information on inserting symbols.

6. Choose **O**ptions to set footnote and endnote formatting options.

In the Note Options dialog box, you can choose where to place the notes, the number format you want to use, which number to start with, and whether or not to restart numbering at the beginning of each new section.

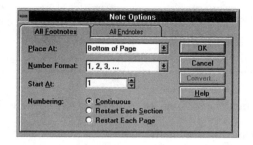

7. Choose OK to return to the Footnote and Endnote dialog box.

8. Choose OK to return to the document.

Word inserts the footnote or endnote reference mark at the insertion point location and opens a pane at the bottom of the document window.

Footnote reference mark

Footnote text panel

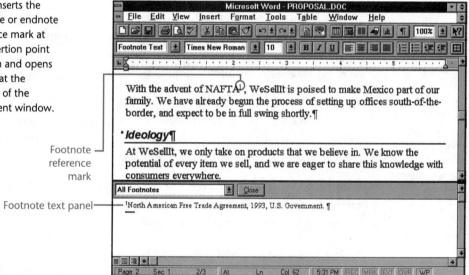

9. Type the footnote or endnote text in the pane at the bottom of the document window. Use character and paragraph formatting to format the text.

10. Choose Close to close the pane and continue editing the document.

7

If you have problems...   In Normal view, you cannot see the footnotes or endnotes correctly positioned in the document. Choose **V**iew **P**age Layout or **F**ile Print Preview to see the footnotes or endnotes.

To delete a footnote or endnote, delete the reference mark.

To quickly display the footnotes or endnotes pane at the bottom of the document window, double-click any footnote or endnote reference mark in the text, or choose **V**iew, **F**ootnotes.

Dividing a Page into Columns

Some documents look best and are easiest to read when divided into columns. The page layout of a newsletter or brochure, for example, usually includes two or more columns. Sometimes, you can fit a document on fewer pages by dividing the document into columns.

Newspaper Columns
Text flows from the bottom of one column to the top of the next column.

With Word, you can split a page into *newspaper columns*. (If you want side-by-side columns instead, create a table or graph. To learn about creating tables, see Lesson 12, "Working with Tables." To learn about creating charts, see Lesson 13, "Working with Graphs.")

With Word, you control the number of columns on a page, the width of each column, the space between columns, and where the text breaks between one column and the next.

Task: Creating Columns of Equal Width

To create two, three, or four columns of equal width, follow these steps:

1. Choose **V**iew, **P**age Layout to change to page layout view.

2. Position the insertion point within the section you want to divide into columns.

 3. Click the Columns button on the standard toolbar. A box with four text columns appears below the toolbar.

You quickly can divide your document into columns of equal width by clicking the Columns button on the Standard toolbar.

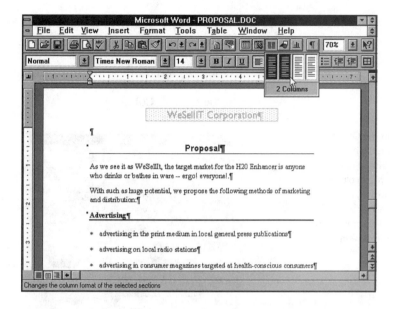

4. Drag the mouse across the text columns to highlight the number you want to create.

When you release the mouse button, Word divides the document into columns.

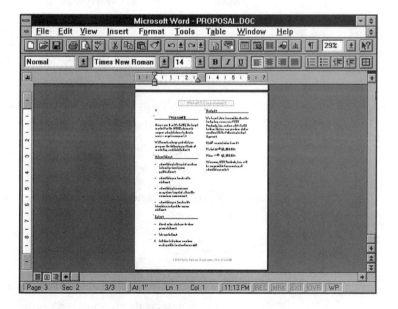

If you have problems...   In Normal view you can only see one column at a time. Change to Page Layout view or Print Preview to see all of the columns in their correct locations.

Task: Creating Columns of Unequal Width

To create up to 11 columns of equal or unequal width, follow these steps:

1. Position the insertion point within the section you want to divide.

2. Choose **F**ormat, **C**olumns.

In the Columns dialog box, you can choose one of the preset column format, or you can set your own using precise measurements.

Choose a column format here

Enter column width and spacing here

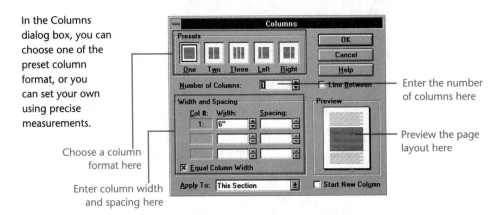

Enter the number of columns here

Preview the page layout here

3. In the Presets area, choose one of the column formats.

4. To customize your columns, do any of the following:

- ■ Enter the number of columns in the **N**umber of Columns text box.

- ■ For each column, enter the column width, and the spacing between columns.

- ■ To create columns of equal width, choose the **E**qual Column Width check box.

- ■ To draw a line between columns, choose the Line **B**etween check box.

5. Choose OK.

Task: Customizing the Column Format

No matter how you create columns, you easily can modify and customize their appearance. You can change the width and spacing, combine column formats on one page or within one section, and you can insert column breaks to balance column lengths.

To change the width and spacing of columns, simply drag the column margin markers on the horizontal ruler.

To insert a column break, follow these steps:

1. Position the insertion point where you want the column to end.

2. Choose **I**nsert, **B**reak.

3. In the Break dialog box, choose **C**olumn Break.

4. Choose OK. Word moves the text immediately following the insertion point up to the top of the next column.

    Note: *In Normal view, column breaks are shown as dotted lines across the page with the words* Column Break *in the middle.*

Task: Controlling Page Breaks

Soft page break

A movable page break that Word automatically inserts and adjusts when the current page is full.

Hard page break

A non-movable page break that you insert when you want Word to start a new page even if the current page is not full.

When the current page is full, Word inserts a *soft page break* into the document to start a new page. If you edit the page, by adding or deleting text, or by changing the page setup or the formatting settings, Word adjusts the text on the page and moves the soft page break accordingly.

If you want to start a new page when the current page is not full, you can insert a *hard page break* into the document. If you want to start a new column before the first column is full, you can insert a *column break*.

To insert a hard page break, follow these steps:

1. Position the insertion point where you want the new page to start.

2. Choose **I**nsert, **B**reak.

3. Choose OK. Word inserts the hard page break at the insertion point location. The text immediately after the insertion point appears at the top of the new page.

7

In Normal view, a soft page break appears as a dotted line across the page. A hard page break appears as a dotted line with the words: Page Break in the middle.

Soft page break indicator

Hard page break indicator

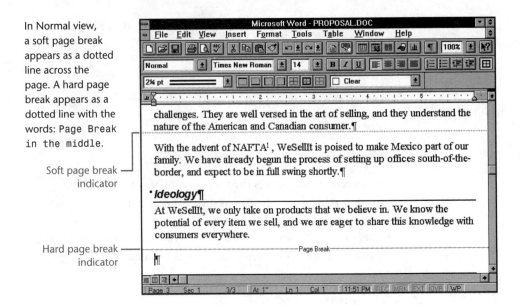

To delete a hard page break, follow these steps:

Position the insertion point on the dotted line that indicates the hard page break and press Delete.

Summary

To	Do This
Change the document view	Choose **V**iew and then choose the view you want to use.
Change document magnification	Choose **V**iew, **Z**oom and then choose the magnification.
Change page size and orientation	Choose **F**ile, Page Set**u**p.
Set Margins	Drag the margin markers to the desired location.
Number pages	Choose **I**nsert, Page Nu**m**bers.
Create headers and footers	Choose **V**iew, **H**eader and Footer.
Create footnotes and endnotes	Choose **I**nsert, Foot**n**ote.
Create sections	Choose Insert, **B**reak and then choose the section break format.
Create columns	Choose **F**ormat, **C**olumns.

On Your Own

Estimated time: 15 minutes

1. Open or create a multipage document.

2. Change to Page Layout view.

3. Magnify the view to 200%.

4. Reduce the magnification to display a whole page on-screen.

5. Change the magnification to one comfortable for editing.

6. Make the document margins wider.

7. Insert page numbers.

8. Create a header.

9. Create a footer.

10. Insert a footnote or an endnote.

11. Make the last page in the document a separate section.

12. Divide the section into two columns.

13. Place a banner heading across the top of the two column section.

14. If necessary, insert page breaks and column breaks so that pages and columns appear well-designed.

7

Part III
Customizing and Adding Nontext Elements to Documents

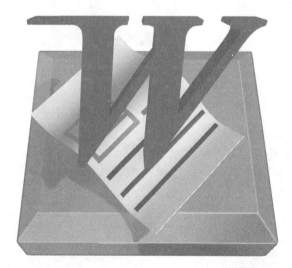

Lesson 8

Customizing Word for Windows

Word for Windows is a flexible program. You easily can adjust many settings and options to suit your own work habits. In this lesson, you learn to customize Word to make the time you spend at your computer more efficient and productive.

Specifically, you learn to do the following:

■ Create and modify templates

■ Create and modify styles

■ Customize shortcut keys and toolbars

■ Set startup options

Using Templates

Style sheet
A collection of styles used to format a particular type of document.

In Lesson 2, "Creating a Document," you learned to create new documents by selecting a document template. Each document template defines page formatting characteristics for a particular type of document, and includes a *style sheet* you can use to quickly apply character and paragraph formatting to the document text.

Word 6 comes with many built-in templates; you simply select the one you want to use in the New dialog box when you create a new document. If none of the built-in document templates are quite right for the documents you create, you can modify one to meet your needs, or you can create a new one.

Task: Modifying a Template

To modify a template, follow these steps:

1. Choose **F**ile, **N**ew.

In the New dialog box, open the template you want to modify.

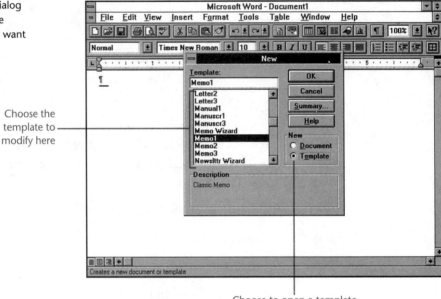

Choose the template to modify here

Choose to open a template file, not a document file, here

2. From the **T**emplate list, choose the template you want to modify.

3. In the New area, choose the T**e**mplate option. If you do not choose the Template option, Word creates a new document file instead of a template file.

4. Choose OK to open the template file.

Title bar

The template file
looks the same as
the document file,
except for the name
Template1 in the
title bar.

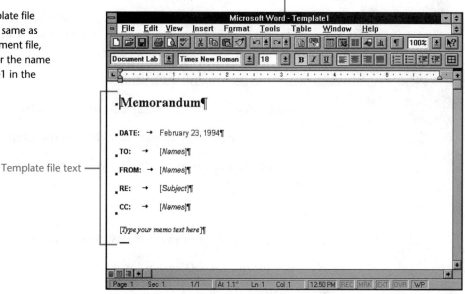

Template file text ———

5. Edit the template file any way you want. You can delete existing text, add text, or change formatting, for example.

6. Choose **F**ile, Save **A**s to save the template file with a new name. (For information on saving, see Lesson 2, "Creating a Document.")

If you have problems...

If you try to save the modified template with the same name as the original template file, Word asks if you want to replace the existing template file. Choose **Y**es to overwrite the existing template file. Choose **N**o to return to the Save As dialog box and give the template file a new name.

Note: *Word automatically adds a .DOT extension to template files, and stores them in the C:\WINWORD\TEMPLATE subdirectory. If you use a different extension or subdirectory, Word may not be able to find the template file.*

7. Choose **F**ile, **C**lose to close the template file. To use the modified template to create a new document, choose **F**ile, **N**ew and select the template name from the **T**emplate list. For more information about creating new files, see Lesson 2, "Creating a Document."

8

Task: Creating a New Template

When you modify a template, you create a new template based on an existing template. If none of the existing templates are close to what you want, you can create a new template from scratch.

To create a new template, follow these steps:

1. Create a new document file, using any document template you want.

2. Insert all the information you want to include in the template.

3. Format the document using the settings you want to include in the template.

4. Choose File, Save As.

5. Change the directory path to C:\WINWORD\TEMPLATE.

6. Name the file using a .DOT extension.

7. Choose OK.

8. Choose File, Close to close the template file. To use the new template to create a new document, choose File, New and select the template name from the Template list.

If you have problems...

If your new template does not appear in the Template list in the New dialog box, you probably forgot to give it a .DOT extension, or to store it in the C:\WINWORD\TEMPLATE subdirectory. Try using the File, Open command to see if the file is stored in the default document directory.

Using the Style Gallery

You can use Word's style gallery to preview templates, apply templates to existing documents, and to see samples of the styles a template contains.

Task: Previewing a Template

When you choose a document template in the New dialog box, a brief description of the template appears. You can find out more about the template and what it contains by previewing it. If you like what you see, you can apply the template to the document currently open on your screen.

To preview a document template, follow these steps:

1. Open a document.

2. Choose Format, Style Gallery.

3. In the **T**emplate list, choose the template you want to preview.

4. In the Preview area, choose **E**xample.

Word displays
a sample of a
document created
using the selected
template.

Choose the template
to preview here

Choose to display
an example here

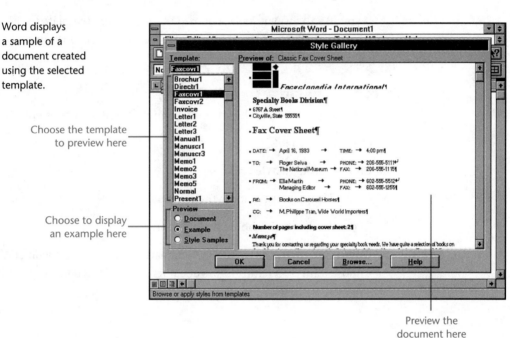

Preview the
document here

5. Choose OK to apply the selected template to the current document, or choose Cancel to return to the current document without changing the style sheet.

Task: Changing a Document Template

You can use the Style Gallery to preview the way an existing document would look if it was formatted using a different document template. You also can use the Style Gallery to change the document template.

8

To preview a document using a different template, follow these steps:

1. Open the document.

2. Choose F**o**rmat, Style **G**allery.

3. Choose the template you want to preview.

4. In the Preview area, choose **D**ocument.

5. If you like the way it looks, choose OK to apply the template to the document. Choose Cancel to return to the document without making any changes.

Task: Previewing a Template's Style Sheet

To display samples of all of the styles in a template, follow these steps:

1. Open a document.

2. Choose F**o**rmat, Style **G**allery.

3. In the **T**emplate list, choose the template.

4. In the Preview area, choose **S**tyle Samples.

5. Choose OK to apply the selected template to the current document. Choose Cancel to return to the document without making any changes.

Task: Using Styles

In Lesson 2, "Creating a Document," you learned to format text by selecting styles from the Style list box. The styles that appear in the Style list box are part of the document template's style sheet. If the styles included in the style sheet are not quite right, you can modify them, create new ones, or copy some from another style sheet.

Style Area
An adjustable column you can display along the left side of your screen in Normal view to identify current paragraph styles.

Task: Examining Styles

One way to find out what style is currently in use is to position the insertion point anywhere within the text and look at the Style list box. The style name appears. If you want to know the current style of every paragraph in your document, you can display the *Style Area* on your screen in Normal view.

To display the Style Area, follow these steps:

1. Choose **V**iew, **N**ormal to change to Normal view.

2. Choose **T**ools, **O**ptions.

3. Click the View tab.

Change the View
option settings to
display the Style
Area on-screen

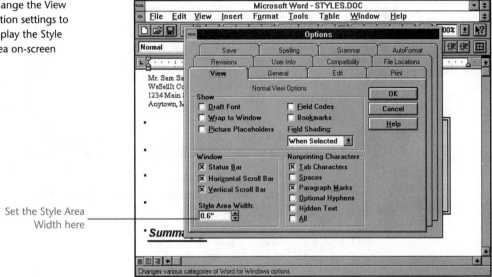

Set the Style Area
Width here

4. In the Style Area Width text box, enter the width you want to use for the Style Area.

5. Choose OK.

If you have problems...

If you do not see the same View options as described here, you probably are not in Normal view. Choose **V**iew, **N**ormal to change to Normal view, and then try again.

8

Word displays the Style Area along the left margin, shifting the rest of the document to the right.

Style names

Style area

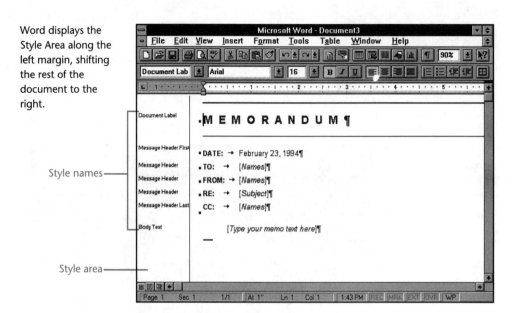

Knowing the style name does not tell you very much about the style. To find out what formatting settings a style contains, follow these steps:

1. Position the insertion point within the style.

2. Choose Format, Style.

In the Style dialog box, you can see the formatting settings for the selected style.

Select a style here

View a description of the style here

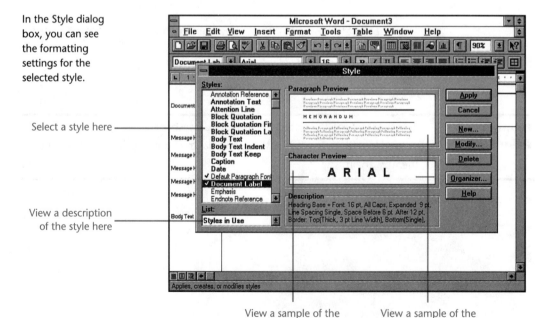

View a sample of the character formatting here

View a sample of the paragraph formatting here

3. In the Description area, you can read the formatting settings associated with the selected style.

   Note: *If the style description begins with the name of another style, it means that all of the formatting settings associated with the other style are also part of the current style. To see a description of the settings associated with the other style, highlight it in the Styles list.*

4. Choose Cancel to close the dialog box and return to the document.

Task: Printing a List of Styles

You also can print a list of the styles associated with the current template, and the style descriptions.

To print a list of styles and style descriptions, follow these steps:

1. Open a document based on the template that contains the styles you want to print.

2. Choose **F**ile, **P**rint.

3. From the **P**rint What drop-down list, choose Styles.

4. Choose OK. Word prints an alphabetical list of all the styles in the current template.

Task: Applying a Style from a Different Document Template

The Style list box on the Formatting toolbar displays a list of all styles associated with the current document template. You can use a style from a different document template to format a paragraph.

To apply a style from a different document template, follow these steps:

1. Position the insertion point within the text you want to format.

2. Choose F**o**rmat, **S**tyle.

3. From the **L**ist drop-down list, choose All Styles to display a list of all available styles.

4. In the **S**tyles list, choose the style you want to apply.

5. Choose **A**pply. Word applies the style to the current text, and returns to the document.

8

Task: Modifying a Style

If a style is not quite right for your needs, you can modify it. However, it is important to remember that when you modify a style the changes are saved with the current document template. That means that all new documents created with that template have the modified style, and text formatted with that style in all existing documents created with that template is modified to reflect the change.

To modify an existing style, follow these steps:

1. Open a document based on the document template that contains the style you want to change.

2. Choose Format, Style to display the Style dialog box.

3. In the Styles list, choose the style you want to change.

4. Choose Modify.

In the Modify Style dialog box, you change the formatting associated with the selected style.

Change the style name here

Preview the style here

Choose to add the modified style to the current document template here

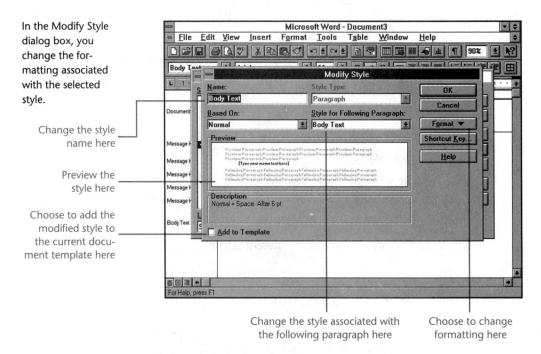

Change the style associated with the following paragraph here

Choose to change formatting here

5. Choose Format. Word displays a list of formats you can modify.

6. Choose the format you want to change.

7. Change the formatting settings and choose OK.

8. Repeat steps 4 through 7 until you have modified all of the formatting you want to change.

9. Choose the **A**dd to Template check box in the Modify Style dialog box.

10. Choose OK to return to the Style dialog box.

11. Choose Close to return to the document.

The style is now modified for use in the current document, but not for future documents.

To save the changes so that the style is changed permanently for use in all documents based on the current template, follow these steps:

1. Choose **F**ile, **C**lose.

2. Word asks if you want to save the changes made to your document. Choose **Y**es if you want to save the changes. Choose **N**o if you do not want to save the changes. This does not affect the changes made to styles.

3. Word asks if you want to save the changes made to the current document template. Choose **Y**es to save the modified styles.

If you have problems... If Word does not ask you if you want to save the changes made to the current document template, you probably forgot to choose the **A**dd to Template check box in the Modify Style dialog box.

Task: Creating a New Style Based on an Existing Style

You sometimes will want to create a style that is similar to an existing style, but keep the existing style as well. To do this, you save the modified style with a new name.

To create a new style based on an existing style, follow these steps:

1. Open a document that contains the style you want to use as a base for the new style.

2. Choose **F**ormat, **S**tyle to display the Style dialog box.

3. Choose **N**ew.

8

In the New Style
dialog box, you can
create a style based
on an existing style.

Enter a new style
name here

Choose the exist-
ing style here

Choose to add the
new style to the
current document
template here

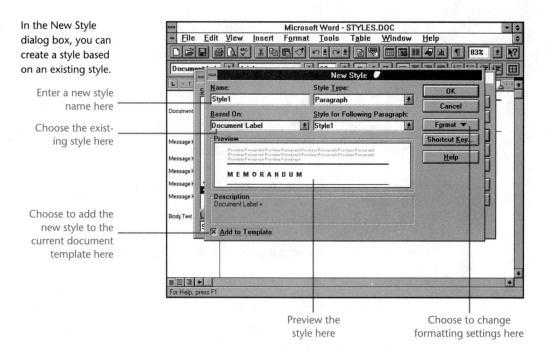

Preview the
style here

Choose to change
formatting settings here

4. In the **N**ame text box, enter a name for the new style.

5. From the **B**ased On drop-down list box, choose the existing style you want to use as a base for the new style.

6. In the **S**tyle for Following Paragraphs drop-down list box, choose the style you want to apply to paragraphs that follow paragraphs formatted with the new style.

7. Choose F**o**rmat to display a list of format options you can change.

8. Choose the format you want to change.

9. Change the formatting settings and choose OK.

10. Repeat steps 7 through 9 until you have modified all of the formatting settings you want to change.

11. Choose the **A**dd to Template check box in the New Style dialog box.

12. Choose OK to return to the Style dialog box.

13. Choose Close to return to the document.

The new style is now available for use in the current document, but not for future documents.

To save the new style for use in all documents based on the current template, follow these steps:

1. Choose **F**ile, **C**lose.

2. Word asks if you want to save the changes made to your document. Choose **Y**es if you want to save the changes. Choose **N**o if you do not want to save the changes. This does not affect the changes made to styles.

3. Word asks if you want to save the changes made to the current document template. Choose **Y**es to save the new style.

Task: Copying a Style from a Different Document

You can copy a style from one document to another. This is useful if you create a new style in one template, but want to make it part of another template as well.

To copy a style, follow these steps:

1. Open a document based on the template that contains the style you want to copy.

2. Choose **F**ormat, **S**tyle.

3. Choose **O**rganizer.

Use the Style Organizer to copy styles from one document to another.

Choose the style to copy here

Choose to clear the **T**o list and open the document to which you want to copy the style here

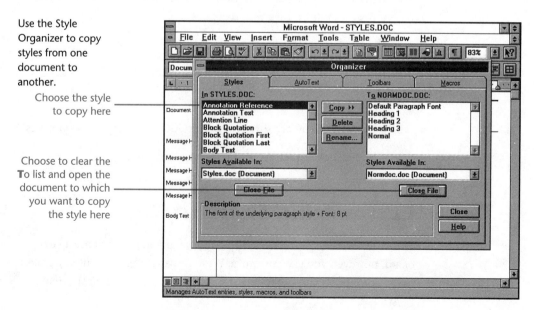

4. On the right side of the dialog box, choose Close File to clear the To list. The Close File button changes to an Open File button.

5. On the left side of the dialog box, choose the style you want to copy from the **In** list.

6. On the right side of the dialog box, choose Open File to display the Open dialog box.

7. Choose the document to which you want to copy the selected style, and then choose OK.

8. Choose **C**opy to copy the selected style from the **In** list to the **To** list.

9. Word asks if you are sure you want to copy the style. Choose **Y**es.

10. Choose **Y**es to save changes to the document.

Task: Deleting a Style

You can delete a style from a document template. The style will not be available for use in new documents created with that template, but existing documents remain unchanged.

To delete a style, follow these steps:

1. Open a document created using the document template that contains the style you want to delete.

2. Choose F**o**rmat, **S**tyle.

3. In the **S**tyles list, choose the style you want to delete.

4. Choose **D**elete.

5. Word asks if you are sure you want to delete the style. Choose **Y**es.

6. Choose Close to return to the current document.

Task: Customizing Shortcut Keys

The easiest way to use Word is with a mouse. If you prefer to use a keyboard, however, you can customize Word by assigning shortcut keystrokes to the commands you use frequently, or by changing existing shortcut keystrokes.

To customize keyboard commands, follow these steps:

1. Choose **T**ools, **C**ustomize.

2. At the top of the Customize dialog box, click the **K**eyboard tab.

You can customize
keyboard shortcuts
to suit your needs.

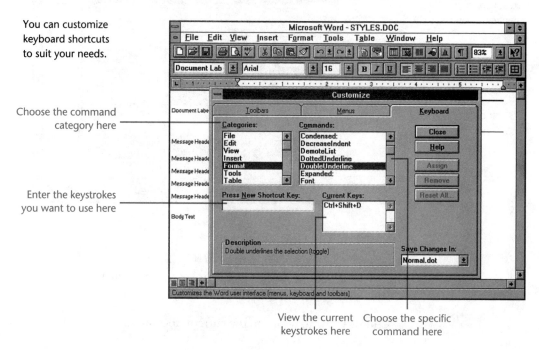

Choose the command
category here

Enter the keystrokes
you want to use here

View the current   Choose the specific
keystrokes here   command here

3. In the **C**ategories list, choose the type of command you want to change.

4. In the C**o**mmands list, choose the specific command to which you want to apply shortcut keystrokes. In the C**u**rrent Keys text box, Word lists the keys currently used to execute the selected command.

5. Position the insertion point in the Press **N**ew Shortcut Key text box, and press the keys you want to use for the shortcut keystrokes. Word displays the keystrokes in the box.

8

Word displays a message indicating whether or not the keys you pressed are already assigned as shortcut keys for a different command.

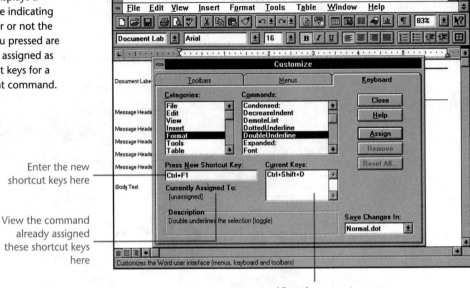

Enter the new shortcut keys here

View the command already assigned these shortcut keys here

View the current shortcut keys here

6. Choose **A**ssign to assign the keystrokes you entered as the new shortcut keys for the selected command.

7. Choose Close to return to the current document.

To remove a shortcut key assignment, highlight the keys in the C**u**rrent Keys list box and choose **R**emove.

Task: Customizing Toolbars

You can customize Word's toolbars by adding buttons, removing buttons, and rearranging buttons. You also can create a new toolbar and place any buttons you want on it.

To customize toolbars, follow these steps:

1. Choose **V**iew, **T**oolbars and select to display the toolbars you want to customize. Choose OK.

2. Choose **T**ools, **C**ustomize.

3. At the top of the Customize dialog box, click the **T**oolbars tab.

To customize toolbars, you can add buttons, remove buttons, or change the order of buttons.

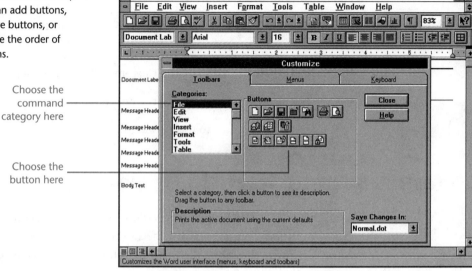

Choose the command category here

Choose the button here

4. Do one of the following:

■ To add a button to a toolbar, choose the type of command in the **C**ategories list, the drag the button to the toolbar on-screen.

■ To remove a button from a toolbar, drag the button off the toolbar. Choose the type of command you want to customize.

■ To change the order of buttons on a toolbar, drag a button to the new location.

5. Choose Close to return to the current document.

To create a new toolbar, follow these steps:

1. Choose **V**iew, **T**oolbars.

2. Choose **N**ew.

3. In the **T**oolbar Name text box, type a name for the new toolbar.

4. In the **M**ake Toolbar Available To: text box, select whether you want to display the toolbar in all documents, or only documents based on the current document template.

5. Choose OK to return to the Toolbars dialog box. Choose OK to return to the current document.

8

To add buttons to the new toolbar, follow these steps:

1. Choose **V**iew, **T**oolbars and select to display the new toolbar on-screen.

2. Choose **C**ustomize to display the Customize Toolbars dialog box.

3. Drag the buttons you want on to the new toolbar.

4. Choose Close to return to the document.

Task: Setting Start-Up Options

You can customize Word by changing various built-in settings that control the way the program runs. Word checks these settings each time it starts, which is why they are called start-up options. You can change them at any time.

You have already changed some start-up options. Suppose that you changed View options to display nonprinting characters on-screen, and you may have changed General options to change the measurement units.

To change start-up options, follow these steps:

1. Choose **T**ools, **O**ptions.

Word has many start-up option settings, divided into twelve categories. To see the options for a category, choose the category's tab at the top of the Options dialog box.

Word displays the settings here

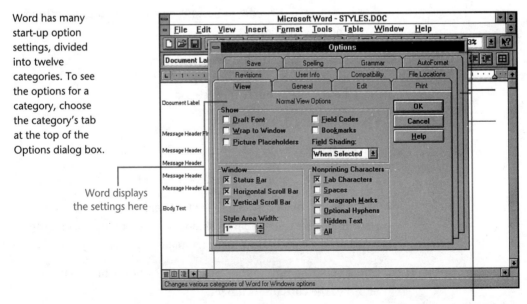

Choose a category tab here

2. Click a tab at the top of the dialog box to display the options settings for that category.

3. Choose Close to remove the dialog box from the screen.

Throughout this book, the start-up options that affect particular tasks are described in detail. The following list provides a brief description of each option category.

■ *View*: Enables you to select the components you want displayed on screen, depending on the current Document view. You can choose such options as nonprinting characters, scroll bars and the Style Area.

■ *General*: Enables you to select such options as whether to use background pagination, help for WordPerfect user, and how many files to display on the File menu. You can choose an alternative color scheme, and change the measurement unit.

■ *Edit*: Enables you to choose settings that affect the way you edit documents, such options as whether or not to turn on drag-and-drop editing, and smart cut and paste.

■ *Print*: Enables you to choose settings that affect the way Word prints files, such as whether to print some nonprinting characters, and whether to support background printing.

■ *Revisions*: Enables you to choose settings for revision marking.

■ *User Info*: Enables you to can change the user identification settings.

■ *Compatibility*: Enables you to adjust settings for files imported from or exported to other applications.

■ *File Locations*: Enables you to set the path to the subdirectories where you want files stored.

■ *Save*: Enables you to choose settings that affect the way Word saves your files, such as how often Word should automatically save, and whether or not it should prompt you for summary information. You also can add password protection to the current document.

■ *Spelling*: Enables you to choose settings that affect the way the Spelling Checker functions. You can create and select user dictionaries, and choose settings such as whether Word should suggest alternatives.

8

- *Grammar*: Enables you to choose settings that affect the way the Grammar Checker functions. You can select and customize grammar and style rules and choose whether to check spelling and show readability statistics.

- *AutoFormat*: Enables you to choose settings that affect the way Word automatically formats documents.

Summary

To	Do This
Open a template file	Choose File, New. Choose the template to modify. In the New area, choose Template. Choose OK to open the template file.
Modify a template	Open the template file. Edit the template file. Save the template file with a new name.
Create a template	Create a document using the text and formatting you want in the template. Save the file using a .DOT extension in the C:\WINWORD\TEMPLATE subdirectory.
Use the Style Gallery	Choose Format, Style Gallery.
Modify a style	Choose Format, Style. Choose the style to change. Choose Modify. Choose Format. Choose the format to change. Change the formatting settings. Choose the Add to Template check box.
Create a new style	Choose Format, Style. Choose New. Enter a style name. Choose Format. Change the formatting settings. Choose the Add to Template check box.
Copy a style	Choose Format, Style. Choose Organizer. Choose the style to copy. Open the file to copy the style to. Choose Copy.
Customize keyboard commands	Choose Tools, Customize Keyboard. Choose the command. Enter the shortcut keystrokes. Choose Assign.
Customize toolbars	Choose Tools, Customize Toolbars. Drag the buttons on or off the toolbars.
Create a new toolbar	Choose View, Toolbars New. Type a name for the new toolbar.
Set start-up options	Choose Tools, Options. Click a tab. Change settings. Choose Close.

On Your Own

Estimated time: 25 minutes

1. Use the Style Gallery to preview some of Word's built-in templates.

2. Apply a template to an existing document.

3. Create a new document template.

4. Create a new document based on the new document template.

5. Modify the document template.

6. Display the Style Area on-screen.

7. Format a paragraph using a style from another document template.

8. Modify a style.

9. Create a new style based on the modified style.

10. Copy the new style to the new document template.

11. Assign shortcut keystrokes to use for applying a dotted underline.

12. Create a new toolbar that contains five of the buttons you use most often.

13. Modify your start-up options so that the five most recently opened files appear at the bottom of the File menu.

14. Modify your start-up options to have Word automatically create backup copies, and to automatically save every five minutes.

8

Making Your Work Easier

Much of word processing involves performing the same tasks repeatedly. In this lesson, you learn how to make your work easier by letting Word automatically format documents, and by using macros and AutoText to automate some of the repetitive tasks that take up so much of your time.

Specifically, you learn to do the following:

- Format documents automatically with AutoFormat

- Create preformatted documents with Wizards

- Store data for use with AutoText

- Automate functions with macros

Task: Automatically Formatting Documents

AutoFormat
A Word 6 feature that automatically applies paragraph styles to an unformatted document.

With *AutoFormat*, Word applies paragraph styles to your document. It determines which paragraphs should be headings, which should be body text, and which should be lists. In addition, Word corrects the document by replacing some characters, such as hyphens or dashes, with symbols, such as bullets or em dashes.

To automatically format a document, follow these steps:

1. Open the unformatted document.

2. Choose F**o**rmat, **A**utoFormat.

Word informs you that it is about to automatically format the current document.

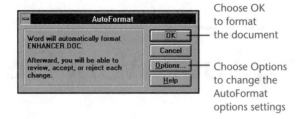

Choose OK to format the document

Choose Options to change the AutoFormat options settings

3. Choose **O**ptions to display the AutoFormat options dialog box.

By default, all Auto-Format options are selected. Choose the ones you want to deselect, then choose OK.

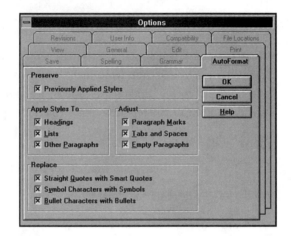

4. Choose OK to return to the AutoFormat dialog box.

5. Choose OK to begin automatically formatting the document.

When the Auto-Format dialog box appears after formatting, it displays additional options.

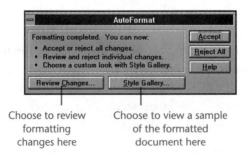

Choose to review formatting changes here

Choose to view a sample of the formatted document here

6. When Word finishes formatting the document, the AutoFormat dialog box appears again. Choose **A**ccept to accept the formatting, and to display the formatted document. You can continue to edit and format the document.

Note: *If you choose to preview the document in the Style Gallery, choose Cancel to return to the document without applying the changes. Choose OK to apply the formatting changes.*

To review each change Word has made to the document, follow these steps:

1. Choose Review, **C**hanges.

You can accept or reject each formatting change.

Highlighted change —

Read a description of the highlighted change here

Choose to find the previous change here

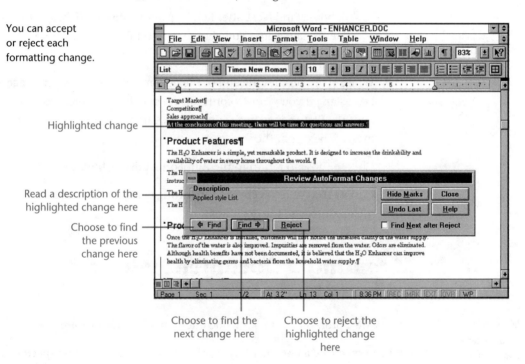

Choose to find the next change here

Choose to reject the highlighted change here

2. In the Review AutoFormat Changes dialog box, do any of the following:

- Choose **F**ind to move back from the insertion point and high-light the previous change in the document.

- Choose **F**ind to move forward from the insertion point and highlight the next change in the document.

- Choose **R**eject to reject the highlighted change.

- Choose Hide **M**arks to hide nonprinting character marks.

- Choose **U**ndo Last to undo the last rejection.

- Choose Find **N**ext after Reject to automatically highlight the next change after you choose to reject the currently high-lighted change.

3. When Word reaches the end of the document, it displays a message box asking if you want to continue the search. Choose OK to high-light the first change in the document. Choose Cancel to clear the message box from the screen.

4. Choose Close to return to the AutoFormat dialog box.

5. Choose **A**ccept to accept the formatting changes. You can continue to edit or format the document.

Task: Creating a Document with a Wizard

Wizard
An automated tem-plate that leads you step by step through the creation of a document.

To create a professional looking document quickly, use a *wizard*.

When you create a document by using a Wizard, Word asks you specific questions about how you want the document to look, then it automati-cally formats it and enters certain text.

Word comes with Wizards for creating many different document types, including letters, agendas, fax cover sheets, newsletters, and resumes. Some Wizards, such as business letters, come prewritten! All you have to do is sign your name.

To create a document by using a Wizard, follow these steps:

1. Choose **F**ile, **N**ew. The New dialog box appears.

2. In the **T**emplate list, choose the document wizard for the document type you want to create.

3. Choose OK to start the wizard.

Each wizard asks a series of questions designed to gather the information Word needs to create the document.

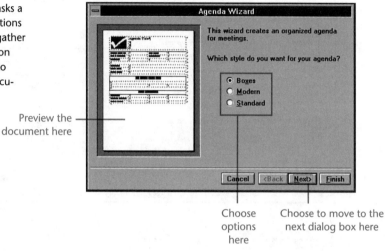

Preview the document here

Choose options here

Choose to move to the next dialog box here

If you have problems...   Wizards are very slow. If you find yourself waiting what seems to be a long time for something to happen, don't worry—Word takes its time formatting Wizards.

---

4. Word begins a series of dialog boxes. Answer the questions by choosing options and typing text. Word suggests answers for some of the questions. If necessary, type over the existing text.

5. Use the buttons at the bottom of the dialog boxes as follows:

   ■ Choose **N**ext to display the next dialog box.

   ■ Choose **B**ack to go back to the previous dialog box.

   ■ Choose **F**inish when you have completed all of the dialog boxes.

6. Word creates the document using the information you entered, and displays it on-screen.

9

You can save, print, edit, and format documents created with Wizards the same way you would any document.

Here, a document created with the Agenda Wizard is displayed in Full Screen view.

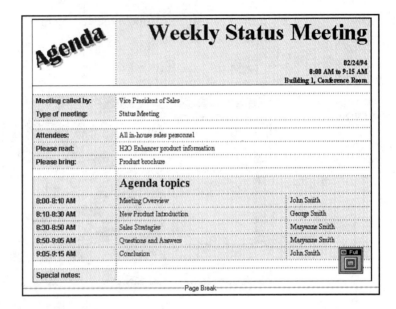

Inserting Data with AutoText

AutoText
A Word feature you can use to store and recreate text or data that you frequently insert into documents.

If you use and reuse the same phrase, block of text, or graphics image repeatedly in many different documents, you can save the data using *AutoText* so that you do not have to keep recreating it.

With AutoText, you create an entry once, and then insert it as many times as you want into as many documents as you want. You can edit, delete, rename, and print AutoText entries.

Task: Creating an AutoText Entry

To create an AutoText entry, follow these steps:

1. Open a document where the data already appears, or where you want to insert the data.

2. Select or type the data.

3. Choose **E**dit, Auto**T**ext.

If you have problems...   If AutoText is dimmed on the Edit menu, you have not selected the data. Return to the document, select the data, and then choose **E**dit, AutoTe**x**t.

The selected data appears in the AutoText dialog box.

Type or edit the AutoText entry shortcut code here

Preview the AutoText entry here

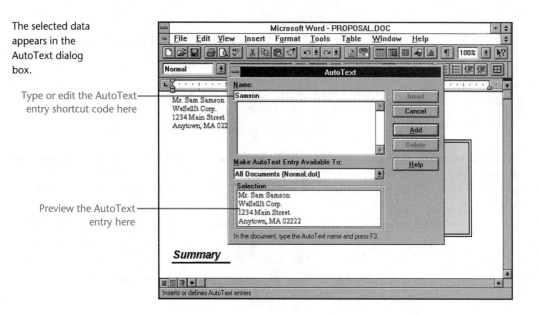

4. In the **N**ame text box, enter the shortcut code you want to use for this AutoText entry. Word automatically enters the first few words of the selected data, but you can edit it. Try to use a short, descriptive term.

5. Choose **A**dd. Word stores the AutoText entry.

Note: *If you want to be able to insert the AutoText entry into all documents, be sure to choose All Documents (NORMAL.DOT) from the **M**ake AutoText Entry Available To drop-down list. If you want to limit the documents into which you can insert the entry to those created with the current template, choose that template from the **M**ake AutoText Entry Available To drop-down list.*

Task: Inserting an AutoText Entry

To insert an AutoText entry into a document, follow these steps:

1. Position the insertion point where you want the AutoText entry to appear.

9

2. Do one of the following:

■ Type the AutoText entry's name and click the AutoText button on the Standard toolbar. Word replaces the name with the entire AutoText entry.

■ Type the AutoText entry's name and press F3. Word replaces the name with the entire AutoText entry.

■ Choose **E**dit, AutoText, highlight the AutoText entry and choose **I**nsert. With this method, you can choose to insert the entry as plain text or as formatted text.

If you have problems...   If Help For WordPerfect Users appears when you press F3, choose **T**ools, **O**ptions General and deselect the Help For **W**ordPerfect Users option check box.

Task: Editing an AutoText Entry

You easily can edit, delete, rename, and print AutoText entries.

To edit an AutoText entry, follow these steps:

1. Insert the AutoText entry you want to modify into a document.

2. Edit the entry in the document.

3. Select the entry.

4. Choose **E**dit, AutoText.

5. In the **N**ame list box, select the original AutoText entry.

6. Choose **A**dd.

7. Word asks if you want to redefine the selected entry. Choose **Y**es. Word stores the edited data in place of the original data.

To delete an AutoText entry, follow these steps:

1. Choose **E**dit, AutoTe**x**t.

2. In the **N**ame list box, select the name of the entry you want to delete.

3. Choose **D**elete.

4. Choose Close.

Note: *Word does not confirm the deletion of an AutoText entry, and the action cannot be undone with the **E**dit, **U**ndo command. Be sure that you want to delete the entry before you choose **D**elete. If you accidentally delete an entry, open a document that contains the data, and create a new entry.*

To rename an AutoText entry, follow these steps:

1. Insert the AutoText entry you want to modify into a document.

2. Select the entry.

3. Choose **E**dit, AutoTe**x**t.

4. In the **N**ame list box, select the entry you want to rename.

5. Choose **D**elete. The entry disappears, but the data is still selected in the document.

6. Enter the new name in the **N**ame list box.

7. Choose **A**dd.

To print a list of the AutoText entries you have stored, follow these steps:

1. Open a document that contains an AutoText entry, or into which you can insert an AutoText entry.

2. Choose **F**ile, **P**rint.

9

You can print a list
of AutoText entries
and names.

Choose to print AutoText
entries here

Summary

3. In the **P**rint What list box, choose AutoText Entries.

4. Choose OK. Word prints a list of AutoText entry names and contents.

Using Macros

Macro

A series of actions
that you record and
play back to accom-
plish specific tasks.

With Word, you can create *macros* that store a series of actions, key-strokes, and commands. You play, or run, the macro when you want to execute the series.

Word comes with built-in macros ready to use, or you can record your own. When you record your own macro, you can assign it a shortcut key, menu command, or toolbar button to use to play it back. Macros are useful for simplifying functions that you must perform often. If you use a macro, you do not have to worry about mistyping information in a dialog box, or forgetting the actions you need to complete a lengthy task.

Task: Using Word's Built-In Macros

When you install Word, the sample macros are stored in the MACRO60.DOT file in the C:\WINWORD\MACROS subdirectory. If you did not install the macros, you can use Setup to do so at any time.

To make the sample macros available for use in all documents, follow these steps:

1. Choose File, Templates.

You use the Templates and Add-ins dialog box to make Word's sample macros available for use in all documents.

Choose Add to select the MACRO60.DOT file

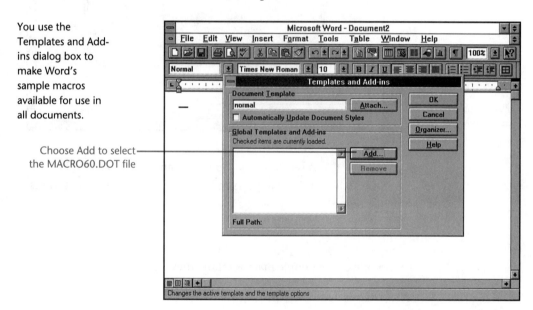

2. Choose Add.

3. In the Add Template dialog box, change to the C:\WINWORD\MACROS subdirectory.

4. Choose the MACRO60.DOT file in the File Name list.

9

You will find the
MACRO60.DOT file
in the C:\WIN-
WORD\MACROS
subdirectory.

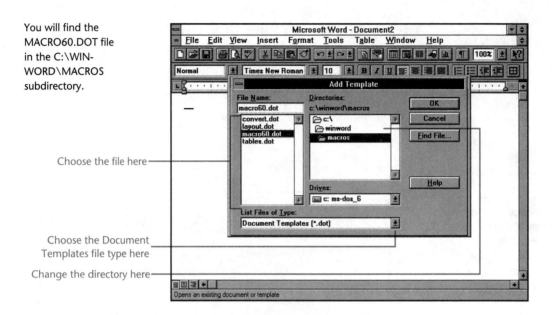

Choose the file here——

Choose the Document
Templates file type here——
Change the directory here——

5. Choose OK to return to the Templates and Add-ins dialog box. The
MACRO60.DOT file appears in the **G**lobal Templates and Add-ins
list box.

6. Choose OK.

To run one of the sample macros follow these steps:

1. Choose **T**ools, **M**acro.

In the Macro dialog box, you see a list of all the sample macros. Highlight one to see its description.

Choose a macro here——

View a description here——

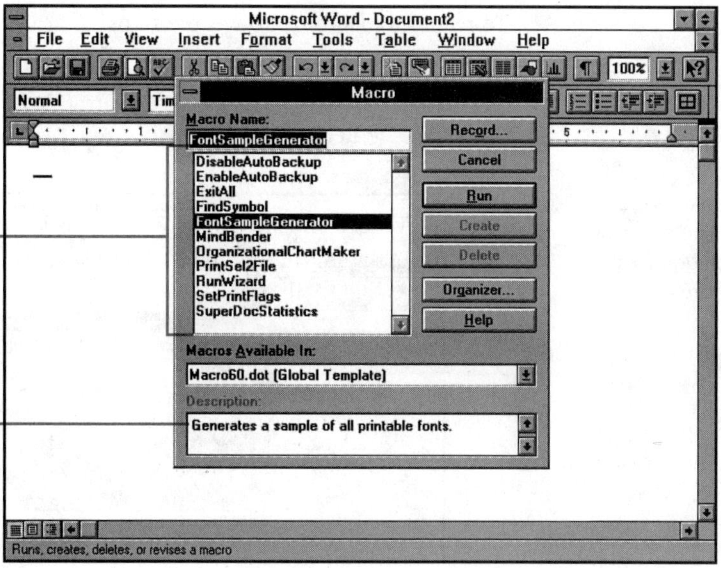

---

2. In the **M**acro Name list box, choose the macro you want to run. Notice that a description of the selected macro appears in the Description area at the bottom of the dialog box.

3. Choose **R**un.

4. If the macro prompts you with dialog boxes, make your choices or enter the appropriate text.

Task: Recording Macros

You can record your own macros by turning on the macro recorder, performing the function you want to record, and then stopping the macro recorder.

9

To record a macro, follow these steps:

1. Choose **T**ools, **M**acro.

2. Choose Rec**o**rd.

In the Record
Macro dialog box,
you give your
macro a name and
a description, and
assign it to a
shortcut.

Enter a macro name here

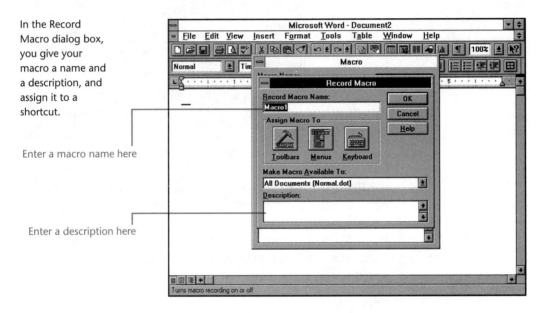

Enter a description here

3. Enter a name in the **R**ecord Macro Name text box. Do not use spaces.

4. Enter a description of the macro in the **D**escription text box.

5. Choose OK. The Macro Recorder is activated.

While the Macro Recorder is on, the Macro Record toolbar is displayed, and the mouse pointer shows a picture of a cassette tape.

Click here to stop

Click here to pause

Mouse pointer

REC button

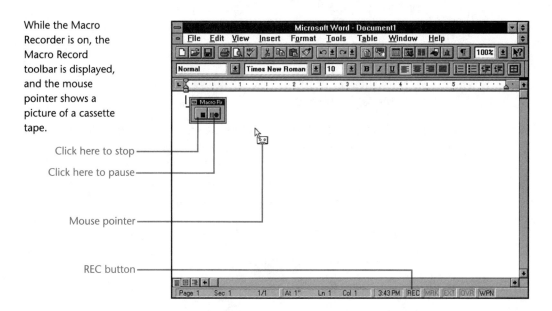

9. Perform the actions you want to record in the macro. You can use the mouse to choose commands, buttons, and dialog box options. You can use the keyboard to enter and manipulate text in the document.

10. When you have completed all of the actions you want to record, click the Stop button on the Macro Record toolbar.

Task: Assigning a Shortcut to the Macro

You can assign a shortcut-key combination to a macro, a menu command, or a toolbar button. Then, to run the macro, you simply use the shortcut.

You can assign the shortcut when you first record the macro by choosing the shortcut in the Record Macro dialog box, or you can assign the shortcut at any time by using the Customize dialog box.

To assign a shortcut key combination to a macro, follow these steps:

1. Choose **T**ools, **C**ustomize.

9

2. Click the **K**eyboard tab at the top of the Customize dialog box.

3. In the **C**ategories list, choose Macros.

4. In the Macr**o**s list, choose the macro you want to assign to a shortcut key combination.

5. Position the insertion point in the Press **N**ew Shortcut Key text box, and press the shortcut key combination you want to use.

6. Choose **A**ssign.

7. Choose Close to return to the document.

To assign a macro to a toolbar button, follow these steps:

1. Choose **T**ools, **C**ustomize.

2. Click the **T**oolbar tab at the top of the Customize dialog box.

3. In the **C**ategories list, choose Macros.

4. In the Macr**o**s list, point at the name of the macro you want to assign to a toolbar.

5. Click and drag the macro name to the toolbar. The Custom Button dialog box appears.

Choose a button for your macro from the Custom Button dialog box.

Choose a button here———

Enter a name for the button here

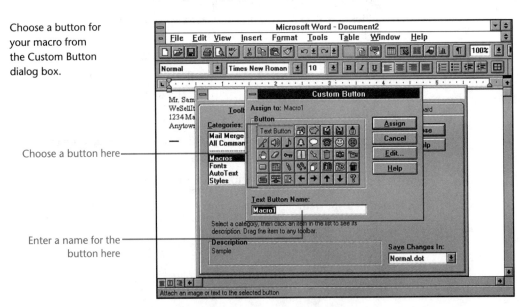

6. Choose the button you want to use. If necessary, enter a name for the button in the **T**ext Button Name text box.

7. Choose **A**ssign.

8. Choose Close to return to the document.

To assign the macro to a menu command, follow these steps:

1. Choose **T**ools, **C**ustomize.

2. Click the **M**enus tab at the top of the Customize dialog box.

3. In the **C**ategories list, choose Macros.

4. In the Macr**o**s list, choose the name of the macro you want to assign to a menu command.

5. In the Change What Men**u** list box, choose the menu to which you want to add the macro command.

6. In the **P**osition on Menu, choose where to place the new command.

7. In the **N**ame on Menu text box, enter or edit the name that appears. Leave the ampersand in place before the letter you want to use as the hot key for executing the command.

8. Choose **A**dd to add the macro command to the menu.

   Note: *For more information on customizing keystrokes and toolbars, see Lesson 8, "Customizing Word for Windows."*

9. Choose Close to return to the document.

Task: Using Your Macros

To run the macro, you can use the shortcut you assigned, or you can follow these steps:

1. Choose **T**ools, **M**acro.

2. Choose All Active Templates from the Macros **A**vailable In list box.

3. Choose the macro you want to run in the **M**acro Name list box.

4. Choose **R**un.

9

To delete the macro, follow these steps:

1. Choose **T**ools, **M**acro.

2. Choose All Active Templates from the Macros **A**vailable in list box.

3. Choose the macro you want to run in the **M**acro Name list box.

4. Choose **D**elete.

5. Word asks if you are sure you want to delete the macro. Choose **Y**es.

Summary

To	Do This
Automatically format a document	Choose F**o**rmat, **A**utoFormat.
Create a document with a wizard	Choose **F**ile, **N**ew. Choose the Wizard. Choose OK. Answer the questions in the dialog boxes. Choose **F**inish.
Create an AutoText entry	Enter and select the data in a document. Choose **E**dit, AutoText. Enter a name. Choose **A**dd.
Insert an AutoText entry	Position the insertion point. Choose **E**dit, AutoTe**x**t. Choose the entry. Choose **I**nsert.
Print a list of AutoText entries	Open a document. Choose **F**ile, **P**rint. Choose to print AutoText entries.
Record a macro	Choose **T**ools, **M**acro. Choose **R**ecord. Enter a macro name. Choose OK. Perform the actions. Click the Stop button on the Macro Record toolbar.
Run a macro	Choose **T**ools, **M**acro. List macros available in All Active Templates. Choose the macro. Choose **R**un.

On Your Own

Estimated time: 20 minutes

1. Create a document using the NORMAL.DOT template.

2. Format the document automatically.

3. Review the changes made by Word.

4. Save the document.

5. Create a Fax cover letter using a Wizard.

6. Save the document.

7. Create a business letter using a Wizard. Have Word supply the letter's contents.

8. Create an AutoText entry to use for adding your name and address to the top of letters and other documents.

9. Use the AutoText entry to insert your name and address into a document.

10. Record a macro to insert the AutoText entry into a document.

11. Assign the macro to a toolbar button.

12. Use the macro to insert the AutoText entry into a document.

13. Use one of the sample macros to print a list of Word fonts.

9

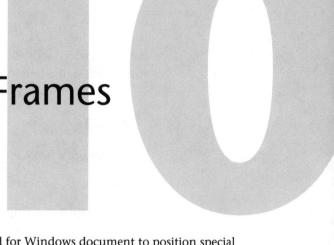

Lesson 10

Working with Frames

You use *frames* in a Word for Windows document to position special objects and to help organize text on a page. Frames can hold many kinds of objects, but usually are used to hold graphics, tables, or text.

You can place a frame anywhere on a page, with text above, below, or flowing around it. In addition, you can move, resize, and delete frames.

In this lesson, you learn to do the following:

- Create a frame

- Size and position a frame

- Format a frame

- Delete and remove a frame

Understanding Frames

Frame
A box that surrounds a picture or text within a document.

In Word, you use a *frame* to define an area on a page that you can manipulate independently from the rest of the document's contents. A frame can contain text or graphics you can format separately from the document around it.

The view you use to display a document determines the way frames appear on-screen. In Print Preview or Page Layout view, framed items appear on-screen the way they will print. You can use a mouse to position and size the frame.

In Normal view or Outline view, frames do not appear the same size or at the size in which they will print. If you try to use a mouse to position or size the frame, the frame's contents change, but the frame itself does not.

Creating a Frame

You can create a frame in the following two ways:

- By adding a frame to an existing item

- By inserting an empty frame into a document

Either way, you should change to Page Layout view before creating the frame. To change to Page Layout view, choose **V**iew, **P**age Layout.

Task: Adding a Frame to an Item

To place a frame around an existing item, follow these steps:

Select the item and then choose **I**nsert, **F**rame. Word surrounds the selected item with a frame. If the item is text, Word wraps the text to fit within the frame.

Word automatically wraps the text to fit within the frame.

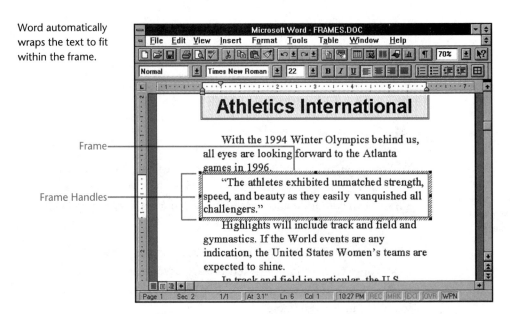

Task: Inserting an Empty Frame

You can place an empty frame in a document and add text or graphics to it later. This is useful if you are designing a document and want to hold a place for the frame, but you are not sure exactly what information you are going to insert in the frame.

To insert an empty frame, follow these steps:

1. Make sure nothing is selected in the document.

2. Choose **I**nsert, **F**rame. The mouse pointer changes from an I-beam to a plus sign.

3. Position the mouse pointer at the location in which you want to place the top left corner of the frame.

4. Click and drag the mouse pointer to the location where you want to place the bottom right corner of the frame. A dotted line outlines the frame.

As you drag the mouse to draw the frame, a dotted line indicates the frame's size and position.

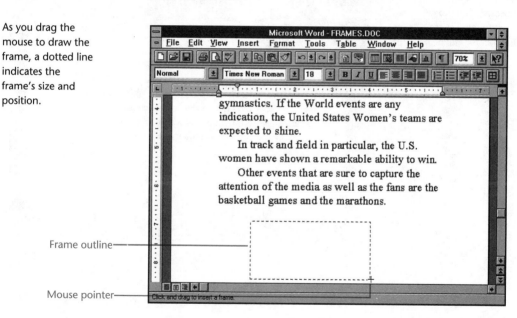

Frame outline—

Mouse pointer—

5. Release the mouse button to position the frame.

Note: *You can format a frame using borders shading. For more information about formatting, see Lesson 5, "Dressing Up Your Text."*

Changing the Size of a Frame

You easily can change the size of an existing frame, whether it is empty or not. If you want to change the size by sight, you quickly can use the mouse to drag the frame. If you know exactly how large the frame should be, you can use precise measurements to change its size.

Task: Resizing a Frame Quickly

To quickly change the size of a frame, follow these steps:

Handles

Small black boxes that appear around the edge of a selected frame.

Drag the handles that appear around the edge of a selected frame to change the size of the frame.

1. Point at any side of the frame until the mouse pointer changes to a four headed arrow.

2. Click the mouse button to select the frame. Eight *handles* appear around the edge of the frame.

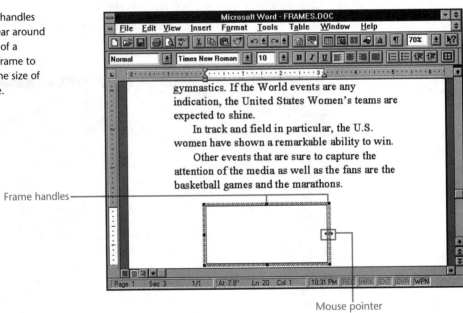

Frame handles

Mouse pointer

3. Point at any of the handles. The mouse pointer changes to a two-headed arrow.

4. Drag the handle to resize the frame. A dotted line indicates the new size.

10

> **Note:** *To change both the height and width of the frame at the same time, drag a corner handle.*

5. Release the mouse button when the frame is the correct size.

If you have problems... If the frame moves rather than the size of the frame changing, you are not dragging a handle. Point at a handle so that the mouse pointer is a two-headed arrow, not a four-headed arrow, and try again. You can choose **E**dit, **U**ndo to return the frame to its original position.

Task: Resizing a Frame Precisely

You can change the size of a frame using precise measurements. This is useful if you need a frame to fit an exact object, such as a photograph, or a bar code.

To resize a frame precisely, follow these steps:

1. Position the insertion point inside the frame.

2. Choose **F**ormat, Fra**m**e.

With the Frame dialog box, you can control the size and position of a frame.

Specify the frame width here ——

Specify the frame height here ——

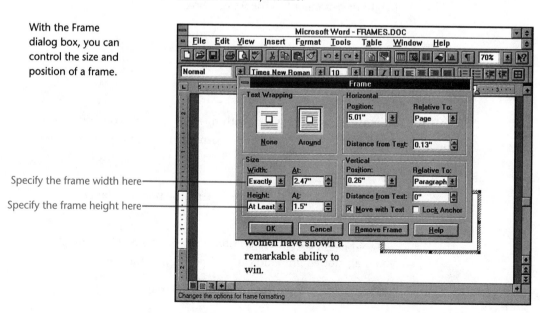

3. In the **W**idth list box, choose one of the following options:

   ■ Auto to automatically adjust the width of the frame to fit its contents

   ■ Exactly to adjust the width of the frame to the exact measurement entered in the **A**t text box

4. If you chose Exactly in the **W**idth list box, enter the exact width of the frame in the **A**t text box.

5. In the Hei**g**ht list box, choose one of the following options:

   ■ Auto to automatically adjust the height of the frame to fit its contents

   ■ At Least to adjust the height of the frame to no smaller than the measurement entered in the **A**t text box

   ■ Exactly to adjust the height of the frame to the exact measurement entered in the **A**t text box

6. If you chose At Least or Exactly in the Hei**g**ht list box, enter the height measurement in the **A**t text box.

7. Choose OK.

Task: Positioning a Frame

You can move a frame anywhere within the document. You quickly can move the frame by dragging it, or you can align it precisely on the page.

To move a frame quickly, follow these steps:

1. Point at any edge of the frame. The mouse pointer changes to a four headed arrow.

2. Click and drag the mouse pointer to the new frame location. As you drag, dotted lines indicate the position of the frame.

3. Release the mouse button to position the frame.

To change the horizontal alignment of a frame, follow these steps:

Note: *By default, Word aligns a frame horizontally relative to the width of the page, placing the frame .13 inches from the surrounding text.*

1. Position the insertion point within the frame.

2. Choose Format, Frame.

3. In the Position list box of the Horizontal area, choose the alignment you want for the frame, or enter a precise measurement.

4. In the Relative To list box of the Horizontal area, choose one of the following options:

■ Margin to align the frame relative to the left or right margins

■ Page to align the frame relative to the left or right edge of the page

■ Column to align the frame relative to the left or right edge of a column

5. In the Distance from Text box, enter the amount of white space you want to leave between the frame and the surrounding text.

6. Choose OK.

Here, a frame is aligned to the left in relation to the edge of a column.

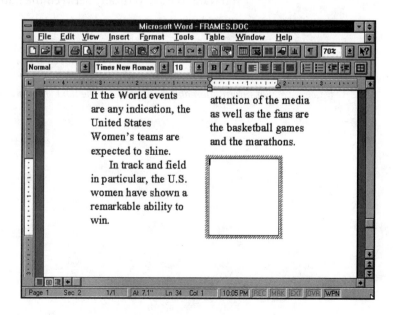

To change the vertical alignment of a frame, follow these steps:

Note: *By default, Word aligns a frame vertically after the preceding paragraph mark.*

1. Position the insertion point within the frame.

2. Choose Format, Frame.

3. In the Position list box of the Vertical area, choose the alignment position you want for the frame, or enter a precise measurement.

4. In the Relative To list box of the Vertical area, choose one of the following options:

   - Margin to align the frame relative to the top or bottom margins

   - Page to align the frame relative to the top or bottom edge of the page

   - Paragraph if you entered a precise measurement in the Position list box. Word positions the frame at exactly the distance you entered, relative to the preceding paragraph mark

5. In the Distance from Text box, enter the amount of white space you want to leave vertically between the frame and the surrounding text.

6. Choose OK.

Note: *When you align frames, the text they are anchored to moves with them. For information about anchors, see the next section in this lesson.*

Here, the frame is aligned vertically 1 inch away from the preceding paragraph, and is spaced .15 inches from the surrounding text.

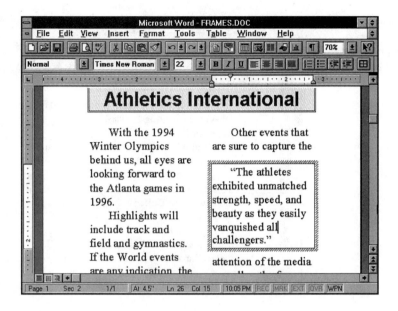

Anchor

To attach a frame to a specific location on a page or to a specific paragraph of text.

If you need to be sure that a frame is always positioned with specific text, or always positioned at a certain location on the page, no matter what happens to the surrounding text, you can adjust the frame's *anchor*. This is useful if you have not yet finished editing the document. If you add or delete text, you do not have to worry about where the frame will end up.

All frames are anchored to a paragraph, but you can change the anchor by locking it or by removing it.

An anchor icon
indicates the
location of a frame's
anchor on-screen.

Anchor

Frame

> With·the·1994·Winter·Olympics·behind·us,·
> all·eyes·are·looking·forward·to·the·Atlanta·
> games·in·1996.·¶
>
> ⚓ Highlights·will·
> include·track·and·field·
> and·gymnastics.·If·the·
> World·events·are·any·
> indication,·the·United·
> States·Women's·teams·
> are·expected·to·shine.·¶
>
> "The·athletes·
> exhibited·unmatched·
> strength,·speed,·and·
> beauty·as·they·easily··
> vanquished·all·
> challengers."¶
>
> In·track·and·field·in·particular,·the·U.S.·
> women·have·shown·a·remarkable·ability·to·win.·¶
> Other·events·that·are·sure·to·capture·the·

Note: *To see the location of anchors on-screen, click the Show/Hide Marks button on the standard toolbar, or choose **T**ools, **O**ptions View, and choose the **O**bject Anchors check box.*

To anchor a frame to a location on the page, follow these steps:

1. Position the frame exactly where you want it on the page.

2. Position the insertion point within the frame.

3. Choose F**o**rmat, Fra**m**e.

4. Deselect the **M**ove with Text and Loc**k** Anchor text boxes.

5. Choose OK.

You can set Word so that a frame always will appear on the same page as the text to which it is anchored, and no matter what page it is on, it will be in a fixed location.

To keep a frame in a fixed position on the same page as an associated text paragraph, follow these steps:

1. Position the insertion point inside the frame.

2. Choose F**o**rmat, Fra**m**e.

3. Choose the Lock Anchor check box.

4. Deselect the **M**ove With Text check box.

5. Choose OK.

A small padlock beside the anchor icon in the document indicates that the frame is locked into a fixed position on the page.

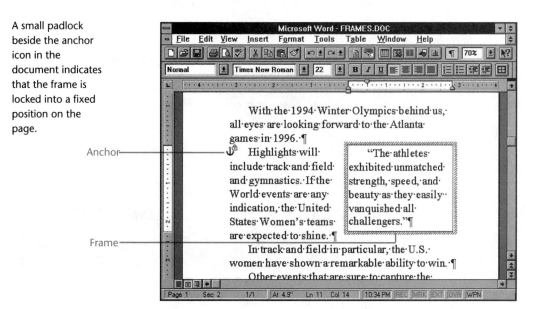

Anchor

Frame

To enable a frame to move vertically as you add or delete text above the frame, follow these steps:

1. Position the insertion point inside the frame.

2. Choose Format, Frame.

3. Choose the **M**ove With Text check box.

4. Deselect the Lock Anchor check box.

5. Choose OK.

By default, Word wraps text around the outside of a frame. You can set Word to position text above and below the frame, however. To change the flow of text around a frame, follow these steps:

1. Position the insertion point within the frame.

2. Choose Format, Frame.

3. In the Text Wrapping area of the Frame dialog box, choose one of the following options:

   - ■ **N**one to position text above and below the frame, but not beside it

   - ■ Around to wrap text around the frame

4. Choose OK.

Here, Word wraps text around the frame.

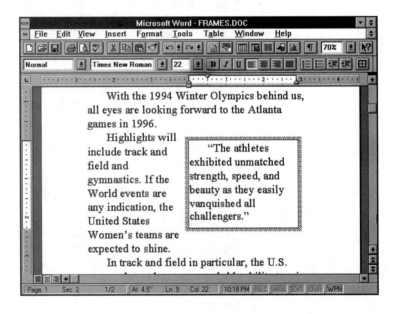

Here, Word
positions the text
above and below
the frame.

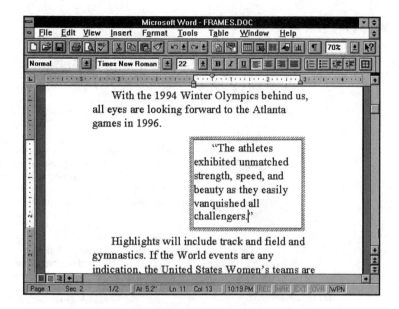

Task: Deleting or Removing a Frame

To delete a frame, follow these steps:

1. Select the frame.

2. Press Delete. Word deletes the frame.

If you have problems...

 If you wanted to remove the frame, but deleted it accidentally, choose **E**dit **U**ndo immediately, and follow the steps for removing a frame.

To remove a frame, follow these steps:

1. Position the insertion point within the frame.

2. Choose **F**ormat, Fra**m**e.

3. In the Frame dialog box, choose **R**emove Frame. Word removes the frame. The contents flow in with the preceding text.

Summary

To	Do This
Create a frame	Choose **I**nsert, **F**rame.
Resize a frame	Drag a handle.
Move a frame	Drag the edge of a frame.
Align a frame	Choose Format, Frame. Choose Position. Choose Relation option.
Keep a frame in a set location	Choose Format, Frame. Deselect the Lock Anchor check box and the **M**ove with Text check box.
Lock a frame on a page with text	Choose Format, Frame. Choose the Lock Anchor check box.
Let a frame move with text	Choose Format, Frame. Choose the **M**ove with Text check box.
Format text in a frame	Choose the text. Apply formatting.
Delete a frame	Select the frame. Choose Delete.
Remove a frame	Select the frame. Choose Format, Frame. Choose **R**emove Frame.

On Your Own

Estimated time: 15 minutes

1. Open a document.

2. Insert a frame around existing text.

3. Change the size of the frame.

4. Move the frame to a different location on the page.

5. Align the frame to the right side of the page.

6. Adjust the frame so that the document text wraps around it.

7. Insert an empty frame at the end of the document.

8. Move the empty frame to the middle of the document.

10

9. Lock the frame into position with its associated text.

10. Adjust the frame so that the document text appears above and below it, but not beside it.

11. Enter text in the empty frame.

12. Format the text in the frame.

13. Add a border to the frame.

14. Add shading to the text in the frame.

15. Remove the border from the first frame.

16. Remove the first frame completely.

Drawing with Word for Windows

Word 6 for Windows comes with drawing capabilities similar to those found in drawing software packages. You can use the Drawing toolbar to create shapes, objects, and drawings, and to incorporate text and drawings into a document.

In this lesson, you learn to do the following:

- Use the Drawing toolbar
- Create objects
- Select objects
- Position objects
- Edit and enhance objects

Task: Creating a Drawing

Object
An image, shape, or text created as part of a drawing.

Picture
A graphic image that can be created in Word by using the drawing toolbar to draw objects, or imported from another application.

In Word, you create drawings by using the buttons on the Drawing toolbar to draw *objects*. You can draw objects directly in a document, or you can draw them in a *picture* that you can place into a document.

Note: *In order to see the way a drawing will actually appear in the document, you should change to Page Layout view.*

To display the Drawing toolbar, follow these steps:

1. Choose **V**iew, **T**oolbars.

2. In the **T**oolbars list, choose the Drawing check box.

3. Choose OK. The Drawing toolbar appears across the bottom of the screen, above the status bar.

With the Drawing toolbar, you can create objects directly in a Word document, or in a picture.

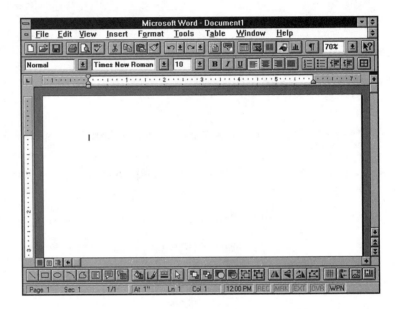

To create a drawing, you choose a button from the Drawing toolbar, and then use the mouse pointer to draw the objects. A drawing can be made up of one object, or many objects.

Selection handles

Small black boxes that appear around the edge of selected objects, used for moving and resizing.

A newly drawn object is automatically selected—it has *selection handles* that you can use to change the object's size and shape. You learn about manipulating objects later in this lesson.

Drawing Lines

With the Drawing toolbar buttons, you can create two kinds of lines:

Arc

A parabolic curve equal to a quarter section of an ellipse or circle.

- Straight lines

- Arcs

To draw straight lines, follow these steps:

1. Click the Line button on the Drawing toolbar.

2. Position the mouse pointer in the document where you want to begin the line. The mouse pointer changes from an I-beam to a plus sign.

3. Drag the mouse pointer from the beginning of the line to the end of the line.

You can use the Line button to draw lines at common angles. Press and hold Shift as you drag the mouse pointer. The line appears progressively at a 30, 45, 60, and 90 degree angle until you release the mouse button.

To draw arcs, follow these steps:

1. Click the Arc button on the Drawing toolbar.

2. Position the insertion point where you want the arc to begin.

3. Click and drag the mouse pointer diagonally from the beginning to the end of the arc.

To make the height and width of the arc equal, press and hold Shift as you drag. The result is a perfect quarter circle.

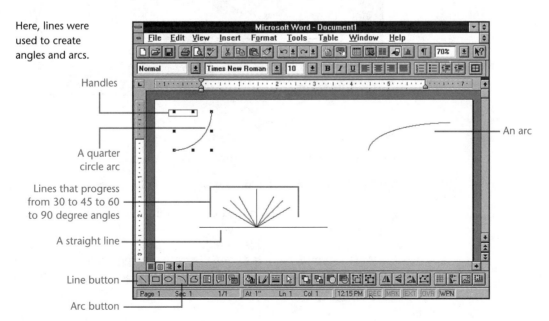

Here, lines were used to create angles and arcs.

Handles

A quarter circle arc

Lines that progress from 30 to 45 to 60 to 90 degree angles

A straight line

Line button

Arc button

An arc

11

Drawing Rectangles

To create a rectangular object, follow these steps:

1. Click the Rectangle button on the Drawing toolbar.

2. Position the mouse pointer where you want to place the top left corner of the rectangle.

3. Drag the mouse pointer to where you want to place the bottom right corner of the rectangle. To create a perfect square, press and hold Shift as you drag.

4. When the object is the size you want, release the mouse button.

Here, a rectangle and a square have been added to the drawing.

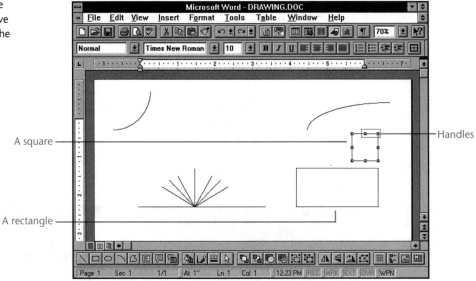

A square ———

A rectangle ———

Handles

Drawing Ellipses and Circles

To create a round object, follow these steps:

1. Click the Ellipse button on the Drawing toolbar.

2. Position the mouse pointer at the location where you want to begin the object.

3. Drag the mouse pointer diagonally from the upper left of the ellipse to the lower right. To create a perfect circle, press and hold Shift as you drag.

4. When the object is the size you want, release the mouse button.

When the object
looks the way you
want, release the
mouse button.

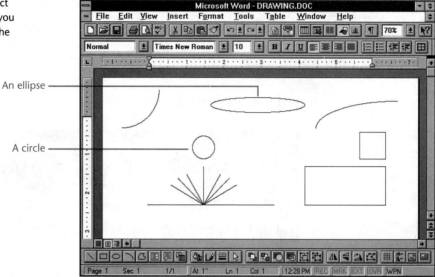

An ellipse —

A circle —

Drawing Polygons and Freeform Shapes

To draw multisided or freeform shapes, you use the Freeform button.
Freeform objects consist of several connected lines, or line segments.
You can use the Freeform button to draw polygons such as triangles
or octagons, or you can use it to draw shapes such as faces, or flowers.

To draw a polygon, follow these steps:

1. Click the Freeform button on the Drawing toolbar.

2. Position the mouse pointer where you want to locate one corner of
the polygon, and click.

3. Move the mouse pointer—don't drag!—to the next corner of the
polygon, and click again. Word connects the corners with a straight
line, creating the first side of the object. To create lines at common
angles, press and hold Shift as you move the mouse pointer.

4. Position the insertion point at the next corner, and click. Word
draws another side.

5. To finish the object, double-click.

To draw a freehand object, follow these steps:

1. Click the Freeform button on the Drawing toolbar.

2. Position the mouse pointer where you want to start the object.

3. Click and drag the mouse pointer, using it like a pencil to draw the object.

4. To finish the object, double-click.

You can create multisided and freeform shapes using the Freeform button.

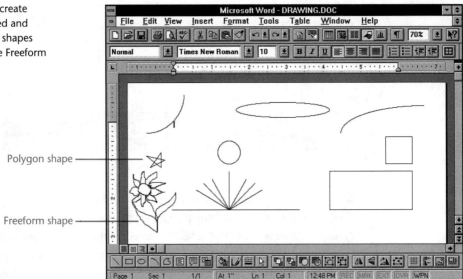

Polygon shape ———

Freeform shape ———

Including Text in a Drawing

Text box
A drawing object that holds text.

Callout
A text box automatically attached to another object by a straight line.

You can incorporate text in a drawing by creating a *text box*, or by adding *callouts*. Each text box or callout can contain more than one paragraph of text. You can format the text by using character and paragraph formatting commands.

Task: Adding Text Boxes to a Drawing

To add a text box to a drawing, follow these steps:

1. Click the Text Box button on the Drawing toolbar.

2. Position the mouse pointer where you want to place the top left corner of the text box.

3. Click and drag the mouse pointer to the bottom right corner of the text box.

4. Release the mouse button. The insertion point appears within the text box.

5. Type, edit, and format the text as you would if it was not enclosed in the text box.

11

Freeform
drawing

Use text boxes
to add words
to drawings

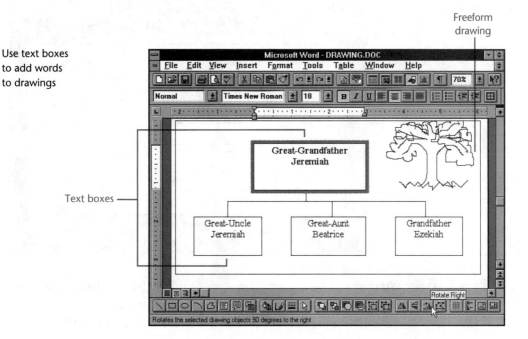

Text boxes —

Note: *When you position the insertion point within a text box, a gray border appears around the box. When you select the text box, handles appear within the gray border.*

Task: Adding Callouts to a Drawing

Callouts are useful for pointing out items of interest in a drawing, or for providing explanatory text. The callout is attached to the drawing by a line that automatically adjusts when you change the position of the callout.

To create a callout, follow these steps:

1. Click the Callout button on the Drawing toolbar.

2. Point at any part of the picture to which you want to attach the callout.

3. Drag the mouse pointer to the place where you want to position the callout box. A line attached to an empty box appears.

4. Type, edit, and format text in the callout box, just as you would if the text was not in the callout box.

Here, a callout is
used to provide
explanatory text.

Callout line ——

Callout text ——

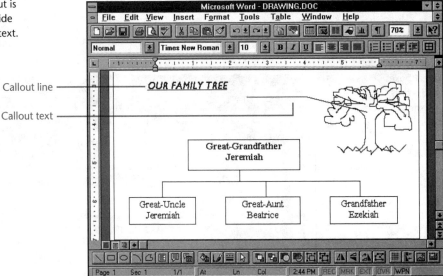

You can change the appearance of the callout box by changing the number and angle of the callout line, by changing the distance between the callout box, the callout line, and the picture, and by adding borders.

To change the appearance of the callout box, follow these steps:

1. Select the callout.

2. Click the Format Callout button on the Drawing toolbar.

In the Format
Callout dialog box,
you can change the
appearance of the
selected callout
box.

Choose the callout
line type here

Set lengths and
distances here

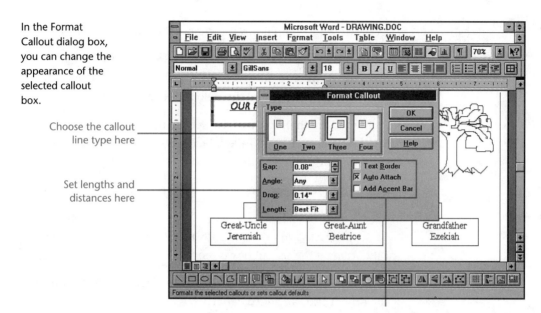

Choose options here

3. In the Type area, choose one of the following callout line types:

   ■ **O**ne to place one horizontal or one vertical line between the
   callout box and the picture.

   ■ **T**wo to place one angled callout line between the callout box
   and the picture.

   ■ Th**r**ee to place one angled and one horizontal line segment
   between the callout box and the picture.

   ■ **F**our to place one angled, one vertical, and one horizontal
   line segment between the callout box and the picture.

4. In the **G**ap text box, specify how far away from the callout box you
   want to place the callout line.

5. From the **A**ngle drop-down list, choose the slant of the angled callout line segment.

6. From the Dro**p** drop-down list, specify the distance between the top of the callout box and the callout line segment next to it.

7. From the **L**ength drop-down list, specify the length of the callout line segment next to the callout box. Choose Best Fit to automatically adjust the line length.

8. Choose the Text **B**order check box to place a simple border around the contents of the callout box.

9. Choose the A**u**to Attach check box to automatically adjust the callout line if the callout box is moved.

10. Choose the Add A**c**cent Bar check box to place a vertical bar next to the callout text, for added emphasis.

11. Choose OK.

Note: *You also can change the line style of the callout line. Changing lines styles is discussed later in this lesson.*

If you have problems...   Unlike text boxes, callout boxes do not automatically have a border. When the insertion point is within the callout box, or if the callout box is selected, a gray border appears, but when you click outside the callout box, the border disappears. If you want a border around the callout box, you must choose the Text **B**order check box in the Format Callout dialog box.

Task: Selecting Objects

To edit or manipulate objects in a drawing, you first must select the objects.

To select an object, follow these steps:

1. Point at any of the object's edges until the mouse pointer changes shape to include a four-headed arrow.

2. Click on one of the edges. Selection handles appear around the selected object.

If you have problems...

If a selected object becomes deselected when you select another object, you are not holding down the Shift key. Press and hold Shift until you finish selecting objects.

11

After an object is selected, you can edit or manipulate the object.

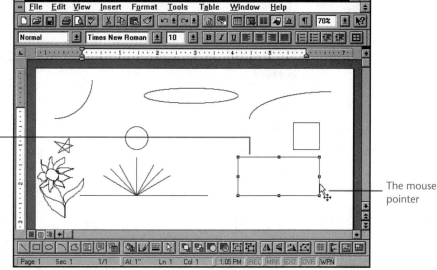

The selected object has handles around it

The mouse pointer

Selecting More than One Object

To select more than one object, press and hold Shift as you point and click each object. Alternatively, you can select an area of the drawing that contains one or more objects.

To select an area of the drawing, follow these steps:

1. Click the Select Drawing Objects button on the Drawing toolbar.

2. Position the selection arrow at the top left corner of the area you want to select.

3. Click and drag the mouse pointer to the bottom left corner of the area you want to select. The area is indicated by a dotted rectangle.

4. Release the mouse button when the area you want to select is surrounded by the dotted rectangle. All of the objects within that area become selected.

5. Click the Select Drawing Objects button again to turn it off.

If you have problems...   If an object you thought was within the selection area does not become selected, you did not surround it completely. The entire object must be within the dotted rectangle in order for it to become selected.

You can use the Select Drawing Objects button to quickly select more than one object at a time.

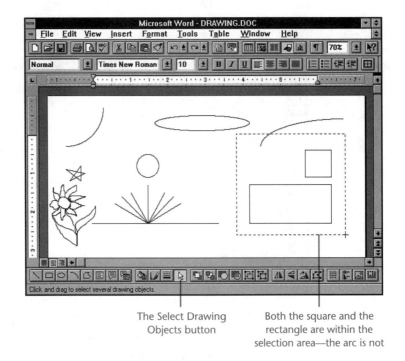

The Select Drawing Objects button

Both the square and the rectangle are within the selection area—the arc is not

Grouping Objects

You can group more than one object, so that they can be manipulated as one. Any action you perform on one object in the group is also performed on all of the objects in the group.

To group objects, follow these steps:

1. Select the objects you want to group.

2. Click the Group button on the Drawing toolbar. A single set of handles appears around the grouped objects.

To ungroup the objects, follow these steps:

1. Select the group of objects.

2. Click the Ungroup button on the Drawing toolbar.

Positioning Objects

With Word, you can position objects in a drawing by moving, copying, and aligning them with each other or with a grid. You also can layer objects to create different effects.

Task: Moving Objects

To quickly move an object, follow these steps:

1. Select the object.

2. Point at any edge of the object so that the mouse pointer is a four-headed arrow.

3. Drag the object to its new location. A dotted rectangle indicates the object's new location.

If you have problems...

If the object changes size rather than position, you are pointing at a handle rather than the object's edge. Choose **E**dit **U**ndo, and then try again.

Tip
To quickly display the Drawing Object dialog box, double-click any drawing object.

To move an object to a precise location on the page, follow these steps:

1. Select the object.

2. Choose F**o**rmat, Drawing **O**bject.

In the Drawing Object dialog box, you can specify exact positions for objects, as well as choose a line style and fill pattern.

Choose to display other Drawing Object options here

Choose to anchor the object to text here

Set the position here

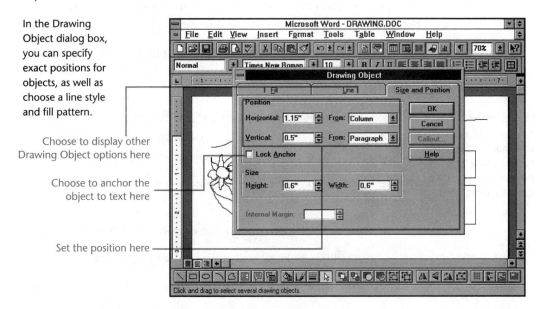

3. Click the Size and Position tab at the top of the Drawing Object dialog box.

4. In the Horizontal text box, enter the distance you want to place the object away from the item in the From drop-down list.

5. From the From drop-down list, choose Margin, Page, or Column.

6. In the Vertical text box, enter the distance you want to place the object away from the item in the From drop-down list.

7. From the From drop-down list, choose either Margin, Page, or Paragraph.

8. To keep an object in the same place relative to the paragraph it is anchored to, enter Paragraph in the From drop-down list box, and choose the Lock Anchor text box.

9. Choose OK.

Task: Layering Objects

Word for Windows documents may look flat, but they can contain text or pictures in three separate layers: a front drawing layer, a text layer, and a back drawing layer.

When you draw objects in a document, they are placed in the front drawing layer, on top of the text layer. If there is text directly behind the object in front, you may not be able to see it. The text layer, in turn, is on top of the back drawing layer, and text may obscure objects behind it.

You can place objects within either the front or back drawing layer in front or in back of each other. You also can move objects from the front layer to the back layer.

Watermark
An image that can be printed on the background of one page or every page in a document.

Layering objects is useful for achieving many different kinds of effects. You can overlap objects in a layer, or you can create a *watermark*, by sending a text box, object, or imported image to the back layer.

To place an object in front of another object in the same layer, follow these steps:

1. Select the object you want to place in front of other objects.

2. Click the Bring to Front button on the Drawing toolbar.

3. Move the object to the desired location in front of any other object.

To place an object behind other objects in the same layer, follow these steps:

1. Select the object you want to place behind the other objects.

2. Click the Send to Back button on the Drawing toolbar.

3. Move the object to the desired location behind any other objects.

11

To move a selected object to the front drawing layer, click the Bring in Front of Text button on the Drawing toolbar.

To place a selected object in the back drawing layer, behind the text layer, select the object and click the Send Behind Text button on the Drawing toolbar. The object moves to the back layer.

To place an object in the text layer, insert a frame around it.

Note: *For information on using frames, see Lesson 10, "Working with Frames."*

Grid

An invisible set of lines that divides the drawing into evenly spaced rows and columns, used for positioning objects.

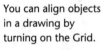

You can align objects in a drawing by turning on the Grid.

Task: Positioning Objects with the Grid

You can align objects and create objects of matching sizes by using the *grid*. When the grid is on, objects "stick" to the nearest gridline in default steps of 1/10 inch horizontally and vertically.

To use the grid, follow these steps:

1. Click the Snap to Grid button on the Drawing toolbar.

Choose to turn the grid on here

Set grid spacing here

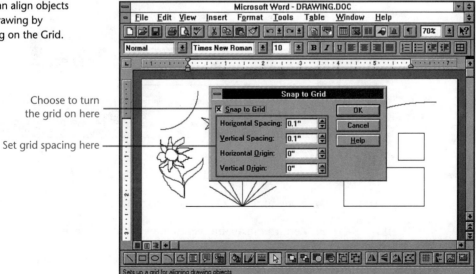

2. Choose the **S**nap to Grid check box.

3. To modify the grid spacing, enter measurements in the Horizontal Spacing and **V**ertical Spacing text bo⁻:es.

4. Choose OK.

To turn off the grid, deselect the **S**nap to Grid check box.

Task: Aligning Objects with Each Other or On a Page

You also can align objects relative to each other, or to an edge of the page.

To align objects in a drawing, follow these steps:

1. Select the objects you want to align.

Use the Align dialog box to make objects even in a drawing.

2. Click the Align Drawing Objects button on the Drawing toolbar.

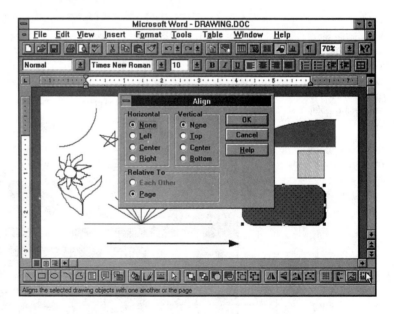

3. In the Horizontal area, choose one of the following:

■ **N**one to use no horizontal alignment

■ **L**eft, to make objects line up evenly on the left side.

■ **C**enter, to make the centers of objects line up evenly.

■ **R**ight, to make objects line up evenly on the right side.

4. In the Vertical area, choose one of the following:

   ■ **No**ne, to use no vertical alignment.

   ■ **T**op, to make the tops of objects line up evenly.

   ■ **C**enter, to make the centers of objects line up evenly.

   ■ **B**ottom, to make the bottoms of objects line up evenly.

5. In the Relative To area, choose one of the following:

   ■ **Ea**ch Other, to align the objects relative to the other objects.

   ■ **P**age, to align the objects relative to the page.

6. Choose OK.

Task: Copying and Deleting Objects

To copy an object, follow these steps:

1. Select the object.

2. Press and hold down Ctrl.

3. Drag the object to its new location. The original object remains in its original place. A copy of the object appears at the new location.

To delete an object, follow these steps:

1. Select the object.

2. Press Delete.

3. In the status bar, Word asks if you are sure you want to delete the selected block. Press Y.

If you have problems... Word does not warn you before it deletes the selected object. If you delete an object accidentally, choose **E**dit, **U**ndo immediately.

*Note: You can use the **E**dit Cu**t**, **E**dit **C**opy, and **E**dit **P**aste commands to move, copy, and delete objects. When you use **E**dit **C**opy, the copy appears almost directly on top of the original. Simply move it to the new location. For more information on using the Edit commands, see Lesson 3, "Revising a Document."*

Editing and Enhancing Drawings

You can change the appearance of drawings in many ways. You can add colors and patterns, change the line style and flip and rotate objects. You can change the size of objects, group objects and layer objects.

To edit existing objects, you first must select them.

Note: *To get a closer look at any area of the drawing, use the View Zoom command. For more information on using Zoom, see Lesson 7, "Setting Up Your Pages."*

Task: Changing the Size of Objects

To quickly change the size of an object, follow these steps:

1. Select the object.

2. Point at any one of the object's handles. The mouse pointer changes shape to a two-headed arrow.

3. Click and drag the mouse pointer until the object is the size you want. A dotted line indicates the new size.

If you have problems... If the object changes position rather than size, you are not pointing at a handle. Choose **E**dit, **U**ndo and try again. Make sure the mouse pointer is a two-headed arrow, not a four-headed arrow.

To resize an object proportionately, follow these steps:

1. Select the object.

2. Point at one of the corner handles.

3. Press and hold down Shift.

4. Click and drag the mouse pointer diagonally. The height and width of the object change by the same amount.

5. When the object is the size you want, release the mouse button and the Shift key.

To resize an object precisely, follow these steps:

1. Select the object.

2. Choose F**o**rmat, Drawing **O**bject.

3. In the Drawing Object dialog box, click the Size and Position tab.

4. In the Size area, enter the precise Height and Width measurements you want to use for the object.

5. Choose OK.

Task: Changing Lines Styles and Colors

In Word, you can use different lines styles and colors to create objects. You can select a line width, a dashed line, or a transparent line. You can turn a line into an arrow, round the corners of objects, and you can add a shadow to an object.

You can set default line styles and colors to use to create objects, or you can change the outlines of existing objects. To change the outline of an existing object, select the object first. To change the default settings, be sure that nothing is selected in the drawing.

Note: *If you are changing the default settings, the name of the dialog box you use is "Drawing Defaults." If you are changing the settings of an existing objects, the name of the dialog box is "Drawing Objects." Both offer the same options.*

To quickly choose a line style, follow these steps:

1. Click the Line Style button from the Drawing toolbar.

Choose a line style from the list that appears when you click the Line Style button on the Drawing toolbar.

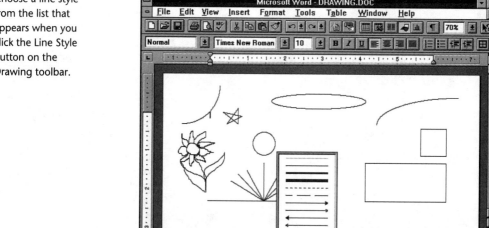

2. Choose the line style you want to use.

To choose a line color quickly, click the Line Color button on the Drawing toolbar.

Choose a line color using the Line Color button on the Drawing toolbar.

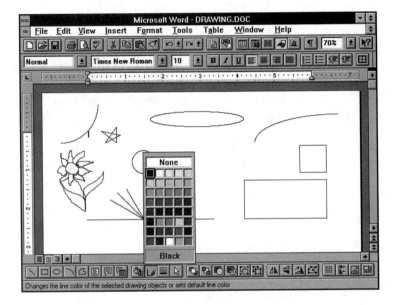

To choose additional line style and color options, follow these steps:

1. Choose F**o**rmat, Drawing **O**bject.

2. In the Drawing dialog box, click the **L**ine tab.

Choose additional line style and color options in the Drawing dialog box.

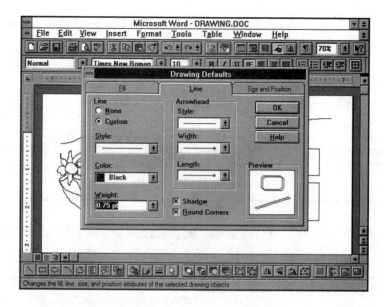

3. In the Line area, choose the line style and color options for outlining and drawing objects as follows:

■ Choose **N**one to make the outline of an object invisible.

■ From the **S**tyle drop-down list box, choose the line type.

■ From the **C**olor drop-down list box, choose the line color.

■ From the **W**eight drop-down list box, choose or specify the thickness of the line.

4. In the Arrowhead area, choose the line style options for creating arrows as follows:

■ From the St**y**le drop-down list box, choose the line type to use for an arrowhead.

■ From the Wi**d**th drop-down list box, choose the thickness of the arrowhead lines.

■ From the Len**g**th drop-down list box, choose the length of the arrowhead lines.

5. To add a shadow, choose the Shad**o**w check box.

6. To round the corners of shapes, choose the **R**ound Corners check box.

7. Choose OK.

If you have problems...

If the Arrowhead options are dimmed, you have an object selected that is not an arrow. You can only choose Arrowhead options if nothing is selected, or if an arrow object is selected.

Changing line styles can give a new dimension to a drawing. Here, an arrow is added, and the rectangle now has a dashed outline, rounded corners, and a shadow.

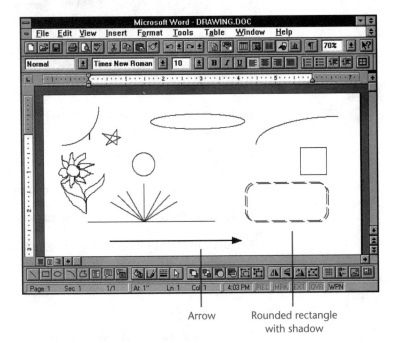

Arrow   Rounded rectangle with shadow

Task: Changing the Fill Color and Pattern

In Word, you can fill objects with color or patterns. Fill patterns enable you to blend more than one color together.

As with line styles, you can change the color or fill pattern of an existing object, or you can select the color or fill pattern before you create an object.

To select a fill color quickly, follow these steps:

1. Click the Fill Color button on the Drawing toolbar.

2. Choose the fill color.

To select a fill color or pattern, follow these steps:

1. Choose F**o**rmat, Drawing **O**bject.

2. Click the **F**ill tab at the top of the Drawing dialog box.

In the Drawing
dialog box, you
can choose a fill
color or blend a fill
pattern from more
than one color.

Choose the fill
pattern here

Choose the fill
color here

Choose the fill
pattern color here

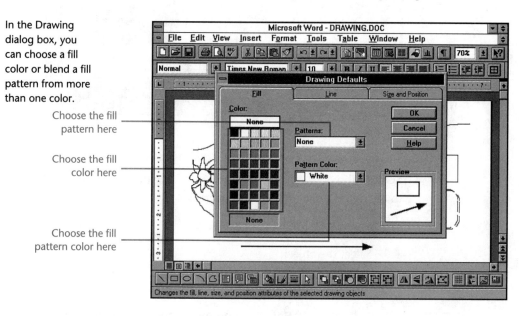

3. In the **C**olor area, choose the fill color.

4. From the **P**atterns drop-down list choose the percentage of pattern color you want to add to the fill color to create the fill pattern.

5. From the Pa**t**tern Color drop-down list, choose the pattern color.

6. Choose OK.

You can use colors
and fill patterns to
add depth and
texture to your
drawings.

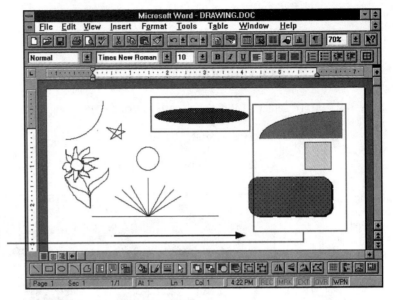

These objects have
different fill patterns

Task: Rotating and Flipping Objects

You can flip objects left to right or upside down. You can rotate objects
to the right in increments of 90 degrees.

To flip an object, follow these steps:

1. Select the object.

2. Click one of the following:

■ The Flip Horizontal button on the Drawing toolbar, to flip the
object from left to right.

■ The Flip Vertical button on the Drawing toolbar, to flip the
object upside down.

To rotate an object, follow these steps:

1. Select the object.

2. Click the Rotate Right button on the Drawing toolbar. The object
rotates 90 degrees to the right.

Task: Changing a Freeform Object

A freeform object created with the Freeform button is comprised of intersecting line segments. Each intersection is marked by a *freeform handle*. The more complex the object is, the more freeform handles it has. To change a freeform object, you move, add, or delete freeform handles.

Freeform handles
Handles used to change the shape of freeform objects.

To change a freeform object, follow these steps:

1. Select the object.

2. Click the Reshape button on the Drawing toolbar. The freeform handles appear.

3. Position the mouse pointer on one of the handles. It changes shape to a plus sign.

4. Drag the mouse pointer to the new location to change the shape of the object.

If you have problems...

Some objects may have dozens of freeform handles. If you cannot distinguish one from another, try using **V**iew, **Z**oom to enlarge the view.

To add a handle, follow these steps:

1. Select the object.

2. Click the Reshape button on the Drawing toolbar. The freeform handles appear.

3. Point anywhere on any line. The mouse pointer changes to include a four-headed arrow.

4. Press and hold Ctrl.

5. Click to insert the new handle.

To delete a handle, follow these steps:

1. Select the object.

2. Click the Reshape button on the Drawing toolbar. The freeform handles appear.

3. Point at the handle you want to delete. The mouse pointer changes to a plus sign.

4. Press and hold Ctrl. The mouse pointer changes to an X.

5. Click to delete the handle.

To hide the freeform handles, click the Reshape icon again.

Task: Creating Pictures

To create a drawing in a picture, follow these steps:

1. Position the insertion point in the document where you want the drawing to appear.

2. Click the Create Picture button on the Drawing toolbar.

   A separate window opens where you can create the drawing by using the features discussed in this lesson.

3. When you are done, click Close Picture on the Picture toolbar. The window closes, and the picture appears in the document, at the insertion point location.

You also can create a picture out of existing objects. Simply select the objects, and then click the Create Picture button.

For information on working with pictures, see Lesson 17, "Working with Other Windows Applications."

To edit a picture, simply double-click it to open the picture window.

Summary

To	Do This
Display the Drawing toolbar	Choose **V**iew, **T**oolbars. Choose the Drawing check box.
Draw objects	Click the button. Drag the mouse pointer to create an object.
Select objects	Click the object you want to select. Press and hold Shift to select additional objects.
Move an object	Point at the object and drag it to the new location.
Copy an object	Point at the object. Press and hold Ctrl and drag the copy of the object to the new location.

To	Do This
Resize or Reshape an object	Select the object. Drag a handle to increase or decrease the object's size, or to change the object's shape.
Delete an object	Select the object. Choose **E**dit, Cu**t** or press Delete.
Rotate an object	Select the object. Click the Rotate Right button.
Flip an object	Select the object. Click the Flip Horizontal or Flip Vertical button.
Group objects	Select the objects. Click the Group button.

On Your Own

Estimated time: 15 minutes

1. Display the Drawing toolbar.

2. Create a round object.

3. Create a rectangular object.

4. Create a multisided or freeform object.

5. Create a text box.

6. Format the text in the text box.

7. Create a callout.

8. Add a border to the callout box.

9. Move the round object to another location on the page.

10. Make a copy of the rectangular object.

11. Change the line style and create another object.

12. Elongate one of the rectangles.

13. Rotate the multisided object.

14. Flip the rectangle either horizontally or vertically.

15. Fill the rectangle with a color or a pattern.

16. Align the objects evenly on a baseline.

17. Layer the objects—placing some in front and some in back.

Working with Tables

In Word, you can use tables to create side-by-side paragraphs and to relate rows and columns of text, numbers, and pictures. With tables, you can create forms, merge documents, create charts, and perform calculations.

In this lesson, you learn the different ways to create, edit, and format tables with Word.

Specifically, you learn to do the following:

- Create tables

Table
A combination of related rows and columns which create cells into which you enter information.

- Enter data in a table

- Edit a table

- Change the appearance of a table

- Perform simple calculations in a table

Understanding Tables

Side-by-side columns
Vertical lines of cells arranged beside one another on a page.

In Lesson 7, "Setting Up Your Pages," you learned to create newspaper-style columns, where text flows from the bottom of one column to the top of the next column. *Tables* also use columns, but these columns are *side-by-side*, not newspaper style.

Row
A horizontal line of cells.

Cell
A rectangular area in a table where a row and column intersect.

In tables, columns are combined with *rows* to create a grid of *cells*, which contain related information.

Perhaps the most easily recognizable table is a spreadsheet, but you can use tables for other purposes such as creating a list of words and their definitions, a schedule of monthly meetings, or even a resume.

Creating Tables

In Word, you can create a table using four different ways:

- You can use the Table Wizard. For information on using wizards, see Lesson 9, "Making Your Work Easier."

- To quickly create a table with columns of equal width that fill the page, you can use the Insert Table button on the Standard toolbar.

- To create a table with columns of a precise width, you can use the **I**nsert Table command from the T**a**ble menu.

- You can create a table out of existing text.

Note: *Give some thought ahead of time to how many columns and rows you need in your table. Don't forget rows for titles and, if applicable, column headings.*

Task: Creating a Table Quickly

To create a table quickly, follow these steps:

1. Position the insertion point in the document where you want to place the table.

2. Click the Insert Table button on the Standard toolbar.

When you click the
Insert Table button,
a box appears from
which you easily
can choose the
number of columns
and rows you want
to include in your
table.

Drag left to right to choose the
number of columns and rows

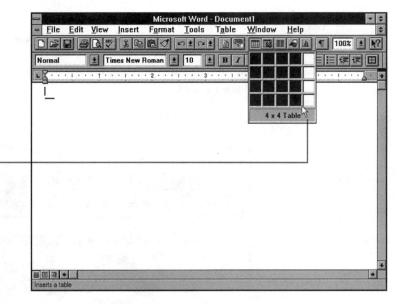

3. Point at the top-left cell in the table box.

4. Click and drag to the right to choose columns and down to choose
rows.

5. When the number of columns and rows you want to include in
your table are highlighted, release the mouse button. The table
appears in your document.

Word creates a
table using the
number of columns
and rows you
select. The columns
are sized to fill the
width of the page.

Rows

Columns

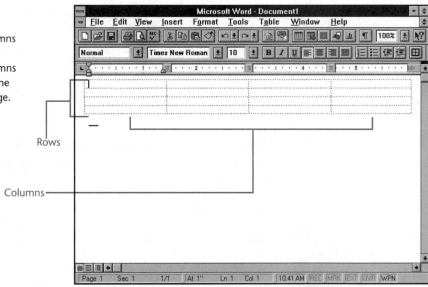

Task: Creating a Table Precisely

To create a table using precise column widths, follow these steps:

1. Position the insertion point in the document where you want to place the table.

2. Choose T**a**ble, **I**nsert Table.

You can specify an exact width for columns in the Insert Table dialog box, or you can leave it set to automatically adjust the width.

Enter the number of columns here

Enter the number of rows here

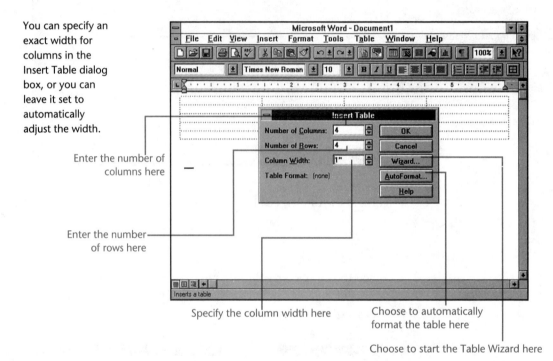

Specify the column width here

Choose to automatically format the table here

Choose to start the Table Wizard here

3. In the Number of **C**olumns text box, enter the number of columns you want in the table.

4. In the Number of **R**ows text box, enter the number of rows you want in the table.

5. In the Column Width text box, specify an exact width for columns, or choose Auto to automatically create columns of equal width across the page.

6. Choose OK to create the table.

Here, Word created a 4-row by 4-column table; the columns are exactly 1-inch wide.

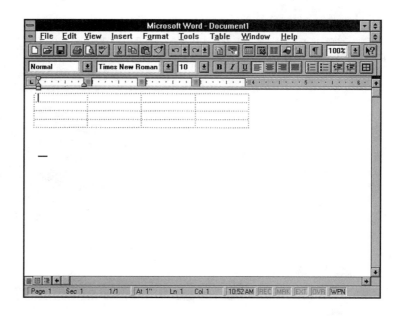

Task: Creating a Table from Existing Text

To create a table from existing text, you must first make sure the text is set up so that it can be converted into columns and rows.

The easiest way to set up the text is to plan for each paragraph to become a separate row. Within the paragraph, separate the text for one cell from the text for another cell with a character that does not appear anywhere else in the paragraph.

To quickly create a table from text, follow these steps:

1. Select the text.

2. Click the Insert Table button on the Standard toolbar.

Alternatively, follow these steps:

1. Select the text.

2. Choose T**a**ble, Con**v**ert Text to Table.

In the Convert Text to Table dialog box, specify the table format.

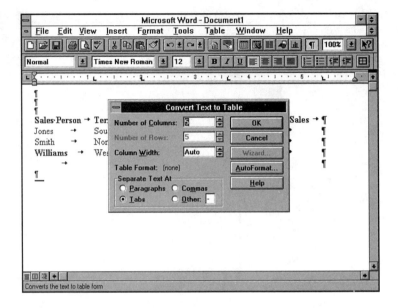

3. In the Convert Text to Table dialog box, Word suggests a format for the table, based on the way you have set up the text. Make changes if necessary.

4. Choose OK.

Task: Viewing Tables

You can create a table in any view. To see the way the table will appear when printed, change to **P**age Layout view or Print Pre**v**iew.

When you insert a table in a document, the horizontal scroll bar shows the width of each column. Notice that the usable width of each column is slightly less than the space between the vertical gridlines. That is because Word leaves some blank space between columns.

Gridlines

Nonprinting dotted lines that define the rows and columns in a table.

You can change the way a table is displayed on-screen. By default, when you create a table, Word displays *gridlines* to show the size and position of each cell. The gridlines do not print. You learn to add printable lines to tables later in this lesson.

To remove the gridlines, choose T**a**ble, Grid**l**ines. To turn them on again, choose T**a**ble, Grid**l**ines again.

If you choose to display nonprinting characters, you can display end-of-text markers at the left end of each cell, and end-of-row markers at the right end of each row.

 To display nonprinting characters, choose **T**ools, **O**ptions View and select the **A**ll check box in the Nonprinting Characters area. You also can click the Show/Hide Marks button on the Standard toolbar.

You can change the way a table is displayed in a document by choosing to display nonprinting characters, and gridlines.

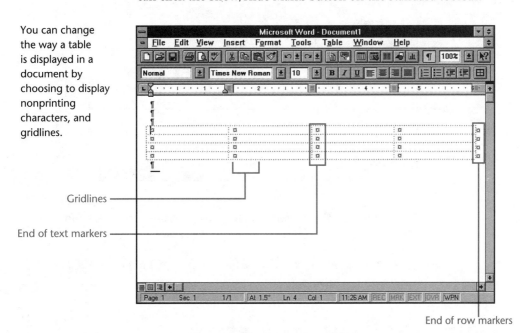

Gridlines

End of text markers

End of row markers

Task: **Entering Data in a Table**

In a table, you enter data into cells. Cells can contain text, numbers, or graphics. You can enter data by typing, importing from another application, or creating a drawing or chart within the cell. In this lesson, you learn to enter text and numbers in tables.

To type data into a table, position the insertion point in the correct cell and type. By default, Word expands the height of the cell to accommodate as much data as you type. It wraps the data in the cell to fit within the column width.

To move to the next cell, press Tab or move the insertion point.

Here a table is used to show sales totals. Notice where Word automatically expands the height of a cell to accommodate the text.

Expanded cell

You can format the data in a table by using Word's character and paragraph formatting commands.

Note: *You can edit data in a table the same way you edit any other data. When you delete data, the empty cell remains in place.*

Changing the Appearance of Tables

You can change the appearance of tables by changing the size of cells, moving rows, columns, and cells, inserting or deleting rows, columns, and cells. You also can format the table by adding character and paragraph formatting, including borders and shading.

Task: Formatting Tables

Word comes with predesigned table formats that specify fonts, character effects, and borders and shading. You can select one of these formats to automatically format your table.

To automatically apply one of Word's built-in formats, follow these steps:

1. Position the insertion point anywhere within the table.

2. Choose Table, Table AutoFormat.

You can automatically apply one of Word's 34 built-in table formats.

Choose a format here—

Modify the format here—

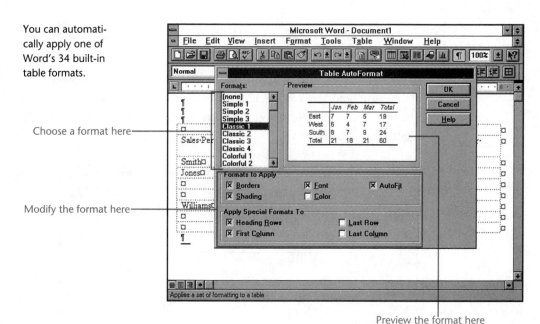

Preview the format here

12

3. In the Formats list, choose the format you want to apply.

4. To modify the format, choose any of the check boxes in the Formats to Apply and Apply Special Formats To areas.

5. Choose OK to apply the format to your table.

You quickly can format a table by selecting one of Word's built-in formats.

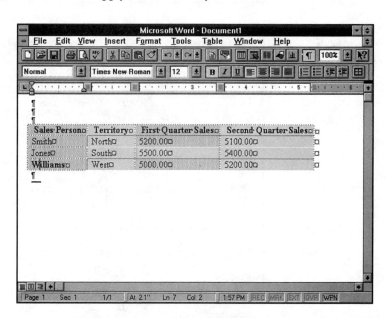

To manually format text in a table, use the character and paragraph formatting commands.

You can change the font, apply font styles and effects such as underlines, italics, and boldface; you can change alignment and add borders and shading. For more information on formatting, see Lesson 5, "Dressing Up Your Text," and Lesson 6, "Dressing Up Your Paragraphs."

In a table, each cell can be formatted with a different look.

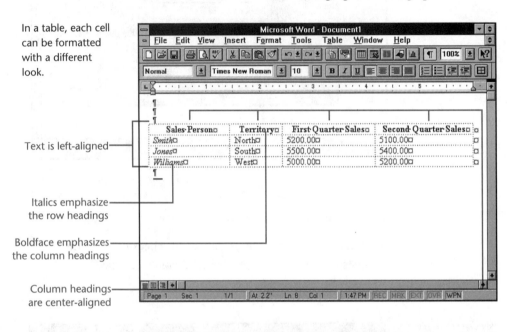

Text is left-aligned

Italics emphasize the row headings

Boldface emphasizes the column headings

Column headings are center-aligned

You can apply borders and shading to customize the look of your table.

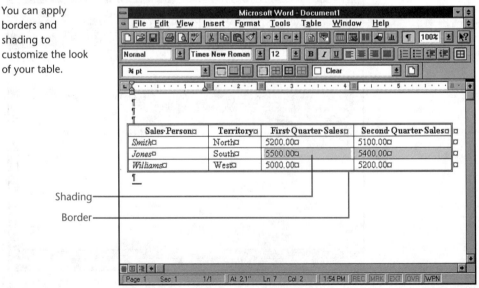

Shading

Border

Task: Changing Column Widths

You can change column widths quickly, by dragging gridlines or the column markers, or you can set precise column width measurements.

To change column widths quickly, follow these steps:

1. Point at a column gridline or a column marker. The mouse pointer changes to include a double-headed arrow.

2. Click and drag left or right to the new location.

When you drag a vertical gridline or a column marker, the overall width of the table remains the same. When you change the width of one column, columns to the right are automatically resized in proportion to their original widths.

To modify the way Word changes column widths, use any of the following methods:

- Hold down Shift while you drag. Only the columns on either side of the gridline are affected. As one becomes wider, the other becomes narrowed.

- Hold down Ctrl while you drag. All columns to the right of the selected gridline become equal in width.

- Hold down Ctrl and Shift while you drag. Only the column to the left of the selected gridline changes width. The overall width of the table is adjusted to accommodate the change in column width.

12

You can display
column widths on
the horizontal ruler.

Drag here to change
column widths

Mouse pointer

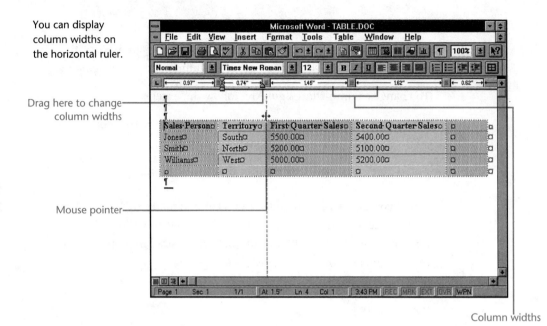

Column widths

To change column widths precisely, follow these steps:

1. Position the insertion point in any cell in the column you want to change.

2. Choose Table, Cell Height and **W**idth.

3. Click the **C**olumn tab at the top of the Cell Height and Width dialog box.

You can set precise
column widths in
the Cell Height and
Width dialog box.

Set the column
width here

Set the space between
columns here

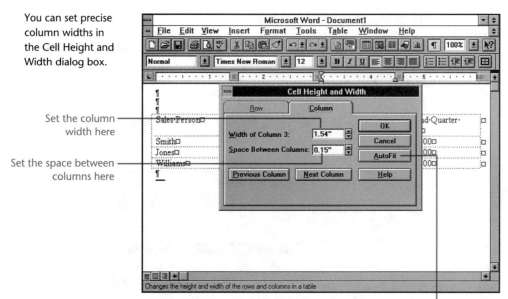

Choose to automatically adjust all column widths here

4. In the **W**idth of Column text box, enter the column width.

5. In the **S**pace Between Columns text box, enter the amount of
   space you want to leave between columns.

6. To change the width of the column to the left of the current
   column, choose **P**revious Column.

7. To change the width of the column to the right of the current
   column, choose **N**ext Column.

8. Choose OK.

Task: Changing Row Heights

By default, Word automatically adjusts the height of rows to accommodate the data entered in the cells in the row.

To change row height, follow these steps:

1. Position the insertion point within the row you want to change. To change all rows, select the entire table.

2. Choose Table, Cell Height and **W**idth.

3. Click the **R**ow tab at the top of the Cell Height and Width dialog box.

You can change row height for the entire table or for selected rows, and you can change row alignment.

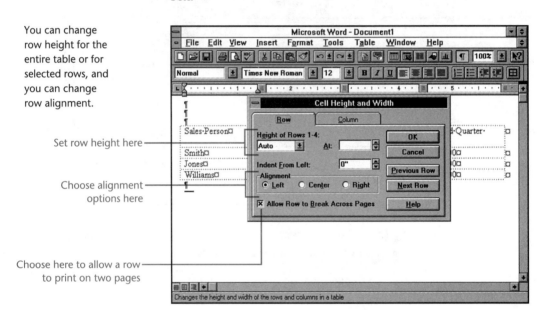

Set row height here

Choose alignment options here

Choose here to allow a row to print on two pages

4. From the Height of Row drop down list, choose one of the following:

   ■ Auto to automatically set the row height

   ■ At Least to set the row height to no less than the specified measurement

   ■ Exactly to set the row height to the specific measurement

5. In the **A**t text box, enter the specific height measurement.

6. To realign the selected row, choose an alignment option.

7. Choose **N**ext Row to set the height for the row below the selected row.

8. Choose **P**revious Row to set the height for the row above the selected row.

9. Choose OK.

Task: Inserting Rows, Columns, and Cells

To insert rows into an existing table, follow these steps:

1. Position the insertion point in the row below the location where you want to insert a row. To insert more than one row, select more than one row.

2. Choose T**a**ble, **I**nsert Rows.

Note: *To add a row to the bottom of a table, position the insertion point in the bottom right cell of the table and press Tab.*

To insert columns into an existing table, follow these steps:

1. Select the column to the right of the location where you want to insert a column. To insert more than one column, select more than one column.

2. Choose T**a**ble, **I**nsert Columns.

Note: *To add a column to the left side of a table, select the end of row markers along the left edge of the table.*

To insert cells into an existing table, follow these steps:

1. Select the cell below or to the right of the location where you want to place a new cell. To insert more than one cell, select more than one cell.

2. Choose T**a**ble, **I**nsert Cells.

You can use the
Insert Cells dialog
box to insert one
cell, or a whole row
or column of cells.

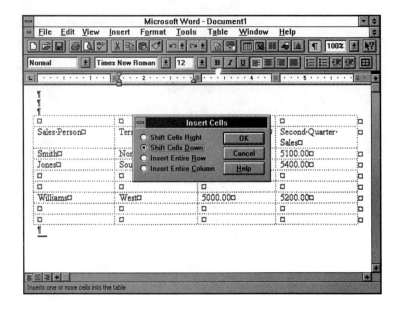

3. In the Insert Cells dialog box, choose one of the following:

- Shift Cells **R**ight to insert one cell to the left of the selected cell

- Shift Cells **D**own to insert one cell above the selected cell

- Insert Entire **R**ow to insert a row of cells above the selected cell

- Insert Entire **C**olumn to insert a column of cells to the left of the selected cell

4. Choose OK.

Note: *To delete a column, row, or cell, select it, and then choose the appropriate **D**elete command from the **T**able menu.*

Task: Moving and Copying Columns, Rows, and Cells

You can move and copy columns, rows, and cells by dragging them, or by using the **E**dit, Cu**t**; **E**dit, **C**opy; and **E**dit, **P**aste commands.

Note: *When you move or copy columns, rows, and cells, the item you move replaces any existing item at the new location. If you do not want to overwrite existing data, make sure to insert the blank space necessary to accommodate the moved item.*

To move or copy a column, row, or cell to a new location, follow these steps:

1. Select the item you want to move. Be sure to select the entire item, including any end-of-text or end-of-row markers.

2. Point at the selected item. To copy the item, press and hold Ctrl.

3. Drag the mouse pointer to the new position.

For information on using the Cut and Paste commands, see Lesson 3, "Revising a Document."

Task: Merging and Splitting Cells

Merge cells
To combine horizontally adjacent cells into one larger cell.

You can *merge* adjacent cells to allow yourself more room for entering data, or creating headings, and you can split merged cells back into multiple cells.

To merge cells, follow these steps:

1. Select the cells you want to merge. They must be adjacent to each other and in the same row.

2. Choose T**a**ble, **M**erge Cells.

To split a merged cell, follow these steps:

1. Select the merged cells.

2. Choose T**a**ble, S**p**lit Cells.

3. In the Number of **C**olumns text box of the Split Cells dialog box, enter the number of cells you want to create out of the merged cell.

4. Choose OK.

Word splits the merged cell as evenly as possible to create the number of cells you specify. If the cell contains data, it tries to split the data evenly, as well.

12

Task: Sorting Data in a Table

You can change the order of rows in a table by sorting the data in the row. Word can sort the data in tables alphabetically or numerically, in ascending or descending order.

To sort data in a table, follow these steps:

1. Select the part of the table you want to sort.

2. Choose Table, Sort.

In the Sort dialog box, you can specify the sort order for sorting a table.

Choose the column to sort by here

Choose the sort type here

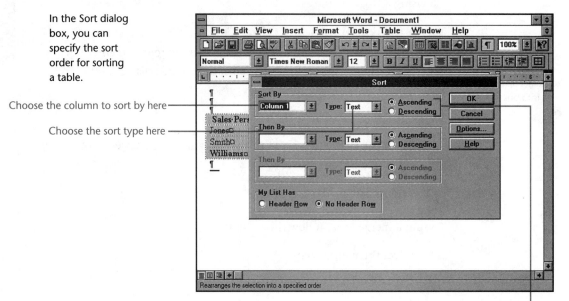

Choose the sort order here

3. In the My List Has area, choose one of the following:

    ■ Header **R**ow if you want Word to ignore the first selected row when it performs the sort. Choose this option if you have a heading you want to leave in place.

    ■ No Header Ro**w** if you want Word to include the first selected row when it performs the sort.

4. In the **S**ort By drop-down list box, choose the column on which you want to base the sort.

5. In the T**y**pe drop down list box, choose to sort text, numbers, or dates.

6. Choose either **A**scending or **D**escending.

7. Choose OK.

Calculating Values in a Table

Formula

An expression that performs mathematical operations on data in cells in a table.

You can use Word to calculate values in a table. Word uses *formulas* to add, subtract, multiple, and divide. It also can calculate averages and percentages, and it can find minimum and maximum values.

When you perform calculations in a Word table, be sure to leave a blank cell available where Word can insert the result. If you are calculating values in rows, leave the blank cell at the end of the row. If you are calculating values in columns, leave the blank cell at the bottom of the column. If you do not leave a blank cell, Word overwrites the data in the current cell.

In a Word table formula, you can use the following operators:

+	Addition
-	Subtraction
*	Multiplication
/	Division
%	Percentage
()	To specify the order of operations
..	To specify a range
:	To specify a range

Note: *If you have experience using a spreadsheet program, such as Excel, you already know how to use Word to perform calculations in a table.*

Task: Adding Numbers

By default, Word assumes that the calculation you want to perform in a table is addition.

12

To add the value of all the cells in a row or column, follow these steps:

1. Position the insertion point in the blank cell where you want the result to appear.

2. Choose Table, Formula.

By default, the formula in the Formula dialog box is for addition.

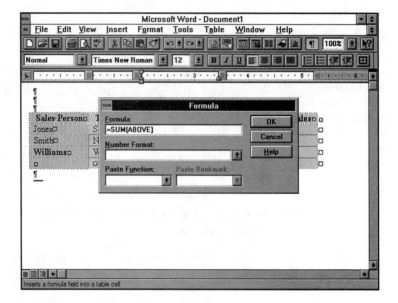

Note: *If the insertion point is at the bottom of a column, Word automatically enters a formula for adding all of the values in the column. If the insertion point is at the end of a row, Word automatically enters a formula for adding all of the values in the row.*

3. Choose OK to add the numbers. The total appears in the blank cell.

Task: Multiplying Numbers

To multiply, you must refer to cells in terms of their positions in the table. Word names columns alphabetically from left to right; it numbers rows consecutively from top to bottom. Individual cells can be identified by the name and number of the intersecting row and column. A1, for example, identifies the cell in the top left corner of the table.

To multiply the data in cell B2 by the data in C2, follow these steps:

1. Place the insertion point in the empty cell where you want the data to appear.

2. Choose Table, Formula.

3. Delete the information in the Formula text box.

4. Type the formula for performing the multiplication: **B2*C2**.

5. Choose OK.

Task: Updating a Value

Word inserts the result of a calculation as a field, not as plain text. You cannot edit the data, because it depends on the other values in the formula.

If you change any of the other values included in the formula, press F9 to update the result.

12

Summary

To	Do This
Create a table	Choose Table, Insert Table. Enter the number of columns and rows.
Display table gridlines	Choose Table, Gridlines View.
Select a cell	Click the cell.
Select a row	Choose Table, Select Row.
Select a column	Choose Table, Select Column.
Select the table	Choose Table, Select Table.
Format a table	Choose Table, Table AutoFormat.
Change cell height or width	Choose Table, Cell Height and Width.
Sort data in a table	Select the data. Choose Table, Sort.
Calculate values	Choose Table, Formula. Enter the formula.
Merge cells	Select the cells. Choose Table, Merge Cells.

On Your Own
Estimated time: 15 minutes

1. Create either a table with at least four columns and four rows, centered on the page.

2. Display the table gridlines.

3. Enter data in the table.

4. Add another sales person to the table.

5. Change the formatting of the data in the top row, such as centering and boldfacing the data.

6. Change the formatting of the data in the first column.

7. Add a row to the top of the table.

8. Merge the cells in the top row and create a title across the top of the table.

9. Add a column on the right. If necessary, change the width of the existing columns to accommodate a new column.

10. Total each salesperson's figures, displaying the totals in the column on the right.

11. Add a double line around the outside of the table.

12. Add printing gridlines to the table.

13. Add a fill pattern to the cell that shows the highest sales figures.

14. Reformat the table using one of Word's built in table formats.

15. Sort the data in the table.

16. Save the table. You can use this information to create a chart in Lesson 13, "Working with Graphs."

Working with Graphs

In many business presentations, charts are used to display statistical information. Charts are an important visual tool for translating numeric data into a format that most people easily can understand.

Word comes with a built-in charting application, called *Microsoft Graph*. You use Graph to create charts out of existing data, or you can enter new data. You can edit charts, enhance charts, and you can copy and paste charts into other applications.

In this lesson, you learn to do the following:

- Create a chart
- Choose a chart type
- Edit a chart
- Enhance a chart
- Edit a datasheet

Understanding Microsoft Graph

Microsoft Graph is a software application program that comes with Word. You use it to create *charts* from data formatted in a table.

Chart
A visual or graphic representation of numeric data. Charts come in many types, including bar charts, pie charts, column charts, and line charts.

Datasheet window
The screen in Graph where you enter and edit the data used to create a chart.

Chart window
The screen in Graph that displays the chart created by using the data in the current Datasheet.

The main Microsoft Graph window contains a Datasheet window and a Chart window.

You can enter data into Graph in three ways:

- You can enter data into Graph directly.

- You can use data already entered in a table in a Word document. For information on creating tables in Word, see Lesson 12, "Working with Tables."

- You can import data from another application, such as Microsoft Excel, or Lotus 1-2-3. For information on importing data, see Lesson 17, "Working with Other Windows Applications."

Graph embeds charts into documents as objects, using Windows' Object Linking and Embedding (OLE). That means that changes made to a chart in Graph are updated in the Word document. In addition, you can start Graph from within Word, simply by double-clicking an existing Chart object. For more information on OLE, see Lesson 17, "Working with Other Windows Applications."

When you start Graph, two windows open on top of the current Word document: a Datasheet window that displays the data used to create the chart, and the Chart window that displays the chart. The chart itself is placed in the Word document, as an object.

Graph menu bar

Datasheet window

Chart window (active)

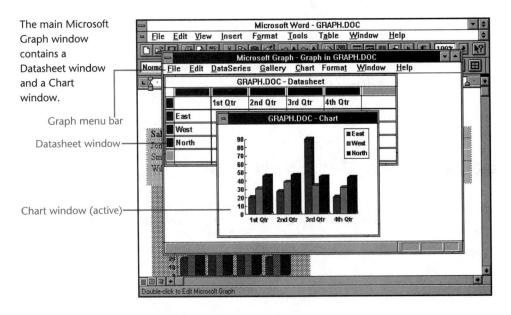

You use the commands on the Graph menu bar for both the Datasheet window and the Chart window. If a command is dimmed, you cannot use it in the active window. The two windows function the same way as other Windows' windows. You can move them and resize them. The title bar on the active window is highlighted. You switch between the windows by clicking in the one you want.

Understanding Charts

Chart format

A variation of a chart type. Side-by-side stacked and 100% stacked are variations of the bar chart type.

A pie chart shows segments of a whole. It can be useful for displaying different segments of a budget.

Charts are useful for enhancing numeric information that may otherwise be boring or difficult to read. For a chart to be effective, however, it is important for you to understand the data you want to display and the information you want to convey before you create a chart.

Different charts are suitable for displaying information in different ways.

13

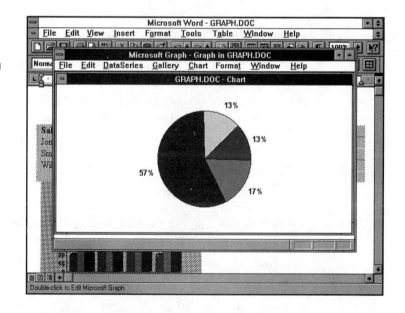

A line chart shows a progression of segments. It can be useful for displaying growth in market share.

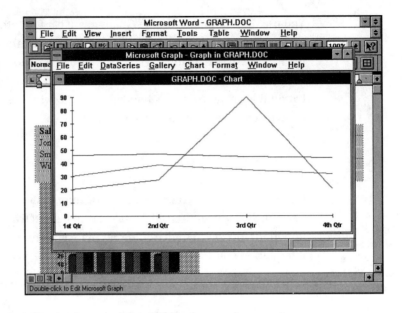

Chart type
A category of charts that Graph can produce.

In Graph, you can format the chart automatically by selecting one of the 12 *chart types*. In addition, you can modify the *chart format* of each chart type, and customize the chart.

For more information about selecting a chart type, and to see samples of each chart, consult the *Microsoft Graph User's Guide*.

Task: Creating a Chart from a Word Table

To create a chart, you can use data displayed in a table in a Word document. By default, Graph creates a 3-D Column chart. You learn later in this lesson how to change chart types, and how to change the chart type default.

To create a chart in a Word document, follow these steps:

1. Open the document that contains the table.

2. To place the chart in a different document, copy the table data into the other document. To place the chart in the original document, continue with step 3.

3. Select the rows and columns in the table from which you want to create the chart. You can select the whole table, or parts of the table.

4. Choose **I**nsert, **O**bject.

5. Click the **C**reate New tab at the top of the Object dialog box.

Graph inserts charts as objects into Word documents.

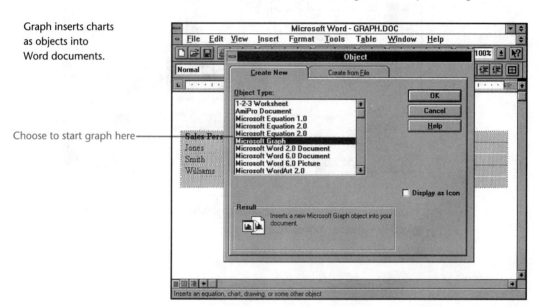

Choose to start graph here

6. From the **O**bject Type list box, choose Microsoft Graph.

7. Choose OK. Microsoft Graph starts with the table data entered in the Datasheet window and a 3-D Column chart in the Chart window.

Graph creates a 3-D Column chart using the selected data.

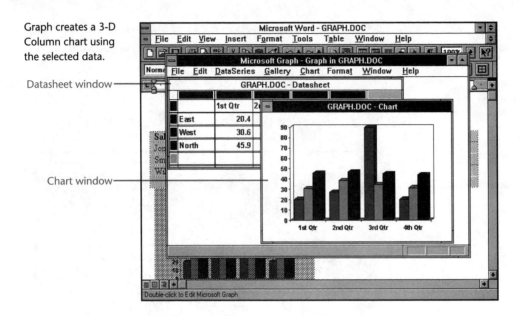

Datasheet window

Chart window

When you exit Graph, the chart is inserted and updated in the current Word document. When you save the document, you save the chart.

To exit Graph, follow these steps:

1. In the Graph window, choose **F**ile, **Ex**it.

2. Graph displays a dialog box prompting you to update the chart in the current document. Choose **Y**es to place the chart in your document. Choose **N**o to exit Graph without updating the chart in the document.

Customizing a Chart

Legend

A box that appears within the chart to identify the data segments. Depending on the type of chart, the legend may identify the segments based on color, shape, or both color and shape.

In Graph, you can create a customized chart by changing virtually any element of the chart. You can change the chart type. You can add, modify, and delete *legends*, gridlines, text, arrows, and background patterns. You can format the text on a chart, and you can change the x- and y- *axes*. You also can adjust the layout and patterns of the *data markers* used to represent the chart data.

You can modify
virtually any
element in any of
Graph's charts.

Add titles

Add and Format text

Add arrows

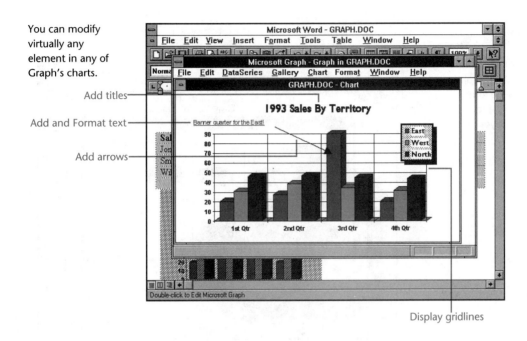

13

Display gridlines

Task: Choosing a Chart Type and Format

To choose a chart type and format, follow these steps:

1. In the Graph window, choose **G**allery.

From the Gallery
menu, choose the
chart type.

Current chart type

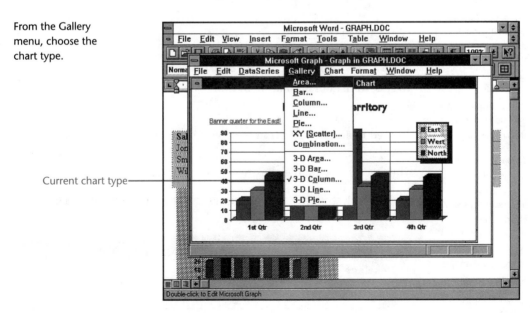

2. From the **G**allery menu, choose the type of chart you want to use.

In the Chart Gallery dialog box, Graph displays the format options for the chart type you select.

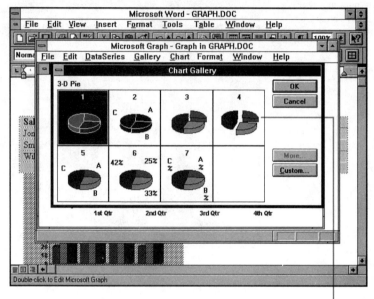

Pie chart format types

Axis

A vertical (y-axis) or horizontal (x-axis) line that provides the scale for plotting data in a chart. Some 3-D charts have a z-axis that runs along the back and side walls of the plot area.

Data marker

The visual image that represents data in a chart. In some charts, the data marker is a dot or symbol. In other charts the data marker is a column, bar, or pie slice.

3. In the Chart Gallery dialog box, choose the format you want to use.

4. Choose OK.

Task: Selecting Items in a Chart

To edit, format, or clear an item from a chart, you must first select the item.

Selected items have selection handles. If the handles are black, you can move, size, or format the item by using the handles. If the handles are white, you must double-click the item to format it.

Table 13.1 describes selection techniques for selecting items in a chart.

Table 13.1 Selecting Items in a Chart	
To select	**Do This**
A single item	Click the item
A data series	Click any data marker in the data series

To select	Do This
A single data marker	Press and hold Ctrl and click the marker
Gridlines	Click any gridline
An axis	Click any tick mark label on the axis
The plot area	Click any empty space in the plot area
The entire chart	Click inside the edge of the window, but outside all chart items.

Task: Working with Legends

A legend in a chart helps to identify what each data marker represents. By default, Graph includes a legend when you create a chart.

A legend identifies the data in the chart.

Legend ———

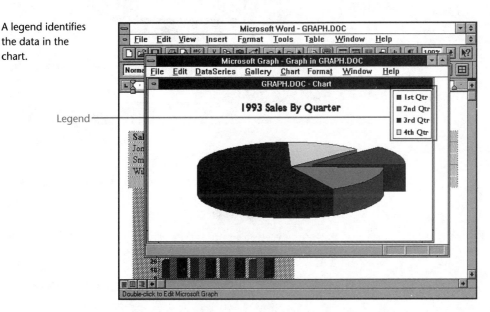

To remove a legend, choose **C**hart, Delete **L**egend.

To insert a legend, choose **C**hart, Add **L**egend.

To move a legend, follow these steps:

1. Select the legend. Black handles appear around it.

2. Drag the legend to the new location.

13

To format a legend, follow these steps:

1. Select the legend.

2. Choose Forma**t**, **L**egend.

Use the Legend
dialog box to
position and format
the legend.

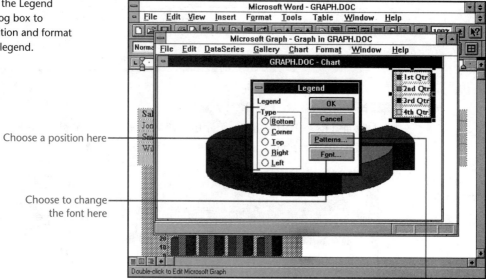

Choose a position here ──

Choose to change ──
the font here

Choose to format the legend area here

3. In the Type area, choose where to position the legend in the chart.

4. Choose one of the following:

■ **P**atterns to select a border style, shadow, and pattern, as well as colors.

■ **F**ont to choose a different font, font size, and font style.

■ OK to return to the Chart window.

Here, the legend has been formatted with a different font, border, pattern, and a shadow.

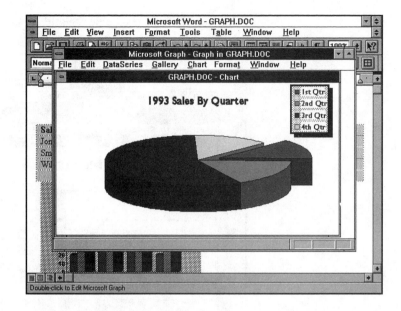

Task: Working with Gridlines

You can add gridlines to a chart to help identify the values represented by data markers.

To add gridlines, follow these steps:

1. Choose **C**hart, **G**ridlines.

In the Gridlines dialog box, you specify the gridlines you want to display.

Specify the horizontal gridlines here

Specify the vertical gridlines here

Specify the 3-D gridlines here (if available)

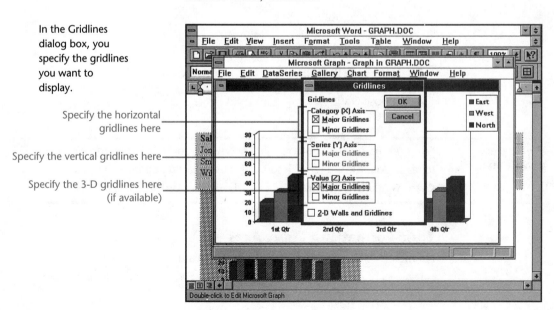

2. Select the check boxes beside the gridlines you want to display.

3. Choose OK.

Here, major gridlines have been added along the x- and y-axes.

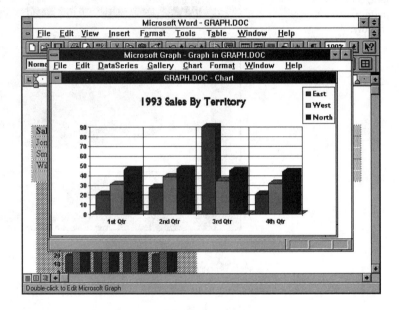

You can change the line style, weight, and color of gridlines.

To format gridlines, follow these steps:

1. Select the gridlines.

2. Choose Forma**t**, **P**atterns.

3. In the Line Patterns dialog box, select the options you want to use.

4. Choose OK.

If you have problems...	If you set too many options for gridlines, it may make the chart more difficult to read. Go back and remove some of the formatting options, or choose **C**hart, **G**ridlines and deselect all check boxes to hide the gridlines.

Task: Formatting Chart Axes

For most two-dimensional charts, you plot values along the y-axis and categories of data along the x-axis. On three dimensional charts, you plot

Tick mark
Marks along the
axis that indicate
a value.

Tick labels
Labels that identify
the value of the tick
marks.

categories along the x-axis, data series along the y-axis, and values along the z-axis.

You can choose which axes appear on a chart, and you can format each axis by changing the scale, adding *tick marks*, and adding *tick labels*.

To add or delete axes from a chart, follow these steps:

1. Choose **C**hart, A**x**es.

If you have problems...

If the Axes command is dimmed on the Chart menu, you have created a pie chart. Pie charts do not have any axes.

---

2. In the Axes dialog box, choose the axes you want to display.

3. Choose OK.

13

To format an axis, follow these steps:

1. Select the axis you want to format.

2. Choose Forma**t**, **S**cale.

3. In the Format Axis Scale dialog box, choose the formatting options for the selected axis. The available options depend on which axis is selected and which type of chart you are using.

4. Choose **P**atterns to change the appearance of tick marks and axis lines and to change the position of tick mark labels.

5. Choose F**o**nt to change the font, font size, font style, and font color.

6. Choose **T**ext to change the tick mark label orientation.

Task: Working with Data Markers

You can control the placement, pattern, and borders of *data markers*, such as the columns in a column chart, or the pie wedges in a pie chart.

To format data markers, follow these steps:

1. Choose Forma**t**, **C**hart.

The options in the
Format Chart dialog
box depend on the
type of chart
selected.

Choose a chart type here

Choose a
data view
here

Set data marker
options here

2. In the Chart **T**ype drop-down list, choose the chart type you want
that contains the data markers you want to change.

3. In the Data V**i**ew area, select the way you want the chart to appear.

4. In the Bar/Column area, set the data marker options you want to
use. For two-dimensional bar or column charts, for example, you
can specify an **O**verlap setting that affects the spacing of data
markers within a category. For any bar or column chart you can
specify a Gap **W**idth setting that affects the spacing of data
markers between categories.

5. Choose OK.

Note: *To find out about the options available for the selected chart type,
press F1 to display help.*

Task: Working with the Plot Area

You can control the color and pattern for the *plot area* and the *plot border*.

To format the plot area, follow these steps:

1. Select the plot area.

2. Choose Forma**t**, **P**atterns.

3. In the Border area, set the border line **S**tyle, **C**olor and **W**eight. Choose **N**one to display no border; choose **A**utomatic to revert to the default setting.

4. In the Area area, choose a fill **P**attern, and **F**oreground and **B**ackground colors. Choose **N**one to display no pattern or color; choose A**u**tomatic to revert to the default setting.

5. Choose OK.

Plot area

The main area of the chart. In two-dimensional charts, the plot area includes the data markers and axes, but not their labels. In three-dimensional charts, the plot area also includes labels and titles.

Plot border

The border around the plot area.

Here, the plot area of a two-dimensional chart is formatted.

13

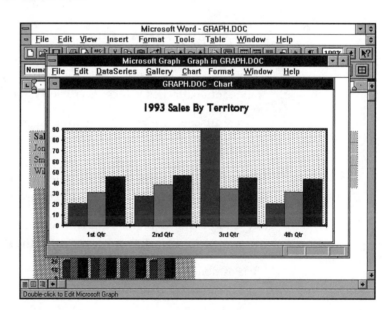

Here, the plot
area of a three-
dimensional chart
is formatted.

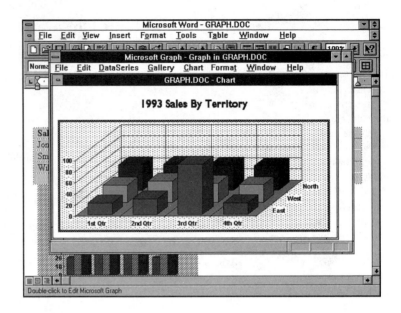

Task: Adding Text to Charts

You can use text in charts to create titles, label axes, and call out specific information. Text can be attached, which means that it is fixed in its location, or unattached, which means you can move it around the chart.

To create attached title text, follow these steps:

1. Choose **C**hart, **T**itles.

2. In the Attach Titles dialog box, select the axis along which you want to place the title, or select to title the entire chart.

3. Choose OK. Graph inserts a Title text box in the chart at the location you specified. Don't worry about the size of the text box.

4. Position the insertion point within the text box, and type the text. If necessary, delete the sample text that Graph inserts. Again, don't worry about the size of the text box, or about the fact that the text seems to disappear as you type it.

5. Press Esc. The title appears in the correct location.

To create attached data label text, follow these steps:

1. Choose **C**hart, **D**ata Labels.

2. In the Data Labels dialog box, choose the type of information you want to show next to each data point in the chart. Choose **N**one to remove a data label.

3. Choose OK.

To create unattached text, follow these steps:

1. Make sure no text is selected.

2. Type the text. It appears in the middle of the chart.

3. Press Esc. Black handles appear around the text.

4. Drag the text to the correct location.

You can edit text in a chart the way you edit text not in a chart. You also can format the text with different fonts, font sizes, font styles, alignments, patterns, and colors.

To format text, follow these steps:

1. Select the text.

2. Choose Forma**t**, **F**ont.

3. In the Chart Fonts dialog box, choose the **F**ont, **S**ize, Style and **C**olor options you want to use.

4. In the Background area, choose one of the following:

   ■ Auto**m**atic to return to the default background setting.

   ■ Tra**n**sparent to enable the information behind the text to show through when the text is on top of other items.

   ■ Opa**q**ue to keep the information behind the text from showing when the text is on top of other items.

5. Choose **P**atterns to format the borders and background patterns of the text box.

6. Choose **T**ext to set text alignment and orientation options for the text box.

7. Choose OK.

    Note: *You can open the Area Patterns or Chart Text dialog box directly from the Format menu.*

Task: Adding Arrows to Charts

You can add an arrow to a chart to call attention to a specific item. Then, you can identify the item by adding text near the arrow.

To insert an arrow in a chart, follow these steps:

1. Make the chart window active.

2. Choose **C**hart, Add A**r**row.

The arrow appears with black handles on either end.

Arrow

Handles

3. To change the size of the arrow, select it and drag either end until it is the correct length.

4. To move the arrow, drag its shaft to the new location.

5. To format the arrow, select it, and then choose Forma**t**, **P**atterns.

Task: Clearing Items from a Chart

You can remove data and custom formatting from a chart. If you clear formats, the selected item returns to the default format. If you clear a data series, the data is removed from the chart, but it remains on the datasheet.

To remove data or custom formatting from a chart, follow these steps:

1. Make the Chart window active.

2. Select the item you want to clear.

3. Choose **E**dit, Cl**e**ar.

4. If the item is a data series, Graph asks if you want to clear the data or the formatting for the series. In the Clear Series dialog box, choose **S**eries to clear the entire series. Choose **F**ormats to clear just the formatting.

13

Task: Copying and Deleting a Chart

You can copy a chart from within Graph, or from within the Word document that contains the chart.

To copy a chart from within Graph, follow these steps:

1. Make the Chart window active.

2. Choose **E**dit, **C**opy Chart.

3. Position the insertion point in the window where you want to place the copy of the active chart. You can place it in a Word document, or in a different application.

4. Choose **E**dit, **P**aste.

To copy a chart from within a Word document, follow these steps:

1. Select the entire chart.

2. Choose **E**dit, **C**opy.

3. Position the insertion point where you want to place the copy of the chart.

4. Choose **E**dit, **P**aste.

To delete a chart, select it, and press Delete.

Task: Changing the Default Chart Type

When you create a chart by inserting a Graph object, the default chart type is 3-D Column. If you usually use a different chart type, a different text font or formatting, you can change the chart default. That way, Graph creates charts using your default settings so that you do not have to make many changes.

To change the default chart type, follow these steps:

1. Create and edit a chart using the settings you want to use as the default.

2. In the Graph window, choose **F**ile, Set as **D**efault Chart.

Entering and Editing Data in the Datasheet

The datasheet is a table-like grid in which you can enter or edit the data that Graph uses to create the chart. You also can change the text and numerical formatting, select the data to include or exclude, and specify the information that appears on the x- or y- axis of the chart.

When you start Graph, the Datasheet window contains either the data you selected in a Word document, or a default example. You can edit the data, or you can enter it by typing, or by pasting it from another application. To make the Datasheet window active, click it.

If you have problems...

If the Datasheet window is hidden behind the chart window, it is not active. Click the Datasheet window to make it active. If you cannot see the Datasheet window, move the Chart window out of the way, or make it smaller.

In the datasheet, data appears in rows and columns. Graph indicates the active cell by surrounding it with a black box. When you move the mouse pointer over cells, it changes to a large plus sign. To make a cell active, click it.

In the datasheet, double lines are used to identify data series—if the double lines run vertically, the data series are in columns, if the double lines run horizontally, the data series are in rows.

The datasheet contains rows and columns of information, similar to a table.

The active cell

A data series

Data series labels

The Datasheet window

The mouse pointer

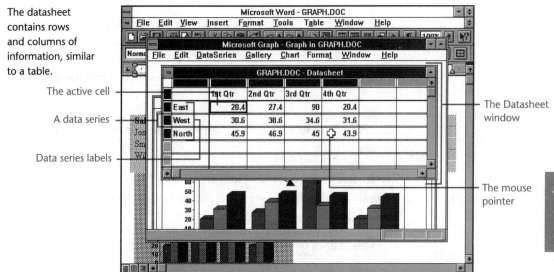

13

Task: Defining a Data Series

A *data series* is a collection of related data points. Because the information in each row and each column of the datasheet is related, you can use either rows or columns of data points as data series.

By default, Graph defines data series as rows. When the data series are defined as rows, the row labels appear in the chart legend. The column labels usually appear along the x-axis. Double lines separate the rows, such as in the data series.

You can change the data series to columns. When the data series are defined as columns, the column labels appear in the legend and the row labels usually appear along the X-axis. Double lines separate the columns, such as in the data series.

To define the data series, follow these steps:

1. Make the Datasheet window active.

2. Do one of the following:

   ■ Choose **D**ataSeries, Series in **R**ows to define the data series in rows.

   ■ Choose **D**ataSeries, Series in **C**olumns to define the data series in columns.

A checkmark appears next to the currently selected option on the DataSeries menu.

Task: Including or Excluding Data from the Chart

You can specify which rows and columns Graph should use from the datasheet to create the chart.

To exclude rows or columns of data, follow these steps:

1. Select the rows or columns you want to exclude. To select cells, click and drag across them.

2. Choose **D**ataSeries, **E**xclude Row/Col.

3. If you did not select an entire row or column, the Exclude Row/Col dialog box appears. Choose to exclude either the current **R**ow, or the current **C**olumn.

4. Choose OK. The rows or columns of data become dimmed, and the data markers are removed from the chart.

To include rows or columns of data that you previously excluded, follow these steps:

1. Select the dimmed rows or columns.

2. Choose **D**ataSeries, **I**nclude Row/Col.

3. If you did not select an entire row or column, the **I**nclude Row/Col dialog box appears. Choose to include either the current **R**ow, or the current **C**olumn.

4. Choose OK. The rows or columns of data are no longer dimmed, and the data markers reappear on the chart.

Task: Applying Numeric Formats

You can apply different number formats to numeric data in the datasheet, either to clarify relationships between numbers or to give the chart a different look. The format you select appears in the chart.

To apply a numeric format, follow these steps:

1. Select the cell or cells you want to format. To select a single cell, click it. To select more than one, drag across them.

2. Choose Forma**t**, **N**umber.

3. From the **N**umber Format list box, choose the format you want to use.

   Note: *To see what the symbols in the Number Format list represent, press F1.*

4. Choose OK.

Task: Applying Character Formats

You can format text and numbers in the datasheet by choosing fonts, font sizes, font styles, and colors. You can format data to emphasize certain information, or to give the chart a different look.

To format the data in the datasheet, follow these steps:

1. Select the cell or cells you want to format.

2. Choose Forma**t**, **F**ont.

3. In the **F**ont list box, choose the font you want to use.

4. In the **S**ize list box, choose the font size you want to use.

5. In the Style area, select the font styles you want to apply.

6. From the **C**olor list box, select the color you want to use.

7. Choose OK.

13

Task: Typing Data in the Datasheet

You can enter data directly into the datasheet by selecting a cell and typing. Leave the upper left cell in the datasheet blank. Type row headings in the first column, starting with the second cell in the column. Type the column headings in the first row, starting with the second cell in the row.

When you type in a cell that already contains data, you replace the original contents of the cell. To edit the contents of a cell without replacing the data, follow these steps:

1. Double-click the cell to display the Cell Data dialog box.

2. Edit the cell data in the text box.

3. Choose OK.

Task: Moving, Copying, and Clearing Cells

To move or copy cell information, follow these steps:

1. Select the cells you want to move.

2. Choose **E**dit, **Cut** to move the cells; choose **E**dit, **C**opy to copy the cells.

3. Position the insertion point in the cell where you want to place the data. If you are pasting more than one cell, position the insertion point in the upper left cell. Graph pastes the cells in the area extending down and to the right of the active cell.

4. Choose **E**dit, **P**aste.

To delete the contents or the formatting of a cell, follow these steps:

1. Select the cells you want to clear.

2. Choose **E**dit, Cl**e**ar.

3. In the Clear dialog box, choose one of the following:

   - Clear **D**ata to delete the data from the cell. New data placed in the cell assumes the cell formatting.

   - Clear **F**ormat to delete the formatting, but retain the data.

   - Clear **B**oth to delete both the data and the formatting.

Task: Inserting and Deleting Rows or Columns

One datasheet can contain up to 4,000 rows and 256 columns. When you insert rows, Graph adds them above the row containing the current active cell. When you insert columns, Graph adds them to the left of the column containing the current active cell. When you delete rows or columns, Graph removes the row or column containing the current active cell.

13

To insert rows or columns, follow these steps:

1. Select the row below or the column to the right of the location where you want to insert a row or column. To insert more than one row or column, select as many as you want to insert.

2. Choose **E**dit, **I**nsert Row/Col.

3. If you did not select an entire row or column, the Insert Row/Col dialog box appears. Choose to insert either **R**ows, or **C**olumns.

4. Choose OK.

To delete rows or columns, follow these steps:

1. Select the rows or the columns that you want to delete.

2. Choose **E**dit, **D**elete Row/Col.

3. If you did not select an entire row or column, the Delete Row/Col dialog box appears. Choose to delete either **R**ows, or **C**olumns.

4. Choose OK.

Summary

To	Do This
Create a chart	Choose Insert, Object. Choose Microsoft Graph.
Choose a chart type	Choose Gallery. Choose the chart type. Choose the chart format.
Add gridlines	Choose Chart, Gridlines. Choose the gridlines.
Add attached text	Choose Chart, Titles. Choose where to attach the titles. Choose OK. Type the text. Press Esc.
Add unattached text	Type the text. Press Esc. Position the text.
Add arrows	Choose Chart, Add Arrow.
Format items	Select the item. Choose Format, Font, Format, Patterns, Format, Text, or Format, Scale.
Choose data to exclude	Select the row or column. Choose DataSeries, Exclude Row/Col.
Insert rows or columns	Choose Edit, Insert Row/Col.

On Your Own

Estimated time: 30 minutes

1. Open a document that contains table data you can use to create a chart. For example, open the document that contains the table created in Lesson 12.

2. Copy the data to another document.

3. Create the chart.

4. See how the chart looks when you change the chart type.

5. See how the chart looks when you change the chart format.

6. Add gridlines.

7. Format the legend.

8. Add a title.

9. Format the title.

10. Add an arrow.

11. Add text to label the arrow.

12. Format the plot area.

13. Edit the datasheet to change the chart data.

14. Add a new data series to the datasheet.

15. Change the data series definition.

16. Apply numeric formats to some cells in the datasheet.

17. See how the chart reflects the changes made to the datasheet.

18. If necessary, choose a different chart type and format.

13

Part IV
Advanced Features and Integration

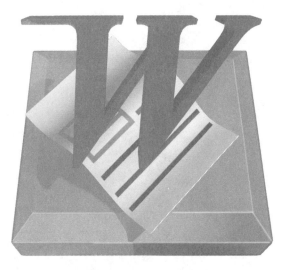

Lesson 14

Using Mail Merge

Merging involves combining variable data with a standard document to create a new document which you can view, print and save.

Most often, merging is used to personalize form letters and to print addresses on envelopes and labels. Although merging can be complex, Word 6 for Windows includes a Mail Merge Helper that guides you through the merge process. Advanced merging procedures are beyond the scope of this book. For more information see Que's *Using Word Version 6 for Windows,* Special Edition.

In this lesson, you learn to do the following:

- Create a main document
- Open or create a data source
- Insert merge fields into the main document
- Conduct a merge

Understanding Merges

Merge
The process of combining information from one document with information from another document to create a new document.

To conduct a *merge*, you need a *main document*, such as the body of a form letter, and a *data source*, such as the names and addresses of the people to whom you are sending the form letter. Then, Word merges the two into a new document, which you can view, print, and save.

Main document
The document that contains the information that does not change.

When Word conducts a merge, it takes the variable data from the data source, and inserts it into a copy of the main document. The main document contains boilerplate text, which doesn't change, and *merge fields* that mark the locations where the variable data will go.

Data source
The file that contains the information that changes in each document.

For Word to know which information to take from the data source, and where to put it in the main document, the information must be organized in a very specific format. Information in a data source is organized into *records*, and each record is organized into *fields*.

The Basic Merge Procedure

Merge field
A code used in the main document to mark the location where variable data information is inserted.

No matter what information you are using in a merge, and no matter what type of document the end result of the merge will be, the basic merge procedure is the same. To conduct a merge, you follow these four steps:

1. Create a main document.

2. Select a data source.

Record
All the variable information for one entry in the data source.

3. Add merge fields to the main document.

4. Merge the data and the document.

Field
One item of information in a record.

In this lesson, you learn to create merged form letters, envelopes, and address labels. Once you are familiar with merging, you will be able to adapt the specific details of these tasks to your own particular merge.

Creating a Main Document

The main document contains the information that is identical in each merged item. For a form letter, that probably includes the date, the body of the letter, the closing, formatting, and some spaces and punctuation marks. For an envelope, the main document may contain your return address and formatting such as the specific page size. For address labels, the only thing in the main document may be formatting, because each label is printed with a different name and address.

When you create a main document, you can use an existing document, if it is already set up and formatted. Usually, the only type of main document you want to create beforehand is a letter to use for a form letter. You can let Word attend to the details of setting up an envelope or mailing labels.

Task: Creating a Main Document for a Form Letter

To create a main document for a form letter, follow these steps:

1. Open the document you want to use for the letter, or create a new one.

2. Choose **T**ools, Mail Me**r**ge.

The Mail Merge Helper prompts you through the steps involved in conducting a merge.

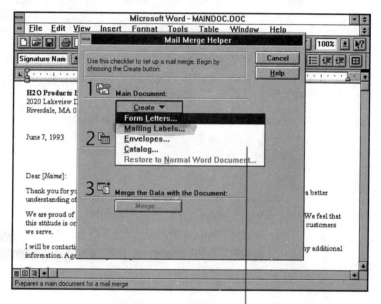

Choose the type of main document to create here

3. In the Mail Merge Helper dialog box, choose **C**reate to drop down a list of document types.

4. Choose Form **L**etters. Word displays a dialog box informing you that you can use the current document, or create a new main document.

5. Because you already opened the document you want to use for the main document, choose **A**ctive Window. Word converts the current document into a merge main document.

The Mail Merge Helper stays open so that you can continue with the next step in the merge procedure: opening or creating a data source.

14

You can opt to use the current document as the main document, or you can create a new document.

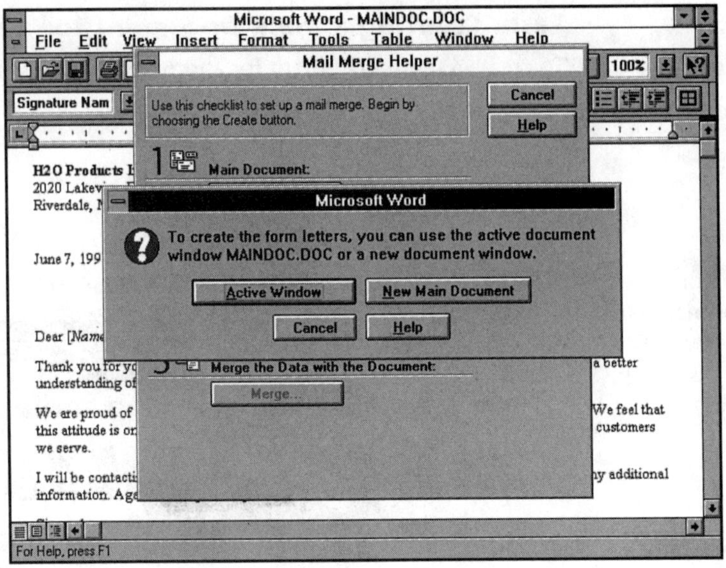

Task: Creating a Main Document for Envelopes or Labels

When you set up a main document for an envelope merge or a label merge, Word automates most of the details. All you need to do is to specify the merge type—either envelopes or labels.

To create a main document for envelopes or labels, follow these steps:

1. Choose **T**ools, Mail Me**r**ge.
2. In the Mail Merge Helper dialog box, choose **C**reate to drop down a list of document types.
3. Choose one of the following:
   - **E**nvelopes to create a main document for an envelope merge.
   - **M**ailing Labels to create a main document for a label merge.
4. Word displays a dialog box informing you that you can use the current document, or create a new main document.

5. In this case, you want to let Word do the work of creating a new main document. Choose **N**ew Main Document. Word creates an empty main document to use for either an envelope merge or a mailing label merge.

The Mail Merge Helper stays open so that you can continue with the next step in the merge procedure: opening or creating a data source.

Task: Opening a Data Source

Most of the work involved in conducting a merge centers on creating a data source. If you already have a data source, such as an Excel file, a Word table, or a database of names and addresses, you are lucky. Word can use these data sources to conduct a merge.

As a data source, you can use data entered in Word tables, or you can import data from another application. If you installed the corresponding conversion filters when you set up Word 6, you can open data files created in the following programs:

■ Word for Windows 1.0 through 6.*x*, Word for Macintosh 3.*x* through 5.*x* and Word for MS-DOS 3.0 through 6.0

■ WordPerfect for Windows or DOS, Version 5.*x*

■ Microsoft Excel

■ Lotus 1-2-3 Release 2.*x* through 3.*x*

■ Microsoft FoxPro, Borland dBASE, and compatible applications

■ Microsoft Access

■ Borland Paradox

For more information on using Word 6 with other applications, see Lesson 17, "Working with Other Windows Applications."

To open an existing data source, follow these steps:

1. Create a main document using the Mail Merge Helper. For information on creating a main document, see the section "Creating a Main Document," earlier in this lesson.

2. In the Mail Merge Helper dialog box, choose **G**et Data.

14

You can choose to get the data from an existing source, or you can create a new source.

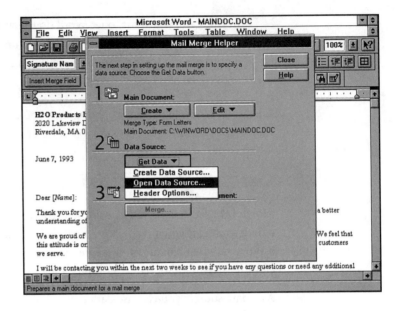

3. Choose **O**pen Data Source.

In the Open Data Source dialog box, specify the file you want to use as the merge data source.

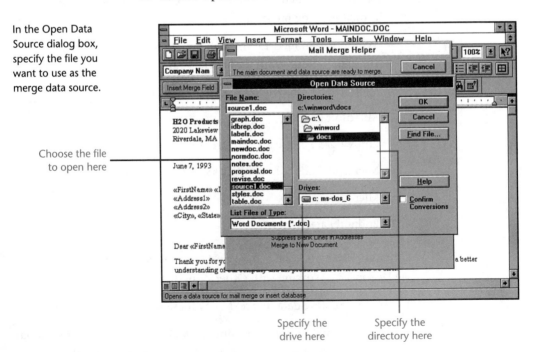

Choose the file to open here

Specify the drive here

Specify the directory here

4. Open the drive and directory that contains the file you want to use as a data source.

5. In the File **N**ame list, choose the file you want to use as a data source. If necessary, choose the file type in the List Files of **T**ype drop-down list.

6. If Word prompts you to specify a data range, enter the range you want to use. If you are using a spreadsheet file, for example, specify the cells you want to use.

7. Word opens the data source file, and then displays a dialog box asking you if you want to set up or edit your main document. Choose from the following options:

   ■ Edit **M**ain Document if you are merging form letters. You already set up the document.

   ■ **S**et Up Main Document if you are merging envelopes or labels. You have not yet set up the document.

14

Creating a New Data Source

If you do not have an existing table or database of information to use as a data source, you can set one up now. Word prompts you through the steps required to define fields and enter data.

It is a good idea to put some thought into the type of data you need for the merge before you start creating the data source. To create the data source, you must define the fields, and then enter the actual data. Although you can edit the data source later, it is helpful to know all of the fields you need right from the start.

Task: Defining the Fields

Field names can be up to 40 characters long. They must begin with a letter, but they can include letters, numbers, and underscore characters. You cannot use spaces, but you can use upper- and lowercase letters.

To define fields for a data source, follow these steps:

1. Create a main document using the Mail Merge Helper. For information on creating a main document, see the section "Creating a Main Document," earlier in this lesson.

2. In the Mail Merge Helper dialog box, choose **G**et Data.

3. From the **G**et Data drop-down list, choose **C**reate Data Source.

In the Create Data Source dialog box, Word displays a list of fields commonly used in merge documents.

Choose a field name here

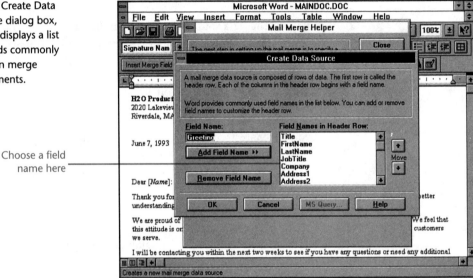

4. From the Field **N**ames in Header Row list, choose a field you *do not* need in your data source.

5. Choose **R**emove Field Name.

6. Repeat steps 4 and 5 until only the fields you need in your data source remain in the Field **N**ames in Header Row list.

7. In the Field Name text box, type the name of a field you need in your data source, that does not already appear in the Field **N**ames in Header Row list.

8. Choose **A**dd Field Name.

9. Repeat steps 7 and 8 until all of the fields you need in your data source appear in the Field **N**ames in Header Row list.

10. To change the order of the fields in the Field **N**ames in Header Row list, select the field name, and then choose the Move up or Move down arrow.

11. Choose OK. Word displays the Save Data Source dialog box.

12. Save your data source file the same way you would save any file. Word saves the file, and attaches it to your main document.

13. Word displays a message prompting you to add data to your data source. Choose Edit **D**ata Source to begin entering data records.

If you have problems...   If you choose Edit **M**ain Document rather than Edit **D**ata Source, Word displays the main document, or the setup options for setting up the main document. Click the Edit Data Source button on the Merge toolbar to return to the data source file.

Task: Entering Data in the Data Source

To enter data in your data source file, follow these steps:

Note: *If you have just completed creating the data source, the Data Form dialog box already may be open on-screen. In that case, skip to step 4 below.*

1. Choose **T**ools, Mail Me**r**ge to display the Mail Merge Helper dialog box.

Now you can choose to edit as well as create a Main Document or a Data Source.

Choose to edit a main document here

Choose to edit a data source here

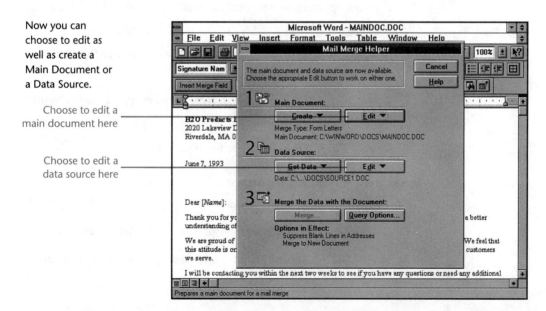

2. In the Data Source area, choose E**d**it to drop down a list of available data source files.

3. Choose the data source you want to edit (chances are it is the only one in the list). The Data Form dialog box appears.

The Data Form dialog box displays a record that contains the fields you specified to include in your data source.

Enter the field information here

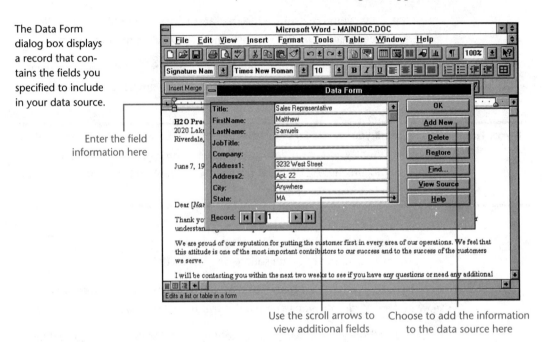

Use the scroll arrows to view additional fields

Choose to add the information to the data source here

4. Type the appropriate data into each field. You can leave fields blank if they do not apply.

5. Choose **A**dd New to add the record to the data source file. Word displays a blank record.

6. Repeat steps 4 and 5 until you have entered every record you want to include in the data source file.

7. Choose OK. Word displays the main document.

Task: Editing a Data Source

To edit the data source, follow these steps:

1. Choose **T**ools, Mail Me**r**ge to display the Mail Merge Helper dialog box.

2. In the Data Source area, choose E**d**it to drop down a list of available data source files.

3. Choose the data source you want to edit (chances are it is the only one in the list). The Data Form dialog box appears, displaying the first record entered in the data source.

Note: *If the main document is open on your screen, you can choose the Edit Data Source button on the Merge toolbar to display the Data Form dialog box.*

Choose to   Choose to update,
delete a   or add a new
record here   record here

You easily can scroll through the records in the data source file, find records and edit records.

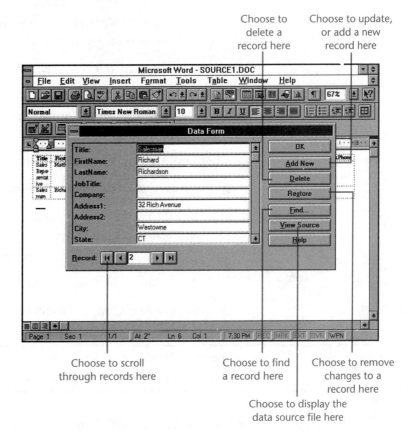

Choose to scroll   Choose to find   Choose to remove
through records here   a record here   changes to a
record here

Choose to display the
data source file here

4. To display a blank record, choose **A**dd New.

5. To display the record you want to edit, do one of the following:

- Type the record number in the **R**ecord text box.

- To display the next record, choose the right pointing arrow.

- To display the previous record, choose the left pointing arrow.

■ To display the first record, choose the arrow pointing left to a bar.

    ■ To display the last record, choose the arrow pointing right to a bar.

■ To find a record, choose **F**ind to display the Find in Field dialog box, and then follow these steps:

- In the Fi**n**d What text box, type the text you know is entered on the record you want to find.

- In the In Fiel**d** text box, type the name of the field that contains the text.

- Choose Find First to display the first record in the data source that contains the specified text.

6. To edit a record, do any of the following:

■ To change data, type the new data into the appropriate field.

■ To save the changes to a record, choose **A**dd New. Word stores the new data, and displays a blank record.

■ To remove the changes made to a record before you choose **A**dd New, choose Re**s**tore.

■ To delete a record, display it, and choose **D**elete.

If you have problems...   If you accidentally delete a record, you must reenter it. Word does not warn you before it deletes a record, and there is no way to undo the deletion.

---

7. When you have finished editing the data source, choose OK. Word displays the main document.

Setting Up Envelopes and Labels

Before you can insert merge fields for envelopes or labels, you must set up the main documents. Setting up the main documents tells Word information such as what kind of printer you are using and how to position the addresses it prints. Once the documents are set up, you can insert the merge fields.

Task: Setting Up an Envelope

To set up an envelope document, follow these steps:

Note: *If you have just completed opening or creating a data source, Word prompts you to setup the main document file. Choose the **S**et Up Main Document button, and skip to step 3 below.*

1. Choose **T**ools, Mail Me**r**ge.

2. In the Main Document area, choose **S**etup.

If you have problems...

If the **S**etup button is dimmed in the Mail Merge Helper dialog box, you have not yet specified a data source. See the sections Opening a Data Source, or Creating a Data Source, earlier in this lesson. If the main document is already set up, go the section on inserting merge fields later in this lesson.

---

3. In the Envelope Options dialog box, click the **E**nvelope Options tab.

In the Envelope Options dialog box, you can set up the envelope to use in the merge.

Set envelope options here

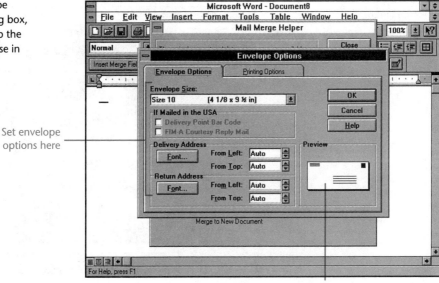

14

Preview the envelope here

4. From the Envelope **S**ize drop-down list, choose the envelope size you want to use. Choose Custom Size to enter your own envelope dimensions.

5. In the Delivery address area and the Return Address area, choose **F**ont and **F**ont to change the font formatting for the address areas of the envelope.

6. Specify the locations where Word should print the delivery and return addresses:

   ■ In the From **L**eft and Fro**m** Left text boxes, enter the distance from the left edge of the envelope where Word should begin printing. Choose Auto to use default positioning based on the envelope size.

   ■ In the From **T**op and F**r**om Top text boxes, enter the distance from the top edge of the envelope where Word should begin printing. Choose Auto to use default positioning based on the envelope size.

7. Click the **P**rinting Options tab at the top of the dialog box.

Specify the printer feed method in the Envelope Options dialog box.

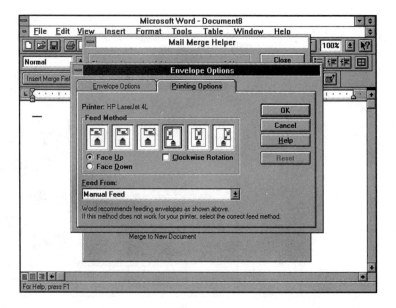

8. Select the Feed Method and **F**eed From options that apply to your printer.

9. Choose OK. The Envelope Address dialog box appears, where you insert the merge fields for envelopes.

Task: Setting Up Labels

To set up a label document, follow these steps:

Note: *If you have just completed opening or creating a data source, Word prompts you to set up the main document file. Click the **S**et Up Main Document button, and skip to step 3 below.*

1. Choose **T**ools, Mail Me**r**ge.

2. In the Main Document area, choose **S**etup.

If you have problems...

If the **S**etup button is dimmed in the Mail Merge Helper dialog box, you have not yet specified a data source. See the sections Opening a Data Source, or Creating a Data Source, earlier in this lesson. If the main document is already set up, go the section on inserting merge fields later in this lesson.

In the Label Options dialog box, you can set up the labels to use in the merge.

Choose printer information here

Choose label information here

Choose to set custom labels here (margin adjust.)

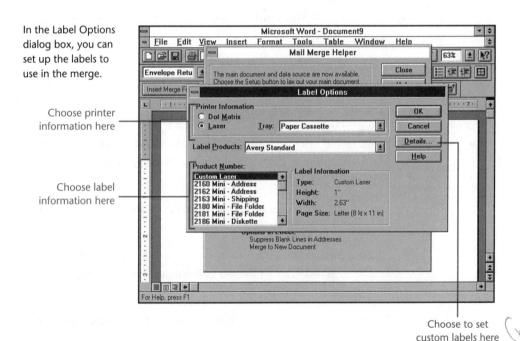

3. In the Label Options dialog box, choose the type of printer you are using to print the labels, and the type of paper tray you are using.

4. From the Label **P**roducts drop-down list, select the brand name label you are using.

5. From the Product Number list select the labels you are using, or select one that has the same dimensions as the labels you are using.

6. Choose **D**etails to see or customize the exact measurements of your labels. Choose OK to return to the Label Options dialog box.

7. Choose OK. The Create Labels dialog box appears, where you insert the merge fields for envelopes.

Inserting Merge Fields

Once you have created and set up a main document and identified the source data, you are ready to insert merge fields into the main document. The merge fields tell Word which information to take from the source data, and where to place it in the main document.

Inserting merge fields is slightly different depending on the type of main document you are using.

Task: Inserting Merge Fields in Form Letters

To insert merge fields in a form letter, follow these steps:

1. Open the main document.

2. Position the insertion point at the location in the document where you want to insert a merge field. For example, position it where the recipient's name should go.

3. Click the Insert Merge Field button on the Mail Merge toolbar to drop down a list of fields.

4. Choose the field you want to insert. Choose the FirstName field, for example. Word inserts the field at the insertion point location.

5. Repeat steps 2 through 4 to insert merge fields at all of the locations in the document where you want to insert data from the data source.

6. Make sure you have included all of the necessary punctuation marks and spaces in the document, such as a comma and a space between the City merge field and the State merge field.

Word inserts the merge field into the main document at the insertion point location.

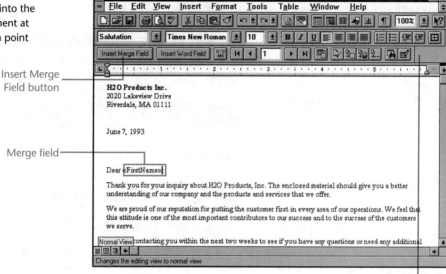

Insert Merge Field button

Merge field

Mail Merge toolbar

7. To remove a merge field, press Ctrl+Shift+F9 to select it, and then press Delete.

8. Edit and format the letter. The formatting you apply to the merge fields will be used by the information insertion in the final merged document.

9. Save the main document.

Task: Inserting Merge Fields in Envelopes or Labels

To insert merge fields for envelopes or labels, follow these steps:

Note: *If you have just completed setting up the envelope main document, the Envelope Address dialog box is already displayed on your screen. If you have just completed setting up the label main document, the Create Labels dialog box is already displayed on your screen. Skip to step 4 below.*

1. Choose **T**ools, Mail Me**r**ge.

2. In the Main Document area, choose **S**etup.

3. In the Envelope Options dialog box or the Label Options dialog box, choose OK. Word displays either the Create Labels dialog box or the Envelope Address dialog box.

14

Both the Envelope
Address and the
Create labels dialog
box look the same;
you insert the merge
fields to use for
printing the
addresses.

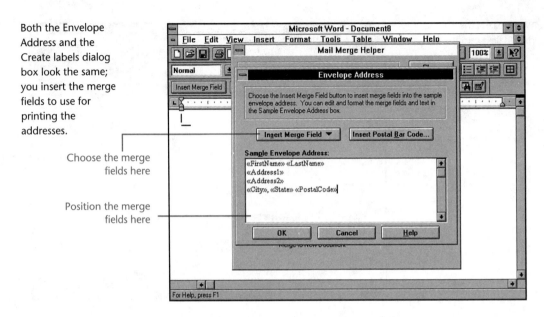

Choose the merge
fields here

Position the merge
fields here

4. Position the insertion point in the Sample area.

5. Choose Insert Merge Field to drop down a list of merge fields.

6. Choose the field you want to insert.

7. Do not forget to type the necessary spaces and punctuation, such as a comma and a space between the city field and the state field.

8. Repeat steps 4 through 6 until you have inserted all of the necessary address fields.

   Note: *If you have a data source file that contains POSTNET bar codes that encode the street address and ZIP code, Word can automatically insert the correct bar code. Choose Insert Postal Bar Code. In the dialog box that appears, select the data source fields that contain the ZIP code and street address, and then choose OK.*

9. Choose OK. Word displays the Mail Merge Helper dialog box.

10. Do one of the following:

    ■ Begin the mail merge. See the section, "Merging" later in this lesson for more information.

    ■ Choose Close to display the main document. You can save the document for future use, or preview the merged documents before printing.

Task: Previewing Merge Documents

It is a good idea to preview the merge documents before you print them. That way, you can fix some errors, such as adjusting punctuation or formatting, or customizing one or two of the documents.

To preview a merge document, follow these steps:

Note: *If the main document is open on your screen, skip to step 2 below.*

1. Choose **F**ile, **O**pen to open the main document.

2. Click the View Merged Data button on the Mail Merge toolbar to see the document as it will appear when merged with the data source information.

3. To see a document as it will appear with any individual record from the data source document, type the record number in the Go to Record box in the center of the Mail Merge toolbar, and press Enter.

If you have problems...   If you enter a record number and nothing happens, it is because you did not change to view the merged data—you are still viewing the data fields. Click the View Merged Data button on the Mail Merge toolbar.

14

---

4. Display each merged document by using the Next record and Previous record buttons on the Mail Merge toolbar.

5. Make any editing or formatting adjustments.

6. Save the document.

Merging the Data and the Main Document

You can merge the documents directly to the printer, or you can save the documents in a file to print later. If you save to a file, Word saves all of the merge documents together in one file, with section breaks in between each one.

Before merging, you can check for errors, you can sort the data source so that the documents are printed in a specific order, and you can select to merge only certain records.

Task: Checking for Merge Errors

To check for errors, follow these steps:

1. Open the Main document window.

2. Click the Check for Errors button on the Mail Merge toolbar.

3. In the Checking and Reporting Errors dialog box, select one of the following:

- **S**imulate the merge and report errors in a new document to check for errors without actually conducting the merge.

- **C**omplete the merge, pausing to report each error as it occurs, to conduct the merge, pausing each time Word encounters a problem, giving you a chance to fix it.

- Complete the merge without pausing. Report errors in a new document, to conduct the merge without pausing at errors.

4. Choose OK.

Note: *To display the Checking and Reporting Errors dialog box from the Mail Merge helper, choose Merge, and then in the Merge dialog box, click the Check Errors button.*

Task: Merging Only Certain Records

You can choose which records to merge by setting limits, or rules. For example, you can choose to merge only records where the address is in New York, or where the last name begins with the letter P.

To merge only certain records, follow these steps:

1. Open the main document.

2. Choose **T**ools, Mail Me**r**ge to display the Mail Merge Helper.

3. Choose **Q**uery Options.

4. Click the **F**ilter Records tab at the top of the Query Options dialog box.

In the Query Options dialog box, you can set filters to allow only certain records to print.

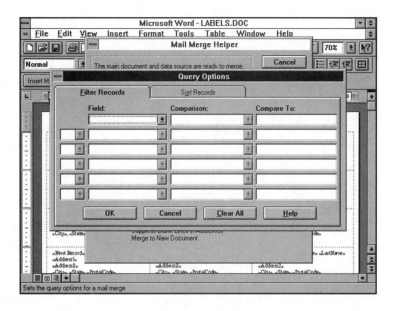

5. From the Field drop-down list, select the field that contains the data you want to compare. Select the State field, for example.

6. From the Comparison drop-down list, select the type of comparison you want to make. Select Equal to, for example.

7. In the Compare To text box type the data you want to compare. Type **NY**, for example.

8. To set additional filters, choose And or Or in the drop-down list box at the far left of the dialog box. If you choose And, Word uses both filters. If you choose Or, Word only uses one.

9. Repeat steps 5 through 8 as many times as you want.

10. Choose OK.

Task: Sorting Data Before Merging

You can sort the data to print the documents in a particular order. You can sort by ZIP code, or by last name, for example. You also can sort by more than field.

To sort data before merging, follow these steps:

1. Open the main document.

2. Choose **T**ools, Mail Me**r**ge to display the Mail Merge Helper.

3. Choose **Q**uery Options.

4. Click the **S**ort Records tab at the top of the Query Options dialog box.

In the Query Options dialog box, you can set Word to sort records before printing.

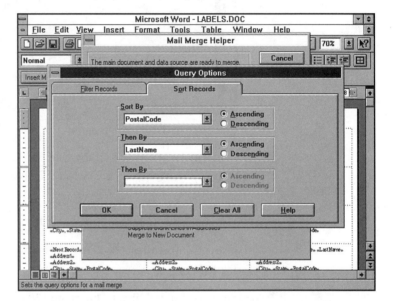

5. From the **S**ort By drop-down list, choose the first field by which you want to sort, and then choose to sort by **A**scending or **D**escending order.

6. From the **T**hen By drop-down list, choose the next field by which you want to sort, and then choose to sort by Asc**e**nding or Desce**n**ding order.

7. From the Then **B**y drop-down list, choose the third field by which you want to sort, and then choose to sort by Ascend**i**ng or Descendin**g** order.

8. Choose OK.

Task: Merging Form Letters, Envelopes, or Labels

To conduct a merge, follow these steps:

1. Open the main document.

2. Do one of the following:

   - Click the Merge to New Document button on the Mail Merge toolbar to store the merged documents in a new document. Word begins the merge immediately, and displays the complete document on-screen in page layout view.

   - Click the Merge to Printer button on the Mail Merge toolbar to print the merged documents. Word begins the merge immediately.

   - Click the Mail Merge button on the Mail Merge toolbar to choose mail merge options. Word displays the Merge dialog box.

3. In the Mail Merge dialog box, choose any of the following:

   - From the Merge To drop-down list box, choose to print the documents or save them in a file.

   - In the Records to Be Merged area, choose All records, or specify a range based on record number.

   - In the When Merging Records area, choose whether or not to print blank lines.

   - Choose Check Errors to check for errors.

   - Choose Query Options to specify filters or a sort order.

4. Choose Merge to begin the merge.

14

Summary

To	Do This
Create a main document	Choose **T**ools, Mail Me**r**ge. Choose **C**reate Main Document. Choose the document type.
Open a data source	Choose **T**ools, Mail Me**r**ge. Choose **G**et Data. Choose **O**pen Data Source. Choose the data source file.
Create a data source	Choose **T**ools, Mail Me**r**ge. Choose **G**et Data. Choose **C**reate Data Source.
Specify data fields	In the Create Data Source dialog box, type field names to add. Select field names to remove.
Enter data records	In the Data Form dialog box, fill out the data fields. Choose **A**dd.
Setup main document	Choose **T**ools, Mail Me**r**ge. Choose **S**etup Main Document. Choose options.
Insert merge fields	Open main document. Position insertion point. Choose Insert Merge Field. Choose a field to insert.
Merge	Open the main document. Choose **T**ools, Mail Me**r**ge. Choose **M**erge. Choose **M**erge.
Check for Errors	Open the main document. Choose **T**ools, Mail Me**r**ge. Choose **Q**uery Options. Enter filter information.
Sort Records	Open the main document. Choose **T**ools, Mail Me**r**ge. Choose **Q**uery Options. Specify Sort fields and sort order.

On Your Own

Estimated time: 30 minutes

1. Create a form letter main document.

2. Create a new data source.

3. Add names and addresses for at least four or five records.

4. Save the data source file.

5. Insert merge fields into the main document.

6. Preview the merged documents.

7. Merge the documents to the printer.

8. Create an envelope main document.

9. Attach the data source file you created for the form letter.

10. Edit the data source file to add a new record.

11. Set up the envelope document.

12. Insert merge fields into the envelope document.

13. Preview the merged documents.

14. Merge the documents into a file.

15. Create a label main document.

16. Use a different source file if you have one, or else attach the same data source file.

17. Set up the label document.

18. Insert merge fields into the label document.

19. Preview the labels.

20. Print the labels.

21. Save all of the main documents and the source file.

14

Lesson 15

Working with Forms

Word 6 provides a feature for creating forms that you can use to gather information of all kinds. You can set up forms that you or others can fill out on a computer. This feature can save hours of time that you might have spent collecting and reentering data.

Word 6 comes with some sample forms that you can use, or adapt for your own needs. You also can design and create your own forms.

In this lesson, you learn to do the following:

- Use Word's sample forms
- Design and assemble new forms
- Use form fields
- Fill in forms

Understanding Forms

Form
A document de-signed for use in collecting and tabulating information.

Forms are a simple method of collecting information. You fill in the blanks, check a few boxes and circle Yes or No, and someone, somewhere has the answers he needs.

Computers made using the information entered on forms easier, because once someone keyed in the data, the computer could tabulate it and use it for purposes such as to generate reports. But collecting the information still involved lots of paper, and lots of time entering data.

Now, Word 6 puts the whole form process on-line. You create the form on-line, you fill out the form on-line and you collect the data on-line. You still can print the forms for distribution, if necessary.

Protected

Set to resist editing.

One of the features that makes form templates different from other document templates, is that they are *protected*. You can only select, enter, and edit information in certain areas on the form. The rest of the form remains intact. That way, someone filling out a form that you create cannot change the form itself.

You can use many of Word's document templates and Wizards to create forms. Some provide the styles you need to do the work yourself, and some actually build the on-line form template. You can use the Fax Wizard, for example, to create a form that can be used for filling out fax cover sheets.

Some of the other templates useful for creating forms include WEEKTIME.DOT, that you can use to create a weekly employee time sheet, PURCHORD.DOT, that you can use to create a purchase order form, INVOICE.DOT, that you can use to create invoice forms.

Using Word's Sample Forms

Forms contain two types of information.

- The text and graphics that appear on the form to tell the form user what information to enter.

Form field

An area on-screen where Word stores information that users enter in an on-line form.

- *Form fields* where the user enters the information.

Word's built-in form templates include both kinds of information. You simply customize the forms for your needs. Many forms are arranged using Word's table features, because tables make it easy to create the side-by-side columns and grids that most forms use. For more information about tables, see Lesson 12, "Working with Tables."

By default, when you installed Word 6, the template files were placed in the c:\WINWORD\TEMPLATES subdirectory. If you did not install all of the document template files, you can use Setup to install them now.

Task: Opening a Template Form

To open an existing form template, follow these steps:

1. Choose **F**ile, **O**pen.

Usually, you find the form templates in the C:\WINWORD\TEMPLATES subdirectory.

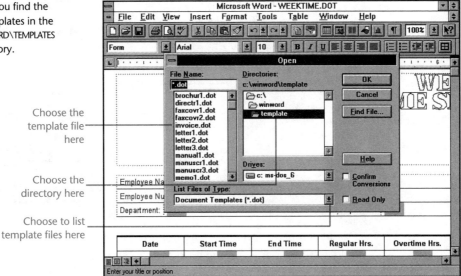

Choose the template file here

Choose the directory here

Choose to list template files here

2. From the List Files of **T**ype list box, choose Document Templates (*.dot).

3. In the **D**irectories area, open the \WINWORD\TEMPLATES subdirectory.

If you have problems...

If the TEMPLATE subdirectory is not in the \WINWORD directory, you may not have installed it. If you installed the template files in a different directory, open that directory now.

---

4. In the File **N**ame list box, choose a form template, such as WEEKTIME.DOT.

5. Choose OK.

15

The template form opens on-screen with shaded boxes marking the form fields.

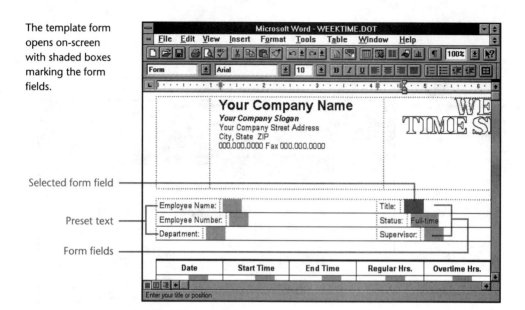

On the template, form fields are indicated by gray shading. When a form field is selected, the shading becomes darker. Some of the text in the template can be edited. You can insert your company name and address, for example.

To move from form field to form field, press Tab, or click to move the insertion point. You can not position the insertion point within the preset text, because the form is protected. Many menu commands are not available, either, because the form is protected.

You can use the form as is. You can substitute your company information, save the form, print it, or fill it out on-screen. Or, you can customize it to meet the specific needs of your company.

Task: Editing a Form Template

Before you edit a form template, you must remove the document protection.

To remove the protection, follow these steps:

1. Choose **F**ile, **O**pen to open the template file on-screen.

2. Choose **T**ools, Un**p**rotect Document. The form fields remain shaded, but you can now edit the preset text.

To customize the template information, follow these steps:

1. Position the insertion point at the beginning of any text you want to change.

2. Type the information using Overtype mode, or delete the existing information before you type.

3. Insert any logos or artwork you want to place in the form, by using the **I**nsert, **P**icture command. For more information on inserting pictures, see Lesson 17, "Working with Other Windows Applications."

You can adapt sample forms to meet your own needs.

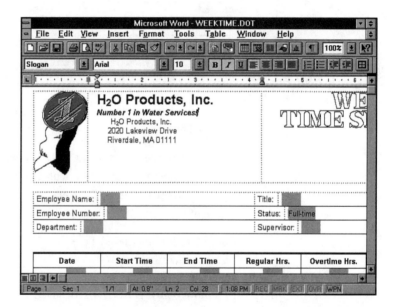

4. When you are done modifying the form, choose **F**ile, Save **A**s to save it with a different name, or **F**ile, **S**ave, to save it with the same name.

   Note: *If you save the file with the same name, you overwrite the existing template file. If you need the original sample template file in the future, use Setup to install it again.*

5. Choose **T**ools, **P**rotect Document.

In the Protect
Document dialog
box, you protect
your form from
unauthorized edits.

Choose to protect
forms here

Enter a
password here

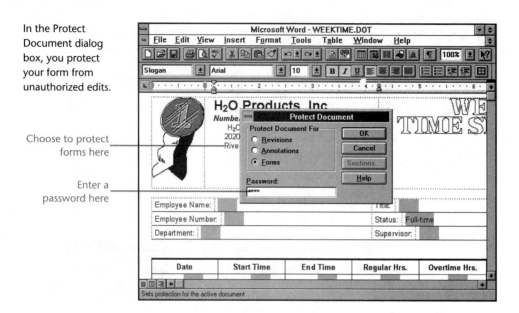

6. In the Protect Document dialog box, choose to protect the Document for **F**orms.

7. In the **P**assword text box, you can type a password to ensure that no one else can unprotect the document and edit it. Word allows only someone who enters the exact password to unprotect the document.

8. Choose OK. If you entered a password, Word prompts you to enter it again, for confirmation.

The form template now is customized, saved, and protected. You can use it to create new form documents.

Note: *To remove the password, choose **T**ools, Un**p**rotect Document. Type the password; the document now is unprotected with no password.*

Using a Form

To use a Word 6 form, you create a new document based on the form template, and then fill it out. Filling out a form on-screen is very much like completing a form on paper. You read the text and fill in the blanks. (You still can print the form and fill it out with a pen or pencil, if necessary.)

Task: Entering Information in a Form

To enter information into a form, follow these steps:

1. Choose **F**ile, **N**ew to create a new document based on the form template.

2. In the **T**emplate list in the New dialog box, choose the form template you want to use.

3. Choose OK.

4. Position the insertion point in the first form field where you want to enter information.

5. Type the information. Some form fields may use check boxes, or drop-down lists, just like Word dialog boxes.

6. Click to move the insertion point to the next form field, or press Tab.

7. Choose **F**ile, **S**ave when you are done filling out the form.

8. Fill out the Save As dialog box to name and store the form document.

9. To print the form, choose **F**ile, **P**rint, and complete the Print dialog box. For more information on printing, see Lesson 2, "Creating a Document."

15

Task: Changing the Way a Form is Saved or Printed

By default, Word saves and prints all of the information that appears on the completed form, including the preset text and the information entered in the form fields. You can choose to save and only the information entered in the form fields.

Saving and printing only the information entered in the form fields is useful for two reasons:

- You easily can use the data with a database program.

- You can print the data on preprinted forms.

To save only the data entered in forms, follow these steps:

1. Choose **T**ools, **O**ptions.

2. At the top of the Options dialog box, click the Save tab.

3. Choose the Save **D**ata Only for Forms check box.

4. Choose OK.

From now on when you save forms, only the information entered in the form fields is saved. The information is saved in comma-delimited format, which means that each field is enclosed in quotation marks and separated by commas with no spaces.

To revert back to saving the whole form, deselect the Save **D**ata Only for Forms check box in the Save Options dialog box.

To print only the data entered in forms, follow these steps:

1. Choose **T**ools, **O**ptions.

2. At the top of the Options dialog box, click the Print tab.

3. Choose the **P**rint Data Only for Forms check box.

4. Choose OK.

From now on when you print forms, only the information entered in the form fields is printed. The information prints in the exact location on the page where the form field would appear.

To revert back to printing the whole form, deselect the **P**rint Data Only for Forms check box in the Print Options dialog box.

Creating a New Form

You can create your own forms in Word 6 by creating a form template, inserting form fields, tables and frames, selecting form field options and protecting the form.

Before you begin creating a form, it is a good idea to think about all of the elements you want to include. If you already have a paper form to base it on, you are one step ahead of the game. Otherwise, look at some other forms, and make notes of all the form fields, text graphics, and other information you want to include.

Task: Creating a Template

A template is a pattern for creating other documents. You modified a sample form template earlier in this chapter to create a customized form. Now, you can use a template to create a new form.

For complete information on creating and modifying templates, see Lesson 8, "Customizing Word 6 for Windows."

To create a new template, follow these steps:

1. Choose File, New.

2. In the New area of the New dialog box, choose the Template option.

3. In the Template list, choose the template on which you want to base your form. You can use any template you want. If you choose a form template, such as INVOICE.DOT, many of the form features are automatically inserted in the new template. Other templates, such as NORMAL.DOT, open as a blank screen.

4. Choose OK.

Laying Out the Form

Laying out the form consists of placing the preset text and graphics into the form template. You must place the text that tells the people filling out the form what information they must enter. You must insert graphics, borders, and shading that you want to appear.

When you begin designing your form, take into consideration the way people will use it. Think of the order in which people will fill out the fields and think about how much information must be entered in each field, for example.

To lay out the form, enter the preset text and graphics in the template where you want them to appear on the form. You can use all of Word's document editing and formatting tools to create the template, including the basic tools of styles, fonts, and paragraph alignment options. Some of the other features you will find most helpful include:

15

- *Tables*: You can insert tables to help align boxes and create repeating rows or columns of information. Tables enable you to set up side-by-side columns. Table cells expand to accommodate different amounts of data. For information on using tables, see Lesson 12, "Working with Tables."

- *Borders and Shading*: You can add outlines, color and fill patterns to table cells or graphics to give your form a professional appearance. For information on using borders and shading, see Lesson 6, "Dressing Up Your Paragraphs."

- *Drawing Tools*: You can use the Drawing toolbar to add shapes and pictures to your form. For information on using the drawing tools, see Lesson 11, "Drawing with Word 6 for Windows."

- *Frames*: You can use frames to position text and graphics on a page and to provide a border around a particular item. For information on using frames, see Lesson 10, "Working with Frames."

- *The Clipboard*: You can use the Clipboard to copy text and graphics from other documents into your form template. For information on using the Clipboard, see Lesson 3, "Revising a Document."

Task: Inserting Form Fields

After you position the preset text and graphics in the form template, it is time to insert the form fields.

To insert form fields, follow these steps:

1. Position the insertion point in the template where you want to place the form field.

2. Choose **Insert, Form** Field.

You can insert form
fields by using the
Form Field dialog
box, or by using the
buttons on the
Forms toolbar.

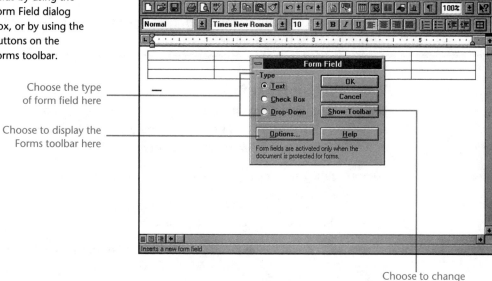

Choose the type
of form field here

Choose to display the
Forms toolbar here

Choose to change
form field options here

Note: *To display the Forms toolbar, choose **S**how Toolbar in the Form Field dialog box. You can use the toolbar buttons to perform most of the tasks required for creating a form.*

3. In the Type area, choose one of the following:

■ **T**ext to insert one of a variety of text fields. Text fields are used to provide for space for entering text answers.

■ **C**heck box to insert fields where users can select options, such as Yes or No, Male or Female, or marital status.

■ **D**rop-down to insert a drop down list of choices from which the user can select a response.

4. Choose Options to display the Options dialog box for the type of form field you selected. Select the options you want to use, and then choose OK.

5. Choose OK. Word inserts the field.

15

If you have problems...

If you cannot see the form field in your template document, the shading option is not turned on. Choose **T**ools, **O**ptions View, and select Always from the Fi**e**ld Shading drop-down list, or click the Form Field Shading button on the Forms toolbar.

Task: Setting Form Field Options

Each type of form field has its own set of options. You can set form field options for each type of form field before you insert the fields, or you can set form field options for each field you insert.

To display the Form Field Options dialog box for a particular field, do one of the following:

- Double-click the field in the template document.

- Choose **I**nsert, For**m** Field. Choose the field type. Choose Options.

- Select the form field in the template document. Click the Form Field Options button on the Forms toolbar.

To set Text Form Field options, follow these steps:

You can specify the type of text a field accepts in the Text For Field Options dialog box.

Select the type of text field here

Specify the field length here

Choose a field format here

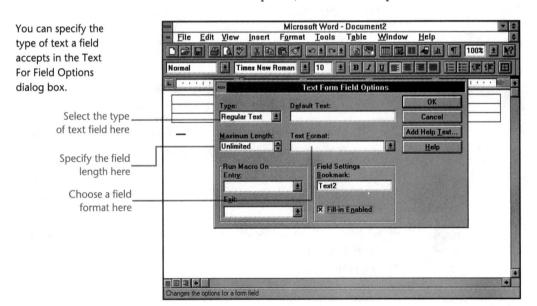

1. From the Ty**p**e drop-down list box, select one of the following:

   - Regular Text to accept any kind of text in the field

   - Number to accept only numbers in the field

   - Date to accept only numbers formatted as dates in the field

   - Current Date to accept only the current date in the field

   - Current Time to accept only the current time in the field

   - Calculation to accept a formula in the field

2. In the **M**aximum Length text box, specify the maximum number of text characters that can be entered in the box. To allow an unlimited number of characters, enter *Unlimited*.

3. In the D**e**fault text box, enter the information you want to appear in the field when the form is opened. The name of the D**e**fault text box changes according to the type of text field you select. If you select Current Date or Current Time, it is not available, because Word automatically defaults to the current date or time. If you select Calculation, it changes to the **E**xpression text box. Enter the default expression you want to use to perform the calculation.

4. From the **F**ormat drop-down list, select the format in which you want information entered in the form field. The name of the Format drop-down list box changes according to the type of text field you select.

5. Choose OK.

15

To set check box form field options, follow these steps:

In the Check Box
Form Field Options
dialog box, you can
specify the size of
the check box.

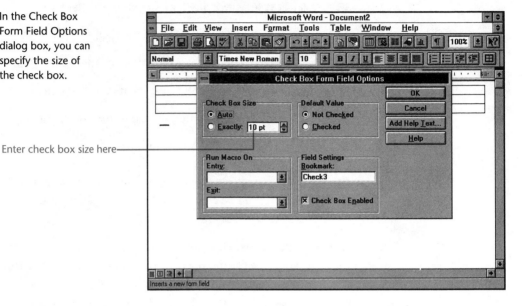

Enter check box size here

1. In the Check Box Size area, choose one of the following:

   ■ **A**uto to automatically adjust the size of the check box to the same point size as the surrounding text.

   ■ **E**xactly to enter an exact point size for the check box. Enter the point size in the text box.

2. In the Default Value area, choose one of the following:

   ■ Not Chec**k**ed to leave the check box blank until an user selects it.

   ■ **C**hecked to display a mark in the box whenever the form is first opened.

3. Choose OK.

To set drop-down list options, follow these steps:

In the Drop-down
Form Field Options
dialog box, you can
enter up to 25
choices to display in
the drop-down list.

Enter the drop-down
list choices here

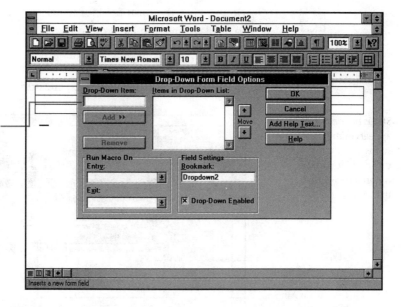

1. In the Drop-down Item text box, type the first item you want to appear in the drop-down list of choices.

2. Choose **A**dd. The item appears in the **I**tems in the Drop-down List text box.

3. Repeat steps 1 and 2 until all of the items you want in the drop-down list are entered.

4. To remove an item from the list, select it in the **I**tems in Drop-down List text box, and choose **R**emove.

5. To rearrange the order in which an item appears in the list, select it in the **I**tems in Drop-down List text box, and choose the Move up or Move down arrow.

6. Choose OK.

Task: Adding Help Text to a Form Field

You can enter text to help a user fill out the form. You can enter text to display in the status bar whenever the insertion point is positioned in a particular field, and you can enter text to display in a dialog box when the user presses F1.

15

To enter help text to display in the status bar, follow these steps:

1. Double-click the form field for which you want to enter help, to display the Form Field options dialog box.

2. Choose Add Help **T**ext.

3. In the Add Help Text dialog box, click the **S**tatus Bar tab.

Status bar help text appears in the status bar whenever the insertion point is positioned within the field.

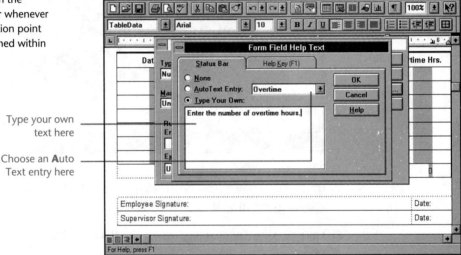

Type your own text here

Choose an **A**uto Text entry here

4. Position the insertion point within the **T**ype Your Own text box, and type the information you want to appear in the status bar when the insertion point is positioned within the current field.

5. If you would rather use an existing **A**utoText entry, select one from the **A**utoText Entry drop-down list box. For information about using AutoText, see Lesson 9, "Making Your Work Easier."

6. Choose OK.

To enter help text to display in a dialog box, follow these steps:

1. Double-click the form field for which you want to enter help, to display the Form Field options dialog box.

2. Choose Add Help **T**ext.

3. In the Add Help Text dialog box, click the Help **K**ey (F1) tab.

Help Key help text
appears in a dialog
box whenever the
insertion point is
positioned within
the field, and the
user presses F1.

Type your own
text here

Choose an **A**uto
Text entry here

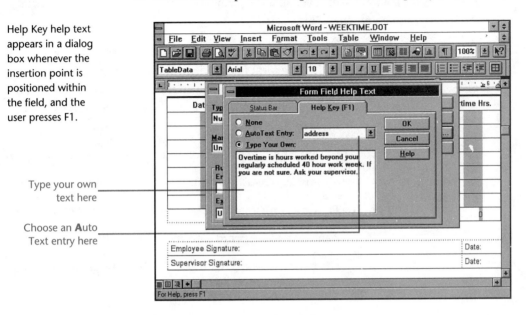

4. Position the insertion point within the **T**ype Your Own text box, and type the information you want to appear in a dialog box when the insertion point is positioned within the current field and the user presses F1.

5. If you would rather use an existing **A**utoText entry, select one from the **A**utoText Entry drop-down list box. For information about using AutoText, see Lesson 9, "Making Your Work Easier."

6. Choose OK.

Task: Formatting Form Fields

Data entered in a form field is displayed according to the formatting applied to the form field. Form fields normally assume the font formatting of the surrounding text. To format a form field independently of the surrounding text, select the form field and apply the font formatting.

15

You can apply paragraph formatting to a paragraph that contains a form field, but not to the form field itself. To Word, a form field is a single character, which assumes the paragraph formatting options of the paragraph in which it is located.

Task: Protecting, Saving, and Testing a Form

After you complete the form template, including all present text and graphics, form fields, and formatting, you need to protect the form, and save it. Protecting the form template ensures that no unauthorized changes are made to the form itself.

To protect and save a form template, follow these steps:

1. Choose **T**ools, **P**rotect Document.

2. In the Protect Document dialog box, choose the **F**orms options.

3. If you want, enter a password, and then choose OK.

4. If you entered a password, Word asks you to confirm the password.

5. Choose **F**ile, Save **A**s.

6. In the Save As dialog box, enter a name for the form template. Make sure that Document Template (*.DOT) appears in the Save File as **T**ype list box.

7. Choose OK to save the form template.

Before you close the template, you can test the form fields to ensure that they work the way you want them to work.

To test the form fields, follow these steps:

1. Choose **T**ools, **P**rotect Document, or click the Protect Form button on the Forms toolbar to make sure your form is protected.

2. Select a form field and enter text.

3. Look at the status bar to see if the help text you entered for that field appears.

4. Press F1 to see if the dialog box help text you entered appears.

5. Test any other fields you want.

6. If you need to make changes, choose **T**ools, Un**p**rotect Document so that you can edit the form.

Summary

To	Do This
Open a sample form	Choose **F**ile, **O**pen. Open the C:\WINDWORD\TEMPLATE subdirectory. Display Document Template files. Choose the file name.
Customize a sample form	Open it. Choose **T**ools, Un**p**rotect Document. Edit the form template.
Protect a sample form	Choose **T**ools, **P**rotect Document. Choose **F**orms. Enter a password.
Save only the form field data	Choose **T**ools, **O**ptions Save. Choose the Save **D**ata Only for Forms check box.
Print only the form field data	Choose **T**ools, **O**ptions Print. Choose the **P**rint Data Only for Forms check box.
Create a new form	Choose **F**ile, **N**ew. Choose to create a template. Choose a document template on which to base the form template.
Enter preset text and graphics	Use all of Word's features to enter and format the preset text and graphics in the form template.
Enter form fields	Position the insertion point. Choose **I**nsert, For**m** Field. Choose the Form Field type. Set the Form Field options. Add Form Field help.
Use a form	Choose **F**ile, **N**ew. Create a document based on the form template. Fill out the form.

15

On Your Own

Estimated time: 30 minutes

1. Open one of Word's built-in sample form templates.

2. Modify the template for use by your company.

3. Save the template with a new name.

4. Create a form document using the modified form template.

5. Fill out the form document.

6. Print the form document.

7. Create a new form template.

8. Insert all three types of form fields.

9. Enter help for all of the form fields that you inserted in the form template.

10. Protect and save the form template.

11. Create a form document using the form template.

12. Fill out the form document on-screen.

13. Print the form document.

Managing Your Documents and Files

Planning and organizing a document is often the most difficult part of writing. That's why Word provides many tools to help you construct and keep track of documents.

In this lesson, you learn to use the tools Word provides for managing lengthy documents, including outlining and indexing. You also learn to manage multiple revisions of a document, and to use Word to find files you may have misplaced on a disk.

Specifically, you learn to do the following:

- Outline a document
- Add bookmarks
- Create cross-references
- Mark revisions
- Compare documents
- Compile a basic index
- Generate a table of contents
- Find files

Outlining a Document

Outline view

An editing mode in Word that you use to create an outline by assigning heading levels to paragraphs and text.

Heading level

A position assigned to a paragraph or text to create an outline in Outline view.

In Outline view, Word adds an Outline toolbar to your screen display, and a heading marker on the first line of the document.

A heading marker

Preparing an outline is a good way to organize a document, particularly a lengthy document. With Word, you can easily construct a multilevel outline. You can than use the outline as a blueprint for writing your document, or you fill in the details within the outline document itself.

In Word, you use *Outline view* to create an outline. Outline view is an editing environment structured specifically for creating an outline. It provides options for assigning and changing *heading levels*.

You can create a document in Outline view, or you can use Outline view to edit an existing document. You can easily switch back and forth from Outline view and other Word views at any time.

To change to Outline view, choose **V**iew, **O**utline.

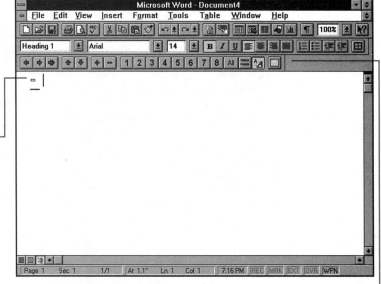

The Outline toolbar

If you have problems... If the Outline toolbar is not displayed on your screen, choose **V**iew, Toolbars and choose the Outlining toolbar check box.

Task: Creating an Outline

To create an outline, you organize paragraphs and text into progressive levels. The levels are based on Word's standard nine heading styles— Heading 1 for main level headings, Heading 2 for first-level subheadings, and so on. You assign heading levels by *promoting* and *demoting* the paragraph.

You can create an outline by typing in all of the headings you know you want to include, then promoting or demoting them to the appropriate level. Or, you can set the level of each heading as you enter it. If you are not sure beforehand where a heading will fall in the outline hierarchy, the first method may be more effective.

To create headings, follow these steps:

1. Choose **V**iew, **O**utline to change to Outline view.

2. Type the text for the first heading you know you want to include.

3. Press Enter. Word starts a new paragraph at the same heading level as the previous paragraph. If you do not want to think about levels yet, just keep typing the text, pressing Enter after each heading.

At first, all of the headings are at the same level. You use the toolbar buttons, the heading markers, and commands to structure your document into an outline.

Style area

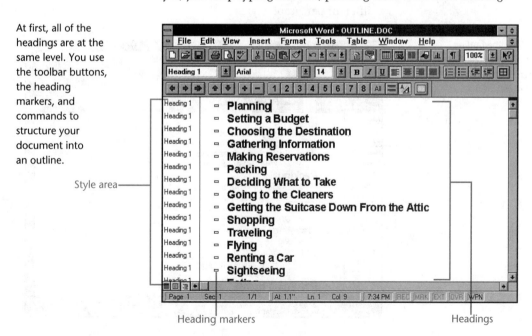

Heading markers

Headings

16

To enter subheadings, follow these steps:

1. Position the insertion point within the heading you want to demote. Or, press Enter to start a new line.

2. Press Tab. Word demotes the heading.

3. Press Enter to start a new line at the same subheading level as the previous line.

4. Continue adding or demoting subheadings. You can create up to nine levels.

There are three simple ways to tell at what level a paragraph is compared to the other paragraphs:

- Look at its position on the page: Heading 1 paragraphs are flush left, and subsequent levels are indented.

- Display the Style area to identify the heading style of each paragraph.

- Look at the formatting. Each level of subheading is formatted using a different paragraph style.

Here, the outline headings have been arranged in three levels.

Heading 1 - Level 1

Heading 2 - Level 2

Heading 3 - Level 3

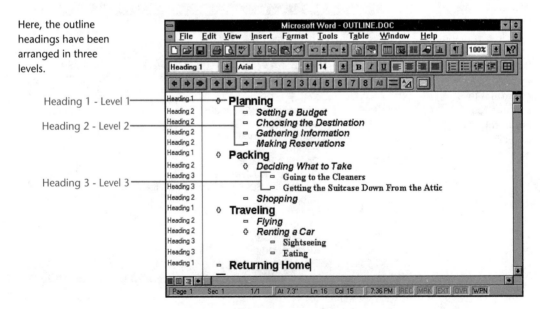

You can promote and demote items in your outline at any time.

 To promote a heading, place the insertion point within the heading and press Shift+Tab.

 To demote a heading, place the insertion point within the heading and press Tab.

If you have problems...	If you promote or demote paragraphs by accident, choose **E**dit, **U**ndo immediately. Word reverts the paragraphs back to their previous level.

Task: Understanding Level Hierarchy

Levels are hierarchical: each level is subordinate to the level above. You can tell whether a heading has subordinates by looking at its heading marker:

- A plus sign indicates that the heading has subordinates.

- A minus sign indicates that the heading has no subordinates.

Often, you want to manipulate subordinates along with their main heading. If you select a heading and all of its subordinates, any action you perform on the heading, affects the subordinates as well.

To select a section of the document comprised of a heading and all of its subordinates, follow these steps:

1. Point at the heading marker at the left end of the heading. The pointer changes shape to a four-headed arrow.

2. Click. After a section is selected, you can promote, demote, or otherwise manipulate it all at once.

Task: Collapsing and Expanding Headings

You can collapse and expand the outline so that only certain levels are displayed. When you collapse the outline, the selected level and all levels above it are displayed; when you expand the outline, the hidden levels also appear.

16

To collapse the entire outline, click the button on the Outline toolbar corresponding to the highest level heading that you want to display. For example, to display only level 1 and 2 paragraphs, click the 2 button.

To expand the entire outline, click the All button.

To expand only one section of the outline, do one of the following:

- Position the insertion point within the highest-level paragraph of the section, and click the Plus button.

- Double-click the highest-level paragraph's outline button.

To collapse only one section of the outline, do one of the following:

- Position the insertion point within the highest-level paragraph of the section, and click the Minus button.

- Double-click the highest-level paragraph's outline button.

Note: *If a collapsed heading contains subordinates, part of the heading text is underlined with gray.*

Here the outline has been contracted to show level 1 and 2 headings only.

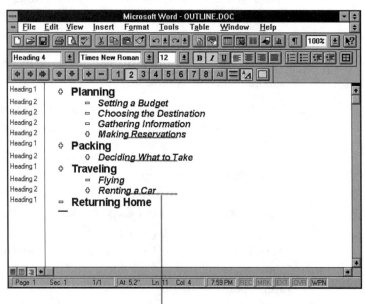

Gray line indicates collapsed subordinate headings

Note: *When you print a document in Outline view, only the displayed paragraphs print. By using Expand and Collapse, you can easily print different variations of the outline.*

Task: Changing the Order of Headings

You can change the order of headings in your outline by moving the paragraphs up or down. Changing the order of headings does not effect the heading levels—you must promote or demote the headings to do that.

 To move a paragraph to the line above the previous paragraph (no matter what the level), position the insertion point in the paragraph you want to move and click the Move up button on the Outline toolbar.

 To move a paragraph to the line below the following paragraph (no matter what the level), position the insertion point in the paragraph you want to move and click the Move down button on the Outline toolbar.

If you have problems...

Moving a paragraph up or down in the outline does *not* change its assigned level. If you find that all your levels are out of order, it's because you moved paragraphs without paying attention to the level of the paragraphs you were putting them between. Use **E**dit, **U**ndo, or promote and demote the paragraphs until they are the correct level.

To move a heading and all of its subordinate headings, click its outline marker to select the section, then drag it to the new location.

Note: *It is easier to drag an entire section if you collapse it first.*

Task: Working with Text in an Outline

As you create your outline, you may come up with ideas for writing part of your document. Instead of entering them as headings, you would like to enter them as text. In Outline view, you can enter body text level paragraphs that are subordinate to all other heading levels.

 To demote a heading to body text level, position the insertion point within the heading, and click the Demote to Body Text button on the Outline toolbar.

16

Word applies the Normal style to the text, and places a small square heading marker at the beginning of the paragraph.

You can enter as much text you like in Outline view. Body text level paragraphs are the lowest level in the outline hierarchy.

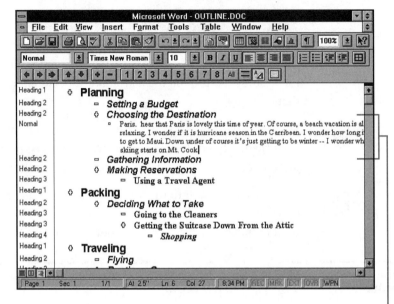

Body text paragraph

If you have problems...   If you only see one line of the body text level paragraph, no matter how much you type, the Show First Line Only button is depressed on the Outline toolbar. Choose it to display all of the text.

Task: Numbering the Outline

You can automatically number the headings in Outline view.

To quickly add numbers to your outline headings, follow these steps:

1. Choose Format, Heading Numbering.

In the Heading
Numbering dialog
box, you can
choose from size
numbering
schemes.

Choose a numbering —————
scheme here

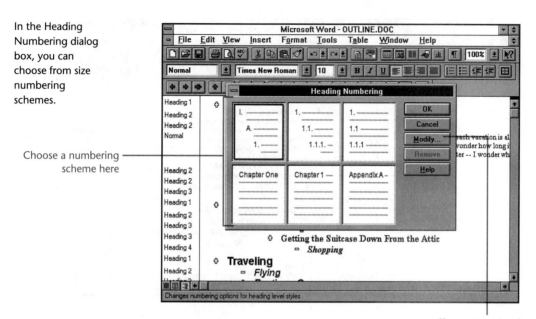

Choose to customize a
numbering scheme here

2. Choose one of the Numbering schemes.

3. If you want, choose **M**odify to customize the numbering scheme,
then choose OK.

4. Choose OK. Word numbers the outline. In the future, if you add,
delete, or move headings, Word automatically renumbers the entire
outline.

16

Word numbers your outline according to the scheme you chose.

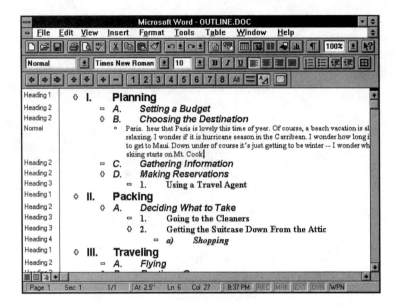

Task: Changing to Normal View

At any time, choose **V**iew, **N**ormal to change to normal view to edit your document.

In Normal view, the document retains the styles and numbering scheme applied in Outline view. If you have nonprinting characters displayed, you see small black rectangles at the beginning of each heading paragraph created in Outline view.

You can change back and forth between Normal view and Outline to develop your document. You can write and format in Normal view, but you may find it easier to add and remove headings, and to rearrange sections in Outline view.

Note: *If you add headings in Normal view, be sure to format them using the Heading styles. That way, when you change back to Outline view, the document retains its structure.*

You can edit your document in Normal view, while retaining the Outline structure.

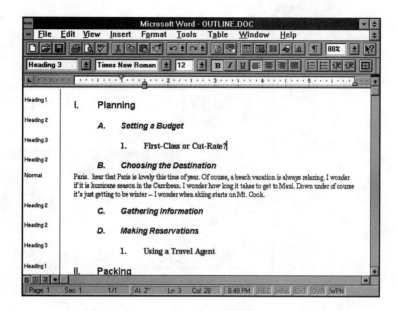

Task: Inserting Bookmarks

Bookmarks

Nonprinting marks that identify specific locations within a document.

You can add *bookmarks* to your text to indicate specific locations or items of interest. Then, if you or anyone needs to find the spot quickly, all you have to do is go to the bookmark.

You can insert up to 450 bookmarks in a document. To add a bookmark, follow these steps:

1. Position the insertion point at the location of interest. To mark a block of text, select the text.

2. Choose **E**dit, **B**ookmark.

16

Bookmark names may be up to 40 characters long. They must start with a letter, and cannot include spaces.

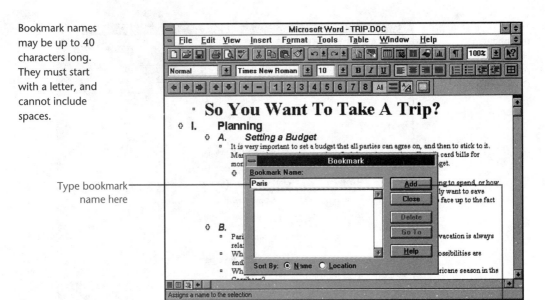

Type bookmark name here

Choose Add to create a bookmark at the insertion point

3. In the **B**ookmark Name text box, type a name that identifies the bookmark.

4. Choose **A**dd.

To go to a bookmark that has been added to a document, follow these steps:

1. Choose **E**dit, **B**ookmark.

2. In the **B**ookmark Name list, choose the bookmark you want.

3. Choose **G**o To. The insertion point moves to the bookmark location.

Note: *To delete a bookmark, select it in the* **B**ookmark Name *list and choose* **D**elete. *Deleting a bookmark deletes the mark, but not the text in the document.*

Task: Using Go To

Go To sometimes appears in dialog boxes in Word; you choose it to go to a particular place or mark in a document. Word also has a Go To command that you can use to move the insertion point directly to a specific location or mark, such as a bookmark, annotation, footnote, or page.

To use Go To, follow these steps:

1. Position the insertion point at the beginning of the document.

2. Choose **E**dit, **G**o To.

With Go To, Word moves the insertion point to the next occurrence of the selected item, or to the specified location.

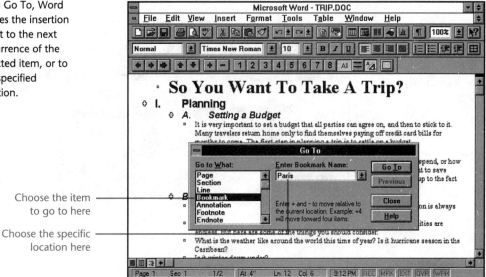

Choose the item to go to here

Choose the specific location here

3. In the Go to **W**hat text box, choose the type of location to which you want to go.

4. In the **E**nter box, either choose the specific location to go to from the drop-down list, or type the location.

5. Choose Go **T**o. Word moves the insertion point directly to the specified item.

16

If you have problems...   If there is no Go To button in the Go To dialog box, choose Next.

Task: Marking Revisions

Revision Marking
Identifying insertions and deletions made to an original document.

When a document is subjected to intense editing and rewriting, it is helpful to be able to track the changes. You may forget who suggested a change, or why a change was made, or even what the original text was about. Word provides a *revision marking* feature that lets you easily identify all changes made to a document.

To turn on revision marking, follow these steps:

1. Open the document you want to revise.

2. Choose **T**ools, Re**v**isions.

To turn on revision marking, choose the Mark Revisions While Editing check box in the Revisions dialog box.

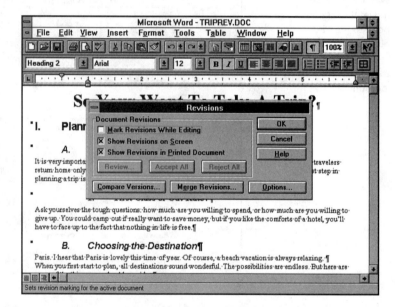

3. Choose the **M**ark Revisions While Editing check box.

4. Choose OK.

   Note: You can quickly turn on revision marking by double-clicking the MRK button on the status bar. When the letters MRK are black, revision marking is turned on.

To use revision marking, simply edit the document. All changes that you make to the document text appear in the default revision marking format:

- If you delete characters, Word leaves them in place, but changes their color and reformats them with strikethrough characters.

- If you insert characters, Word displays them underlined, and in a different color.

To return to regular editing, deselect the **M**ark Revisions While Editing check box in the Revisions dialog box, or double-click the MRK button.

With revision marking, you can identify changes while still seeing the original document text.

Revision marked insertions

Bars in the margin indicate paragraphs that have been revised

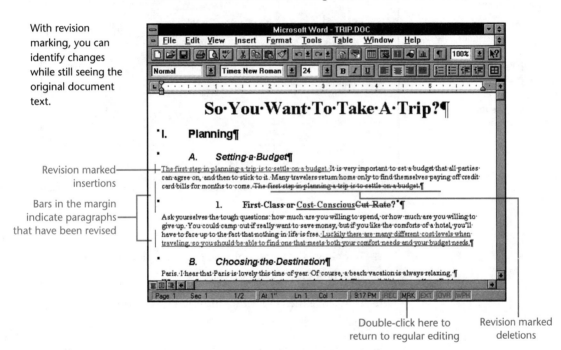

Double-click here to return to regular editing

Revision marked deletions

16

Customizing Revision Marks

By default, revision marking insertions appear in blue with an underline and deletions appear in blue with a strikethrough. You can change the look of revision marks, to distinguish one editor from another.

To change the appearance of revision marks, follow these steps:

1. Choose **T**ools, **O**ptions.

2. Click the Revisions tab at the top of the Options dialog box to display the revision options settings.

If more than one person is editing a document, you can use different revision marks to identify who made which revisions.

Choose the insertion format and color here

Choose the deletion format and color here

Choose the revision indicator you want to appear in the margin here

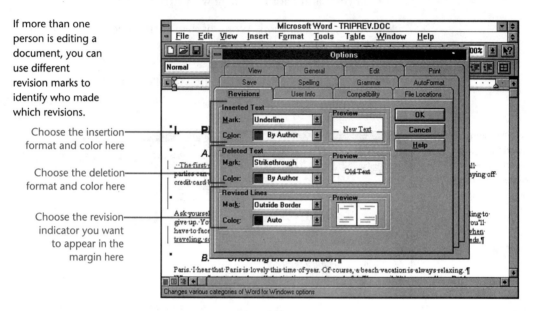

3. Choose from the following:

- To change the format of inserted text, choose a format from the **M**ark drop-down list.

- To change the color of the inserted text, choose a color from the **C**olor drop-down list.

- To change the format of the deleted text, choose a format from the M**a**rk drop-down list.

- To change the color of the deleted text, choose a color from the Co**l**or drop-down list.

- To change the location of the indicator used to mark revised paragraphs, choose a location from the Mar**k** drop-down list.

- To change the color of the indicator, choose a color from the Color drop-down list.

4. Choose OK.

Reviewing Revisions

You can review all edits made with revision marking and decide whether to incorporate the changes into the document.

To review revision marking, follow these steps:

1. Position the insertion point at the beginning of the document.

2. Choose **T**ools, Re**v**isions.

3. In the Revisions dialog box, choose **R**eview. Word finds the first marked revision in the document and displays the Review Revisions dialog box.

4. Choose from the following:

- Choose **A**ccept to incorporate the changes into the document.

- Choose **R**eject to leave the original text intact and remove the revision marks from the selected text.

- Choose **F**ind to highlight the next marked revision in the document.

- Choose F**i**nd to highlight the previous marked revision in the document.

- Choose **U**ndo Last to undo the last change you made using the revisions dialog box.

5. Choose Close to return to the document.

To accept or reject all changes at once without reviewing each one, follow these steps:

16

1. Choose **T**ools, Re**v**isions.

2. Choose from the following:

   - Choose **A**ccept All to accept all of the revisions.

   - Choose Re**j**ect All to reject all of the revision.

3. Word asks you to confirm your action.

4. Choose **Y**es.

Displaying and Printing Revision Marks

By default, Word displays revision marks on-screen, and prints them in a document.

To turn off revision marks so that you cannot see them on-screen, and so that they do not print, follow these steps:

1. Choose **T**ools, Re**v**isions.

2. Deselect the Show Revisions on **S**creen check box so that the marks to not appear on-screen.

3. Deselect the Show Revision in **P**rinted Document check box so that the marks to not print.

Task: Comparing Documents

Compare
To identify differences between two versions of a document.

With Word, you can easily *compare* differences between two copies of the same document.

Comparing documents is useful for keeping documents up-to-date, and for deciding which of two versions has the most effective edits. For example, if you maintain a copy of a document before it has been edited, you can compare the revised version with the original version.

Note: *When you compare documents, the differences between the two are marked with the default revision marking formatting.*

To compare two documents, follow these steps:

1. Open the document you want to use as the source. The source document is the document that you want to be the final, most up-to-date version.

2. Choose **T**ools, Re**v**isions.

3. In the Revisions dialog box, choose **C**ompare Versions.

Use the Compare Versions dialog box like the Open dialog box.

Choose the document to compare here

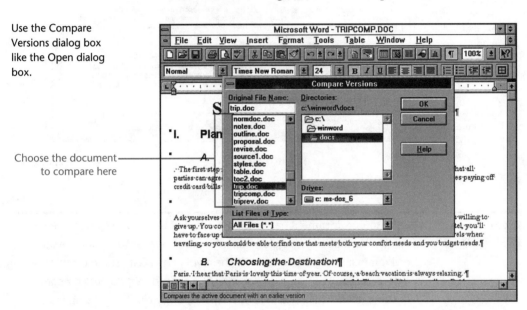

4. In the Compare Versions dialog box, open the document you want to compare to the document already displayed on-screen.

5. Choose OK.

Word compares the documents and inserts into the source document any differences that it finds, using the default revision marking format.

16

To identify the differences between the documents, Word displays text found in the source document as revision-inserted text and text found in the comparison document as revision-deleted text. Text that is the same in both documents is unchanged.

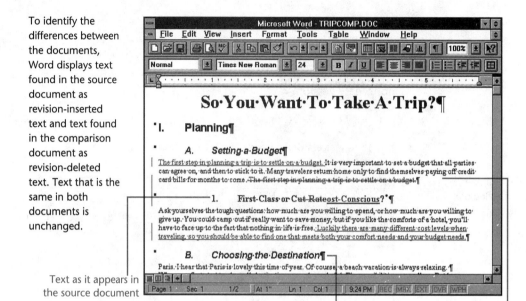

Text as it appears in the source document

Text that appears the same in both

Text as it appears in the comparison document

If you have problems...

If the source document has revision marks in it before you compare documents, Word displays a dialog box informing you that some of the existing revision marks may be covered by the revision marks it uses to display the differences between the two documents. To avoid this, do not compare documents that still contain revision marks, or try changing the appearance of the marks before you compare the documents.

To review the differences between the two documents, use the Review Revisions dialog box. For information on using revision marking, see the preceding section.

Creating an Index

Index

A table compiled by Word to reference the page numbers where readers can locate key words and topics in a document.

Indexing is an art form. A good *index* can make a document more valuable to the reader; a poor index can turn any document into nothing more than trash.

You create an index in Word by identifying the subjects in your document that readers are likely to look for. Word does the rest by compiling a list of those subjects in alphabetical order, and marking each subject in the list with one or more page numbers.

This lesson covers creating basic index entries. Word can create entries, subentries, and referenced entries. For more information on creating complex indexes, see Que's *Using Word Version 6 for Windows,* Special Edition.

Task: Marking Index Entries in a Document

Word marks index entries by placing nonprinting index fields in the document. You can see the field by choosing to display nonprinting characters.

With Word, you can mark two kinds of basic index entries:

- You can mark entries for words and phrases that appear directly in your document.

- You can mark entries for words and phrases that describe a subject covered on a particular page in your document.

In either case, to mark the entry follow these steps:

1. Position the insertion within the text you want to mark. If possible select the exact word or phrase.

2. Press Alt+Shift+X.

You prepare index entries in the Mark Index Entry dialog box.

You can select the entry in the text

Enter or edit the entry here

Choose to mark the entry here

Choose to mark all occurrences of this entry here

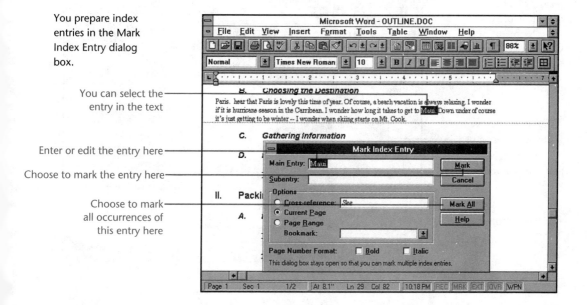

16

3. In the Main Entry text box, enter or edit the text you want to appear in the index. If you selected the entry in the document, Word has automatically entered it already.

4. Choose one of the following:

   ■ **M**ark to mark the entry and return to the document.

   ■ Mark **A**ll to mark all occurrences of the entry in the document, and return to the document.

5. The dialog box remains on-screen. You can continue marking index entries throughout the document.

6. To clear the dialog box from the screen, choose Close.

Task: Compiling an Index

To compile the index once the entries are marked, follow these steps:

1. Position the insertion point where you want the index to appear. Usually you want to place an index at the end of the document.

2. Choose **I**nsert, Inde**x** and Tables.

3. At the top of the Index and Tables dialog box, click the Inde**x** tab.

In the Index and Tables dialog box, you can choose the format to use for compiling the index.

Choose a format here

Preview the format here

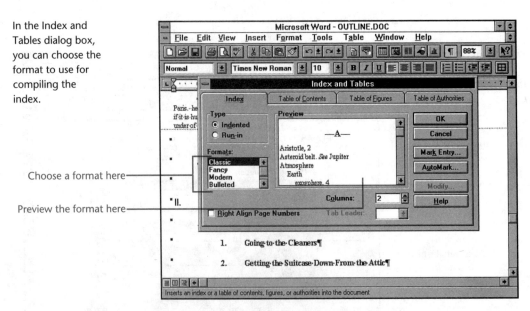

4. In the Formats list box, choose the format you want to use.

5. Choose OK. Word generates the index and inserts it in the document.

If you have problems...	If the index appears with a gray background, you have field shading turned on. Choose **T**ools **O**ptions View to display the View options dialog box. In the Field Shading drop-down list box, choose Never to keep fields from being shaded, or When Selected to shade them only when they are selected.

Task: Updating an Index

If you edit the document after you have generated the index, page numbers and references may change.

To update the index, follow these steps:

1. Position the insertion point anywhere within the existing index.

2. Press F9. Word displays the Update Index dialog box.

3. Choose one of the following:

    ■ Update **P**age Numbers only, if you only need Word to adjust the page numbers

    ■ Update **E**ntire Index, if you made major changes and you want Word to update the entire index

4. Choose OK.

16

Creating a Table of Contents

Table of contents
A table created by Word to identify the names and locations of sections of a document.

Including a *table of contents* with a document helps readers quickly find the information they need. With Word, you can automate the creation of a table of contents.

Note: *Generating a table of contents should probably be the last thing you do before completing your document. You want to complete all sections of the document before you generate a table of contents, including an index, and you want to be sure that you will not have to update the table too many times because of editing changes.*

Word can automatically create a table of contents based on the paragraph styles which you have applied to paragraphs. You simply identify the styles you want to include in the table, and Word does the rest.

Word formats a table of contents by assigning levels to the styles you choose to include. It places the level 1 styles at the first level of the table of contents. It places the level 2 styles subordinate to the level 1 styles. (For more information on understanding level hierarchy, see the section on outlining, earlier in this lesson.)

By default, Word bases a table of contents on its standard Heading styles, but you can identify the styles you want to use.

No matter what styles you use, if you applied styles consistently in your document, then you are ready to use to create a table of contents. Applying consistent styles means that all first-level headings in your document are formatted with the same style, such as Heading 1. All second-level headings in your document are formatted with the same style, such as Heading 2, and so on.

If you created an outline in Outline view, then you know that your style levels are consistent. If you created your document by applying character and paragraph formatting to Normal style text, you will have trouble creating a table of contents.

When you're sure your headings are formatted consistently, you are ready to generate the table of contents.

If you have problems... If your styles are not applied consistently, you have two options. You can go back and apply consistent styles to the headings you want to include in the table of contents, or you can give up trying to create a table of contents.

Note: *Text appears in the table of contents exactly as it appears in the document. Make sure it is formatted the way you want it (and spelled correctly) before you create the table of contents.*

Task: Using Heading Styles To Create a Table of Contents

To generate the table of contents, if you used Word's standard heading styles to format your document, follow these steps:

1. Position the document where you want the table of contents to be placed. Usually, you want the table of contents at the beginning of the document.

2. Choose **I**nsert, Inde**x** and Tables.

3. At the top of the Index and Tables dialog box, click the Table of **C**ontents tab.

In the Index and Tables dialog box, you can choose a format for your table of contents.

Choose a format here

Preview the format here

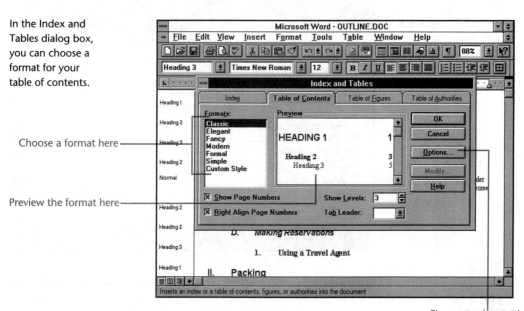

Choose to change the default style options here

4. In the Formats list box, choose one of the preset table of contents formats.

5. If you want to change any of the preset table format settings, choose from the following:

   ■ Choose the **S**how Page Numbers check box to include page numbers in the table

   ■ Choose the **R**ight Align Page Numbers check box to align page numbers along the right indent marker.

   ■ In the Show **L**evels text box, specify how many levels of headings to include in the table.

16

■ From the Tab leader drop-down list box, choose a tab leader character to insert between the page number and the table of contents text.

6. Choose OK to create the table of contents.

Word generates the table of contents and inserts it in your document.

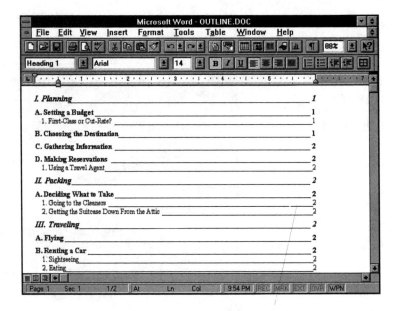

If you have problems...

If the table of contents text appears with a gray background, you have field shading turned on. Choose **T**ools, **O**ptions, View to display the View options dialog box. In the Fi**e**ld Shading drop-down list box, choose Never to keep fields from being shaded, or When Selected to shade them only when they are selected.

Task: Using Other Styles to Create a Table of Contents

If your document was formatted with styles other than the Heading styles, you have to tell Word which styles to use in the table of contents, and what level to assign to each style.

To create the table of contents, follow these steps:

1. Position the document where you want the table of contents to be placed. Usually, you want the table of contents at the beginning of the document.

2. Choose **I**nsert, Inde**x** and Tables.

3. At the top of the Index and Tables dialog box, click the Table of **C**ontents tab.

4. In the Forma**t**s list box, choose one of the preset table of contents formats.

5. If you want to change any of the preset table format settings, choose from the following:

  ■ Choose the **S**how Page Numbers check box to include page numbers in the table.

  ■ Choose the **R**ight Align Page Numbers check box to align page numbers along the right indent marker.

  ■ In the Show Levels text box, specify how many levels of headings to include in the table.

  ■ From the Tab leader drop-down list box, choose a tab leader character to insert between the page number and the table of contents text.

6. Choose **O**ptions.

In the Table of Contents Options dialog box, you can specify the styles Word should use to create the table.

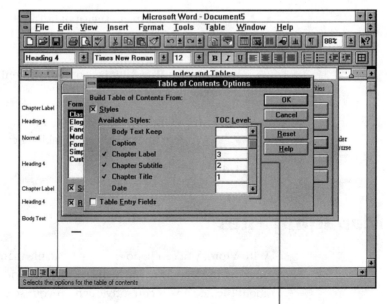

Enter the table of contents levels here

16

7. In the Table of Contents Options dialog box, scroll through the list of available styles until you find the one that corresponds to the level 1 heading in your document.

8. In the TOC **L**evel text box beside the style, enter 1.

9. Scroll through the list of available styles until you find the style that corresponds to the level 2 heading in your document.

10. In the TOC **L**evel text box beside the style, enter 2.

11. Repeat the procedure for as many levels as you want to include in your table of contents, and then choose OK to return to the Index and Tables dialog box.

12. Choose OK. Word creates the table of contents.

Task: Updating a Table of Contents

If you edit the document after you have generated the table of contents, heading titles and page numbers may change.

To update the table of contents, follow these steps:

1. Position the insertion point anywhere within the existing table of contents.

2. Press F9. Word displays the Update Table of Contents dialog box.

3. Choose one of the following:

   ■ Update **P**age Numbers only if you only need Word to adjust the page numbers

   ■ Update **E**ntire Table if you made major changes and you want Word to update the entire table of contents

4. Choose OK.

Managing Files

With Word, you can perform some basic file management tasks without opening the Windows File Manager. You can view and edit information about the document currently open on your screen, and you can view information about a file without opening the document. You can also use Word to search disks for misplaced files.

To view information about a closed file, you use Word's Find File feature.

Task: Finding Files

To search for a file, follow these steps:

1. Choose **F**ile, **F**ind File to open the Find File dialog box.

2. Choose **S**earch.

If you have problems...

If the Search dialog box opens rather than the Find File dialog box, you do not have to choose Search. Continue with step 3.

In the Search dialog box, specify the file you want to find.

Choose to save the search specifications for future use here

Enter the file name and path here

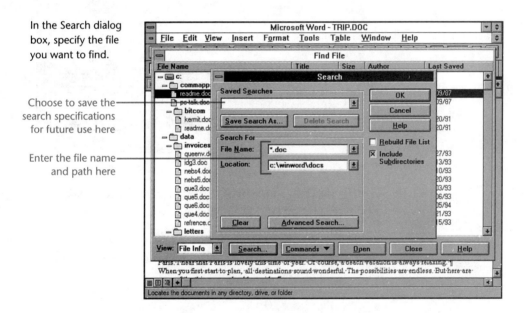

3. In the Search For area, enter the file name in the File **N**ame text box. If you do not know the name, open the drop-down list to choose a file type.

4. Enter a file path in the **L**ocation text box. If you do not know the path, click the arrow next to the drop-down list to choose a disk drive.

16

5. Choose the Include Su**b**directories check box to search the subdirectories of the path entered in the **L**ocation text box.

6. Choose OK. Word searches the specified path, and displays the files it finds in the Find File dialog box.

Word displays an alphabetical list of all files that match the information you entered in the Search dialog box.

Choose a file here

Choose to search for another file here

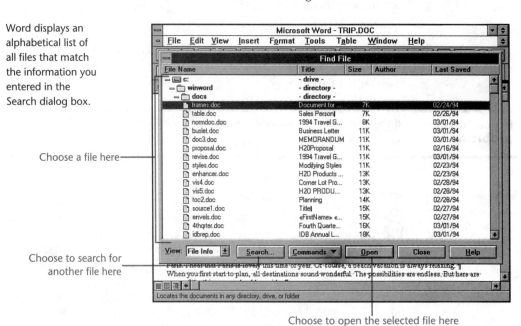

Choose to open the selected file here

Task: Manipulating Files in the Find File Dialog Box

After you find a file in the Find File dialog box, you can preview it, open it, print it, display summary information, copy it, or delete it.

To perform any action on a file, select it in the **L**isted Files list. Then, choose from the following:

■ To open a file, choose **O**pen.

■ To preview the contents of a file, choose Preview from the **V**iew drop-down list.

■ To view the document statistics, choose Summary from the **V**iew drop-down list.

■ To print the file, choose **C**ommands **P**rint. Word displays the Print dialog box.

■ To open the file but not edit it, choose **C**ommands Open **R**ead Only.

■ To open the file's Summary Info dialog box, choose **C**ommands **S**ummary.

■ To delete the file, choose **C**ommands **D**elete. Word asks you for confirmation.

■ To copy the file, choose **C**ommands **C**opy. Word asks you to specify the path to the location where you want the copy stored.

■ To sort the File Name list, choose **C**ommands Sor**t**ing. Word prompts you to specify the sort order.

■ To close the Find File dialog box, choose Close.

Summary

To	Do This
Promote or Demote an outline heading	Click the Promote or Demote button.
Collapse an outline	Click the Outline level button corresponding to the level you want to display.
Expand an outline	Click the All button.
Insert a Bookmark	Choose **E**dit, **B**ookmark. Name the bookmark.
Mark revisions	Choose **T**ools, Re**v**isions. Choose the **M**ark Revisions While Editing check box.
Compare documents	Choose **T**ools, Re**v**isions. Choose Compare Versions.
Mark index entries	Press Alt+Shift+X. Enter the entry. Choose **M**ark.
Generate a table of contents or index	Choose **I**nsert, Inde**x** and Tables. Choose a format.
Find a File	Choose **F**ile, **F**ind File. Choose **S**earch. Specify search criteria.

16

On Your Own

Estimated time: 30 minutes

1. Open a new document.

2. Change to Outline view.

3. Enter outline headings.

4. Promote and demote the headings to create a document outline.

5. Number the outline.

6. Rearrange the outline.

7. Change to Normal view and enter text paragraphs to finish the document.

8. Insert a bookmark.

9. Attach an annotation to the document.

10. Save a copy of the document with a new name.

11. Turn on revision marks and edit the new document.

12. Review the revisions and accept the ones you want to keep.

13. Compare the original document to the revised document.

14. Review the differences and accept the ones you want to keep.

15. Mark index entries in the document.

16. Generate an index.

17. Generate a table of contents.

18. Close the document (or both if both documents still are open).

19. Use Find, File to display all word documents in subdirectories of the \WINWORD directory. If you want, limit the search by using Summary Information.

20. Preview a document from the Find File dialog box.

Working with Other Windows Applications

The capability to import many different file formats is built into Word. That means you can use files and data created with other programs, including word processing, spreadsheet, database, and graphics applications. You also can export Word document files so that someone with a different application program can use them.

Word supports Windows' *Dynamic Data Exchange* (DDE) and *Object Linking and Embedding* (OLE). With DDE and OLE, you can link and embed data from other Windows applications into Word, so that when you update the data in the original application, Windows automatically updates the data in Word. DDE and OLE make using Windows applications a real time saver—you can update data in one application without having to update the same information in Word.

In this chapter, you learn to do the following:

- Import and export text and data
- Import graphics
- Modify imported graphics
- Copy and paste text, data, and graphics
- Link and embed text and data

Importing and Exporting Text and Data

Applications programs use different file formats. Until recently, a person using one application program could not read, edit, print, or otherwise make use of a file created with another application program.

Converters

Software programs that translate data from one file format to another, preserving formatting whenever possible.

Word, however, includes *converters* that enable you to change most application file formats into Word file formats, and vice versa. The result is that you can *import* files from many programs to use in Word, and *export* Word files to use in other programs.

You install converter files when you install Word. If you did not install the converters, you can use Setup to install them at any time.

Import

Make a non-Word file available for use by Word.

Converters do a good job of translating the data entered in files, but you can't translate all of the formatting attributes from one application program into other application programs. Don't be surprised if the imported or exported file is not identical to the original file.

Export

Make a Word file available for use by other application programs.

Task: Importing

When you import a file into Word, it becomes a Word file. You can edit it, format it, print it, and otherwise manipulate it using all of Word's features. To import a file into Word, follow these steps:

1. Start Word.

2. Choose **F**ile, **O**pen. The Open dialog box appears.

Word can import files created with many different applications programs. Click the drop-down arrow in the List Files of **T**ype box to display a list of all files.

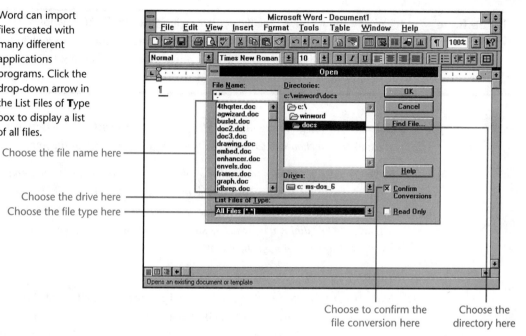

Choose the file name here

Choose the drive here

Choose the file type here

Choose to confirm the file conversion here

Choose the directory here

3. From the List Files of **Type** drop down list, choose to display All Files (*.*).

4. If necessary, choose the drive and directory where the file is located. Word lists the files in the File **N**ame list.

5. In the File **N**ame list box, choose the file you want to import.

6. Choose OK.

What happens next depends on the type of file you are importing.

■ For some files, such as files created with other versions of Word or Word for Windows, Word just imports the file.

■ For some files, such as Microsoft Excel .XLS files, Word displays the Open Worksheet dialog box, where you can specify to import the entire worksheet, or a range of cells.

■ For other files, Word displays the Convert File dialog box, where you can choose the application in which the file was originally created.

17

If you have problems...   If Word cannot convert the file you are trying to import, you may not have installed the correct converted. To see a list of installed converters, look in the Convert File dialog box. If the file type you want to convert is not there, then the converter was not installed.

Note: *When you go to save an imported file, Word may ask you what format to use. You can choose to save it as a Word file, or in its original file format.*

Note: *You can insert files from other applications into Word documents, converting them in the process. Position the insertion point in the Word document where you want the other file to appear, and then choose **I**nsert, **F**ile. Word displays the File dialog box, which is similar to the Open dialog box. Choose the file to import, and then choose OK.*

Task: Exporting

Exporting means converting a Word file into another file format. You might have to export a Word file if someone who uses a different program needs the file. To export, save the Word file in the other file format, and then store it on a floppy disk and give it to the other person.

To export a Word file, follow these steps:

1. Start Word.

2. Open the file you want to export.

3. Choose **F**ile, Save **A**s. The Save As dialog box appears.

Word can export files into many different file formats. Click the drop-down arrow in the List Files of **T**ype box to see a list of applications and file formats.

Enter the file name here

Choose the drive where you want to store the file here

Choose the format of the application to which you are exporting here

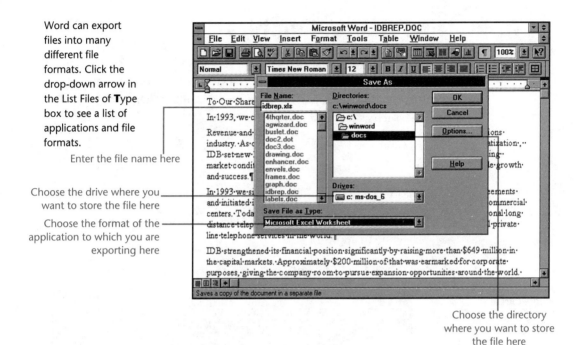

Choose the directory where you want to store the file here

3. In the List Files of **T**ype list box, choose the format in which you want to save the file.

4. If necessary, choose the drive and directory where you want to store the file.

5. In the File **N**ame text box, enter the name you want to give the exported file. Word automatically enters an extension based on the file type you select.

6. Choose OK. Word saves the file in the selected file format.

If you have problems...   If you cannot open the exported file using the other application, you may have selected the wrong file type in the Save As dialog box. Refer to the other application's documentation to find out what file type to select, and then try again.

17

Task: Importing Graphics

You can import graphics files from other applications into Word. You can import clip art files, charts that you create in a spreadsheet program or in Microsoft Graph, and other images created in other graphics applications, such as presentation graphics files.

After you import a graphics file into Word, you can use Word features to edit it.

To import a picture file, follow these steps:

1. Position the insertion point in the document where you want the picture to appear.

2. Choose **I**nsert, **P**icture.

Choose the file you want to import in the Insert Picture dialog box.

Choose the file to import here

Choose the format of the file you are importing here

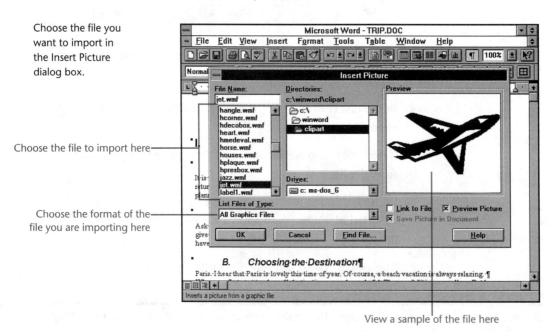

View a sample of the file here

3. Choose the picture you want to import. If necessary, specify the drive and directory where the file is stored. To list files of different types, choose an option from the List files of **T**ype drop-down list.

4. Choose OK.

Word imports the file and displays it in the frame on your screen. You can edit it using commands and the buttons on the Drawing toolbar.

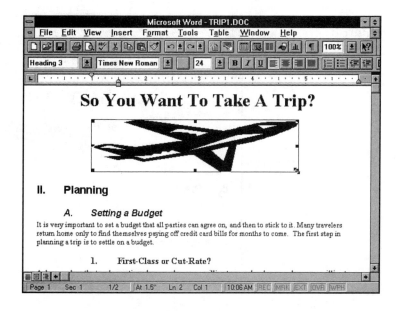

Resizing a Picture

To change the size of a picture in Word, follow these steps:

1. Click the picture to select it. A box with selection handles appears around the picture.

2. Point at any handle. The mouse pointer changes to a two-headed arrow.

3. Click and drag the handle to resize the picture.

4. To resize the picture proportionately so that the length and width grow or shrink equally, drag a corner handle diagonally.

17

You can resize an
imported picture in
a Word document.

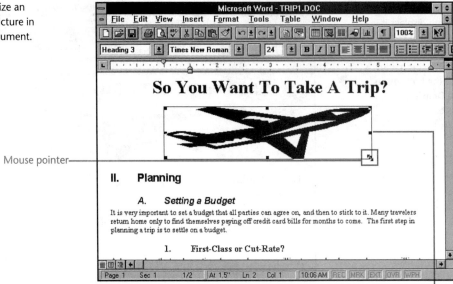

Mouse pointer

Drag a handle to change the size

Scale
A percentage of the
picture's original
size.

You can resize a picture by changing its *scale*.

To resize a picture precisely, or to change the scale, follow these steps:

1. Select the picture.

2. Choose F**o**rmat, Pictu**r**e.

You can change the
scale of the picture
by using the Picture
dialog box.

Enter the scaling
percentages here

3. In the Scaling area in the Picture dialog box, enter the percentages by which you want to change the size of the picture. To shrink the picture to one half it original size, for example, enter **50** in each box.

4. Choose OK.

Cropping a Picture

Crop
To change the area of a picture that appears in a document.

You can crop a picture to show more or less of it in your document.

To crop a picture, follow these steps:

1. Select the picture.

2. Point at one of the handles and press and hold Shift. The mouse pointer changes to a cropping symbol.

3. Drag the handle to change the amount of the picture which appears. A dotted line indicates the amount of the picture which will be cropped.

4. Drag a corner handle to crop two sides of the image simultaneously.

You can crop the picture to show more or less of it.

Cropping symbol

Dotted line indicates the picture area

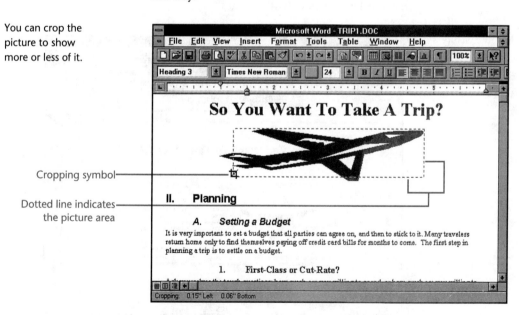

17

To crop an image precisely, follow these steps:

1. Select the picture.

2. Choose F**o**rmat, Pictu**r**e.

3. In the Crop From area of the Picture dialog box, specify the amount of the picture you want to crop. Enter positive numbers to crop in—reducing the area of the picture. Enter negative numbers to crop out—increasing the area of the picture.

4. Choose OK.

Positioning a Picture on the Page

Word treats a picture in a document as if it were a single character in a paragraph. That means that if you add or delete text around the picture, the picture moves. You also can move a picture by dragging it, or by using the Edit commands.

If you want to fix the picture at a certain spot on the page, place a frame around it. Then, you can anchor it, you can format it, and you can change the flow of text around it. For information on using frames, see Lesson 10, "Working with Frames."

Here, the picture is in a frame with a border.

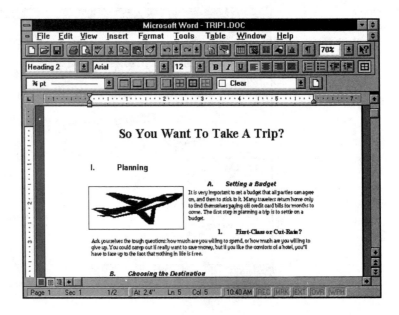

Editing a Picture in a Separate Window

Word actually uses a built-in program called Word Picture to insert pictures into Word documents. With Word Picture, you can edit the picture in a Picture window, separate from the document window.

In the Picture window, you may be able to see the picture object more clearly, and you can more easily use the buttons on the Drawing toolbar to modify the picture, or enhance it. In addition, you can see and re-adjust the picture boundary.

To start Word picture to edit the picture in a separate window, double-click the picture.

Here, the picture appears in a separate window.

Choose to reset the picture boundaries here

Choose to close the window and return to the document here

Picture boundaries

Drawing toolbar

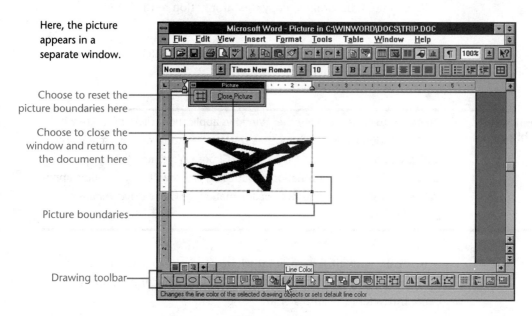

For information on using the Drawing toolbar to edit and enhance the picture, see Lesson 11, "Drawing with Word 6 for Windows."

Task: Copying and Pasting with Other Windows Applications

Windows was designed to provide a consistent operating environment for varied applications. If you use more than one Windows applications, you know how they use similar menus and commands.

17

You can use the Windows Clipboard to exchange data between Windows applications. The same copy and paste commands you use within Word documents also work to copy text, data, and graphics from other Windows applications into Word.

To copy information from another Windows application into Word, follow these steps:

1. Start the other application and open the file that contains the information you want to copy.

2. Select the information.

 3. Choose **E**dit, **C**opy to copy the information to the Windows Clipboard.

4. Switch to Word and open the document in which you want to paste the information.

If you have problems...   To switch to Word from another Windows application, click anywhere within the Word window. If you cannot see the Word window on your screen, press Ctrl+Esc to open the Windows Task List. Choose Word, and then choose **S**witch To. For more information about using Windows to run multiple applications, consult your Windows documentation, or Que's *Using Windows 3.1, Special Edition.*

---

5. Position the insertion point where you want to place the information. You can insert the information into a document, into frame, into a table, or into a chart.

 6. Choose **E**dit, **P**aste. The data is inserted into the Word document.

Importing Linked or Embedded Text or Data

Copying and pasting moves data from one Windows applications to another—but with Windows, you can do more. You can *link* or *embed* text or data between applications. Linking and embedding ensures that if you modify the text or data in the original application, the changes are made in the other application as well.

Link
To electronically join the data pasted into one application with the data in the original application so that changes made to the data in the original application are automatically made to the pasted data, as well.

Embed
To place data from one application in another application as an object. The embedded object can only be edited, displayed, and printed by the original application.

Linking and embedding are important if you use data that needs regular updating, such as spreadsheets or databases. If you place linked or embedded data into Word, you do not have to worry about it becoming outdated—when the data is changed in the original application, it is also changed in Word.

Linking and embedding are also useful for saving disk space, because although an object may appear in more than one document, it is only stored once.

Note: *You can link and embed Word data with other Windows applications using the same basic procedures you use to link other data to Word.*

You can create links between text and data in Windows applications in two ways:

- *Object linking and embedding*: OLE creates links between Word and the original application, and embeds the original data into your Word document as an object. The OLE object contains the original data in the original file format. The original application is responsible for updating, displaying, and printing the linked data.

- *Dynamic data exchange*: DDE links the data in Word with the data in the original application. When you modify the data in the original application, Windows notifies Word and asks to update the linked data.

Both applications must support OLE and DDE in order to create the link. Some older Windows applications may not support these features. All the applications in the Microsoft Office series of applications do. For information about whether your applications support OLE or DDE, consult your documentation.

You have already used OLE with Word. When you create a chart using Microsoft Graph (see Lesson 13, "Working with Graphs"), the chart is automatically linked into the Word document. When you used WordArt to enhance the look of your text, you were embedding the WordArt object into Word. That's why you can start Graph and WordArt simply by double-clicking the object in the Word document, and why changes you make in the original application automatically appear in the object in the Word document.

17

You can create an OLE link with an existing object, or you can use OLE to create the object.

To link an existing object, follow these steps:

1. Start the application that contains the data you want to link or embed, open the file, and select the data.

Here, data is selected in Microsoft Excel.

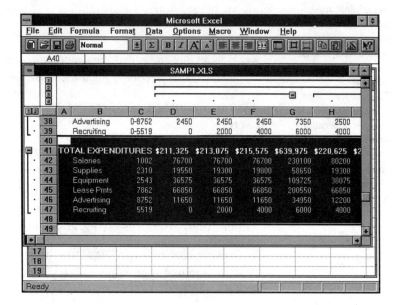

2. Choose **E**dit, **C**opy to copy the selected data to the Windows Clipboard. Do not close the application.

3. Start Word, open the document where you want the object to appear and position the insertion point in the correct location.

4. Choose **E**dit, Paste **S**pecial. The Paste Special dialog box appears.

Different applications support different OLE formats. You can choose the format to use for embedding the object into Word.

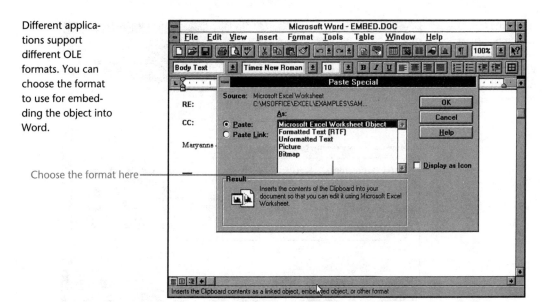

Choose the format here

5. Choose the format to use for embedding the object.

6. Choose OK. Word embeds the data in your document as an object.

Note: *Different applications support different OLE formats. Some of the newer OLE formats provide more sophisticated features than some of the older OLE formats. OLE Embed supports all currently available OLE features. It enables you to embed objects rather than just linking them. OLE Link is not quite as full-featured as OLE Embed.*

17

Here, data from the Excel spreadsheet is embedded in a Word document. It is selected, so it has selection handles.

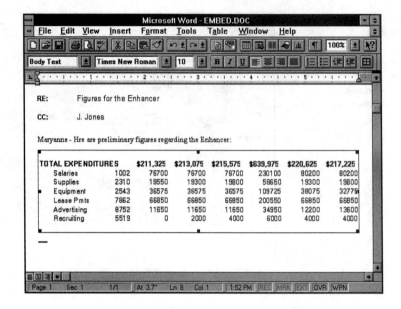

To create an embedded object, follow these steps:

1. In Word, open the document where you want to place the object and position the insertion point in the correct location.

2. Choose **I**nsert, **O**bject. If necessary, click the **C**reate New tab at the top of the Object dialog box.

In the Insert New Object dialog box, Word lists all of the Windows applications on your system that support OLE.

Choose the application you want to use to create an object here

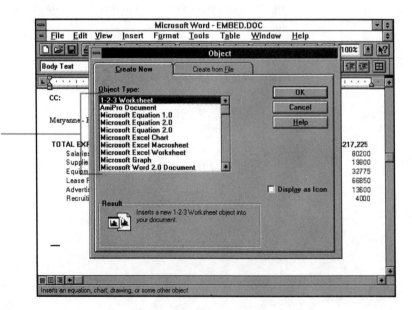

4. Choose the object and choose OK. Word switches to the application you selected.

5. Create the object you want to embed, and then choose **F**ile, **U**pdate to paste it into your Word document. Choose **F**ile, Save **A**s to save the file to disk.

6. Close the application and switch to Word.

When you update the file in the original application, it is not saved to disk. To save it to disk, choose **F**ile, Save **A**s.

Choose Update here

Choose Save As here

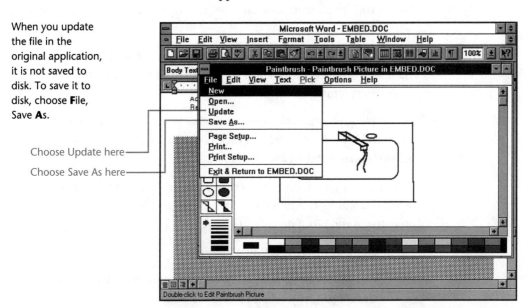

The object is embedded in your Word document. You can manipulate it using the selection handles.

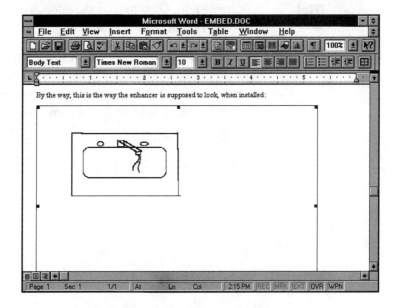

17

If you have problems... If the object does not appear in your Word document, you may not have saved it. You must choose **F**ile, Save **A**s in the original applications to save the file to disk.

You must edit the data in an embedded object in its original application. To start the application, double-click the object in the Word document. When you are done making changes, choose **F**ile, **U**pdate in the original application.

You can manipulate the embedded object in Word by using its selection handles. For more information on editing objects, see the section on importing pictures earlier in this lesson.

Note: *The applications that come built-in to Word, such as Graph and WordArt, might function a bit differently than other Windows applications when it comes to linking and embedding.*

You can create DDE links between a file in another application and a Word document. When data changes in the other application, it is updated in the Word document.

To link data using DDE, follow these steps:

1. Start the application that contains the data you want to link to Word, open the file, and select the data.

2. Choose **E**dit, **C**opy to copy the selected data to the Windows Clipboard. Do not close the application.

3. Start Word, open the document where you want the data to appear, and position the insertion point in the correct location. To insert the data into a table, position the insertion point in the first cell. To insert the data in an empty frame, select the frame.

4. Choose **E**dit, Paste **S**pecial. The Paste Special dialog box appears.

5. Click the Paste Link option button.

6. Choose the formatting you want to use for inserting the data.

7. Choose OK.

Here, spreadsheet data from Excel was linked into a Word table.

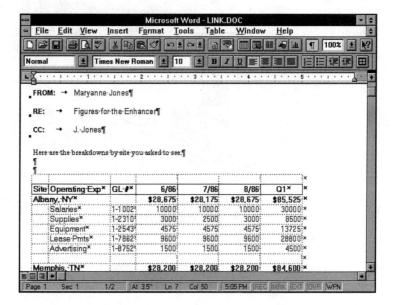

Data edited in the original application is updated automatically as long as Word is open. By default, Word is set to automatically update links whenever you open a Word document that contains a DDE link. You can set Word to prompt you to update the links each time.

To modify the link options, follow these steps:

1. Open the document that contains the links.

2. Choose **Edit**, **L**inks. The Links dialog box appears.

17

You can manage
your links by using
the Links dialog
box.

Choose the link here

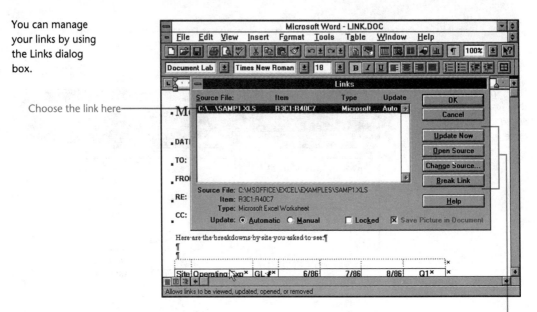

Choose the link option here

3. Choose any of the following:

- **M**anual to set Word to prompt you to update links

- **A**utomatic to automatically update the links whenever you open the document

- Lo**c**ked to lock the link

- **U**pdate Now to update the links now

- **O**pen Source to launch the source application

- Cha**n**ge Source to change the source application

- **B**reak Link to cancel the DDE

Using Imported Data

You can use data imported into Word to augment and enhance Word documents, or to save you time you might otherwise spend reentering existing data.

Here are just a few ways you can use imported data in Word:

- You can use database records as a data source for a mail merge.

- You can use database records to create a monthly schedule.

- You can use slide graphics files from a presentation program to illustrate a presentation handout.

- You can use spreadsheet data to create tables and charts.

To use a database file as a data source in a mail merge, see Lesson 14, "Using Mail Merge." To create a chart using data from a spreadsheet, copy and paste the data into a Word document, and then use it to create a chart in Graph. For more information see Lesson 13, "Working with Graphs."

Here, a column chart has been created in Word using the same Excel spreadsheet data seen in an earlier example.

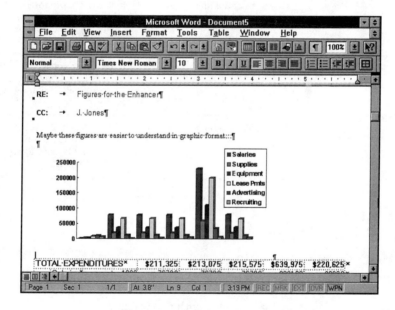

17

Summary

To	Do This
Import a file	In Word, choose **F**ile, **O**pen. Choose the file to import.
Export a File	In Word, choose **F**ile, Save **A**s. Choose the export file format. Enter the file name.
Import a picture	Choose **I**nsert, Picture. Choose the file.
Copy and paste data from another application	In the other application, select the data. Choose **E**dit, **C**opy. In Word, choose **E**dit, **P**aste.
Embed an existing object	In the other application, select the data. Choose **E**dit, **C**opy. In Word, choose **E**dit, Paste **S**pecial. Choose the OLE format.
Create an embedded object	In Word, choose **I**nsert, **O**bject. Choose the other application. In the other application, create the object to embed. Choose **F**ile, **U**pdate.
Link data	In the other application, select the data. Choose **E**dit, **C**opy. In Word, choose **E**dit, Paste **S**pecial. Click the Paste Link option button.
Insert database data	Choose **I**nsert, **D**atabase. Choose **G**et Data. Choose the file. Choose the file format. Choose to insert the data. Specify the data.

On Your Own

Estimated time: 30 minutes

1. Import a file from any other Windows application.

2. Save the file with a new name.

3. Export a Word document for use in another application.

4. Open the file with the other application.

5. Insert one of Word's clip-art pictures into a document.

6. Resize and crop the picture. Fix its position on the page.

7. Copy and paste data from another application file into a Word document.

8. Embed data from another application file into a Word document. If necessary, create the object.

9. Start the other application from Word to edit the object.

10. Link data from another application file into a Word document.

11. Link spreadsheet data into a Word table.

12. Create a chart using spreadsheet data.

13. Import a database file.

14. Conduct a merge using the database file.

17

Index

J-K

L

multiple document windows, 70-72

multiplying numbers (in tables), 284-285

N

narrowing text search, 81-82

navigating in help, 32

newspaper columns, 170

nonprinting character marks
  displaying, 123, 271
  hiding, 204

nonprinting tab marks, 132

NORMAL template, 36

Normal view
  as default view, 152
  changing to Outline, 372-373

numbered lists, 145

numbering
  outlines, 370-372
  pages, 161-162

numbers, 145-146

numeric formats (charts), 309

numerical characters, sorting, 147

O

objects
  aligning, 252-253
  changing outlines, 255
  copying, 253
  creating embedded objects, 410-414
  deleting, 253
  editing embedded objects, 412
  flipping, 260
  grouping in drawings, 248
  invisible outlines, 257
  layering, 250-251
  linking, 408
  moving, 249-250
  positioning, 249-253
    with grid, 251
  precisely moving, 249
  resizing, 254
  rotating, 260
  selecting in drawings, 246-248
  sizing, 254
  ungrouping in drawings, 248

OLE (Object Linking and Embedding), 288, 395, 407

on-line help, 28

opening
  a data source for merges, 321-323
  documents, 37-38, 53-55
    from different drives or directories, 54-55
    from File menu, 55-61
    in several windows, 75
  files, 392-393
  form templates, 345-346
  several document windows, 70
  Summary Information dialog box, 393
  Windows Task List, 406

operators, Word table formula, 283

ordering headings, 369

orientation (pages), changing, 157-158

Outline toolbar, 364

Outline view, 152
  creating outlines, 364

outlines
  changing for objects, 255
  collapsing, 368
  creating, 365-367
  documents, 364-373
  expanding, 368
  invisible object outlines, 257
  numbering, 370-372
  text, 369-370

Overtype mode (text), 41
  turning on, 24

overwriting existing template file, 181

P

page layout view, 153
  creating frames, 222
  dropped caps, 113

page numbers (headers or footers), 164

page setup, 151-175

pages
  changing size and orientation, 157-158
  dividing into columns, 170-173
  numbering, 161-162

page breaks, 173-174

panes (split windows), 70
  activating, 74
  changing size of, 74
  footnotes and endnotes, 169
  restoring to single pane, 74
  working a document in two panes at once, 73

paragraph marks
  displaying, 122-123
  viewing, 56

paragraphs
  aligning, 125-127
  applying styles with AutoFormat, 201
  bordering, 140
  boxing, 142
  changing tab stops, 132
  determining levels, 366
  dropped caps, 112
  formatting, 121-149
  indenting, 127-131
  inserting line breaks for starting new lines, 57
  moving, 369
  promoting or demoting (creating outlines), 365
  setting line spacing, 135-137
  starting new lines, 56
  starting new paragraphs, 56

passwords, removing from forms, 348

perfect circles, 240

perfect squares, 240

PgDn key, moving the insertion point, 41

PgUp key, moving the insertion point, 41

picas, 124

pictures
  creating drawings within, 262
  cropping, 403-404
  editing in a separate window, 405
  importing, 400
  positioning, 404
  resizing, 401-403

pie charts, 289

placing
  headers and footers on different pages, 165
  objects, 250-251

plot area (charts), 301

Word 6 for Windows QuickStart Disk Pack Order Form

If a disk is not included with this book, then you can use this form to order the *Word 6 for Windows QuickStart Disk Pack*, which contains approximately 30 pages of additional exercises that build on the examples presented in the lessons and Visual Index. These "hands-on" exercises enable you to further your learning of Word 6 for Windows by practicing with existing documents (rather than creating new documents from scratch). In addition, the *Word 6 for Windows QuickStart Disk Pack* includes a 1.4M high density 3 1/2-inch disk that contains the following items:

- Sample files used in the chapters of *Word 6 for Windows QuickStart*. These files include the examples shown in the Visual Index at the beginning of *Word 6 for Windows QuickStart*.

- Practice files that you will use in the approximately 30 pages of additional exercises supplied with the *Word 6 for Windows QuickStart Disk Pack*.

The easiest way to order your *Word 6 for Windows QuickStart Disk Pack* is to pick up the phone and call

    1-800-428-5331

between 9:00 a.m. and 5:00 p.m. EST.

For faster service, please have your credit card number available.

ISBN	Item	Unit Cost
1-56529-791-1D	*Word 6 for Windows QuickStart Disk Pack*	$7.95*

The unit price includes the shipping and handling charges for domestic orders. For overseas shipping and handling, add $2.00 per disk pack. Price subject to change.

If you need to have the *Word 6 for Windows QuickStart Disk Pack* NOW, we can ship it to you so that you will receive the disk pack overnight or in two days for an additional charge of approximately $18.00.

Que Corporation
201 W. 103rd Street
Indianapolis, Indiana 46290
Orders: 1-800-428-5331; **Sales FAX:** 1-800-448-3804;
Customer Service FAX: 1-800-835-3202